ATROPOS PRESS
new york • dresden

CHE GUEVARA and the Economic Debate in CUBA

Luiz Bernardo Pericás

Original title: Che Guevara e o debate econômico em Cuba
First Brazilian edition: 2004
Cover design: Patrícia Murtinho Pericás, Hannes Charen
Translation: Rodrigo Sardenberg
Revision of the English version: Vanessa Binder
Foreword: Michael Löwy
Bookflap text translated from Italian by: Bettie Lippitt Gambaccini

ATROPOS PRESS
New York • Dresden

US: 151 First Avenue # 14, New York, N.Y. 10003
Germany: Mockritzer Str. 6, D-01219 Dresden

ISBN 978-0-9819462-8-3

CONTENTS

FOREWORD

By Michael Löwy

Luiz Bernardo Pericás' book is an important contribution to the understanding of Che Guevara's economic ideas. He shows, very aptly, that the debate, among well-known European Marxist economists such as Ernest Mandel (with Guevara) and Charles Bettleheim (against him), concerned not only the specifics of the Cuban road to Socialism, but more general problems of Marxist economic theory and practice. Whether or not the law of value persists in a socialist economic process; the relationship between planification and market; the economic autonomy of enterprises and their « rentability ». It discusses the paradigmatic character of the Soviet model of «really existing Socialism», which Che did not accept. Although Ernesto Guevara knew very little of Leon Trotsky's ideas, Luiz Alberto Moniz Bandeira correctly emphasizes, in his preface to the Brazilian edition, the similarity of his concepts to those of the theoretician of permanent revolution.

Che Guevara's arguments in defense of socialist planification, and against the corrupting use of market instruments were very powerful and persuasive. In my view, however, a major deficiency in his discourse was that his thoughts about the relationship between democracy and planning were insufficient. His argument that planning, rather than market categories, were extremely important acquires new relevance in light of the dominant neoliberal vernacular with its "market religion". But the key political questions remain: Who does the planning? Who determines the major options of the economic plan? Who prioritizes production and consumption? Without a genuine democracy — that is, without (a) political pluralism, (b) open discussion of priorities, and (c) the population's freedom to choose between the various economic propositions and platforms being debated, planning is inevitably transformed into a bureaucratic and authoritarian system of "dictatorship over needs" (as is amply demonstrated by the history of the former Soviet Union). In other words, the economic problems created by the transition to socialism are inseparable from the nature of the political system. The Cuban experience over the last three decades reveals the negative consequences of the absence of democratic socialist institutions. However, Cuba has managed to avoid the worst bureaucratic and totalitarian aberrations of the other states of so-called "actually existing socialism."

This debate relates to the problem of the revolution's institutions. Guevara rejected bourgeois democracy, but — notwithstanding his anti-bureaucratic and egalitarian sensibility — he hardly had a clear vision of socialist democracy. In *Socialism and Man in Cuba* (1965), he acknowledges that the revolutionary state may make mistakes, thereby provoking a negative reaction among the masses and forcing the state to make corrections (he cites the sectarian policy of the party under the leadership of Anibal Escalante in 1961–1962). But, he notes, "Clearly this mechanism is not adequate for insuring a succession of judicious measures. A more structured connection with the masses is needed...." At first, he seems to be satisfied with a vague "dialectical unity" between the leaders and the masses. But a few pages later he confesses that he is nowhere near finding an adequate resolution to the problem of effective democratic control: "This institutionalization of the revolution has not yet been achieved. We are looking for something new…." [1]

We know that, in the final years of his life, Ernesto Guevara had gone a long way in distancing himself from the Soviet model, in his rejection of the "imitation and copy" of "actually existing socialism." But a good part of his last writings, and particularly his critical comments on the 1963 edition of the Soviet *Handbook of Political Economy,* have remained unpublished.

It wasn't until 2006 that these critical notes were published in Cuba: Ernesto Che Guevara, *Apuntes Criticos a la Economia Politica*, Ocean Press, Editorial de Ciencias Sociales, La Habana, 2006, 397 pages. It was written during his stay in Tanzania and Prague, in 1965-66, after the failure of his mission in Congo and before leaving for Bolivia. This document remained "invisible" for four decades. After the dissolution of the USSR, some Cuban researchers were allowed to consult these writings, and take limited notes. Only now, forty years later, they have finally been published in Cuba, together with some other material from the same period.

At last, this extremely significant material is available to interested readers. It reveals his intellectual independence, and his search for a radical alternative to the Soviet model of "really existing socialism". His opposition to Stalinism is apparent: the notes contain this blunt statement: "Stalin's great historical crime was to have depreciated Communist education and instituted the unfettered cult of authority."

Guevara continues to defend planning as the key element in the process of building socialism, because it "liberates the human being from his condition of economic thing". Again, who should make the plans? In

---

[1] Guevara, "El Socialismo y el hombre en Cuba", *Obras 1957–1967*, Paris, Maspero, 1970, vol. 2, pp. 369, 375.

the debate from 1963-64, he did not answer this question. These critical notes from 1965-66 contain some new insights. One important paragraph shows that, in his later political writings, Guevara came close to developing a complete theory of socialist democracy, a democratic planning process in which the people themselves, the workers, "the masses," to use his terminology, will make the major economic decisions. "In contradiction to a conception of the plan as an economic decision by the masses, conscious of the peoples' interests, we are offered a placebo, in which only the economic factors determine the collective fate. This is a mechanistic, non-Marxist technique. The masses must be able to direct their fate, to decide which share of production will be assigned respectively to accumulation and consumption. Economic technique must operate within the limits of this information and the consciousness of the masses must ensure its implementation."[2]

One can consider these notes an important stage in Guevara's path towards a radical alternative to the Soviet (Stalinist) model. In October 1967, the assassins' bullets of the CIA and its Bolivian allies interrupted this work of "heroic creation" — as José Carlos Mariátegui would say — of a new revolutionary socialism and a new democratic communism.

---

[2] Ernesto Che Guevara, *Apuntes criticos a la Economia Politica*, Ocean Press, Editorial de Ciencias Sociales, La Habana, 2006, pp. 132-133

AUTHOR'S NOTE

It's important here to say a few words about the nature of this work and its main goals. This is certainly not a biographical sketch about Che Guevara, nor is it a linear narrative of the first few years of the Cuban Revolution. My intent, using the figure of Guevara as a starting point, is to analyze the main discussions on the island's industrialization, trying to make an accurate correlation between the objective reality of that specific historical moment and the economic debate taking place in the socialist world and inside Cuba at the time, without, however, incorporating every aspect of that country's economy. Thus, I was cautious to use bibliography and documents from the mentioned period, as well as the most recent relevant publications. I also interviewed scholars, experts in socialist economy and members of the Cuban government who participated in its economic development at the beginning of the revolution.

Books that discuss the Cuban Revolution often follow a traditional chronological structure and emphasize the political and social aspects of Castro's government. In turn, the works about Guevara's ideas often dissociate his theories from their concrete historical context, idealizing his image without relating his elaborations to the current political environment and to the different lines of economic thought of the time. Che, after all, is usually seen more as a revolutionary and theoretician of guerrilla warfare than as an economist. In this book, beginning with an examination of crucial themes in Che's economic thought and of the Cuban industrial development, I strive to draw a detailed portrait, using important statistical data on the Cuban economy combined with an analysis of the economic ideas shared by Guevara and his group within that specific context. Although I am aware of the importance of agriculture and its relationship to Cuba's industrial sector, it will not be addressed here. Nor will I make a comparative study of different historical processes or between Cuban planning and that of other socialist countries. I will focus instead on the debates over centralization and decentralization, the different approaches to management of enterprise and the influence of reformist economists on this historical period.

The island experienced several important events in the first few years of the Revolution, from the invasion of the Bay of Pigs and the "missile crisis" to the establishment of the new Communist Party — the latter, only occurring after a purification of the Integrated Revolutionary Organizations (ORI) and of the Unified Party of the Socialist Revolution (PURS), and the pronouncement of the socialist character of the new regime. These facts are crucial for understanding contemporary Cuban History, which permeates this work. However, they are not directly related to the chosen theme, despite the fact that all aspects of the political and economic life of a nation are intrinsically connected, an integral component of the dynamics that characterize any historical moment.

So, what's the purpose of studying the limited period of the Cuban revolution? It was precisely during that time that the new paths taken by the regime were established. The transition to socialism required a national effort in order to rebuild the country according to new standards, and to consolidate a new industrial policy. That was the period when this book's main theme — the economic debate — took place. The discussions about the transition became both, a part of the broader debate taking place in the socialist world, and of the Cuban problem. In that sense, the influence of Marxist trends, such as Stalinism, Khrushchevism, Titoism, Trotskyism and Maoism, debated within the Cuban ruling summit, and in the intellectual circles of the country at that time, were also present in the ideological sphere. For that reason, it is important to resume the discussions about those trends and study their influence, not only for historical balance but also for a greater understanding of the sense and the depth of the discussions about the transition and their specific relationship on our continent.

Why is Che Guevara the focus of this study? It is well known that Guevara was the main debater and strongly encouraged the economic discussions of that period. He also produced the majority of published writings on the "economic debate" at that time. It must be recalled as well, that using central figures as the lead in their research, allows historians to analyze historical settings in a more detailed fashion. Such are the cases of Adam B. Ulam and his *Lenin and the Bolsheviks,* C. V. Wedgwood and the trilogy *The King's Peace, The King's War* and *The Trials of Charles I,* and several works by Christopher Hill, such as *God's Englishman: Oliver Cromwell and the English Revolution, Milton and the English Revolution* and *Lenin and the Russian Revolution.* Therefore, I am using Guevara as the focal point of this work, and as the platform to discuss several questions surrounding the economic debate in Cuba, and in the socialist sphere.

Guevara believed that it would be necessary to create a "new man" at the same time that technology and technical skills were developed. But what would man's role in building socialism be? How should the trade unions act? Where would the consciousness factor come in? What would the best approach to the island's economic development be? What were the main ideas in the theoretical sphere about the transition to socialism? Those are the questions that I will discuss throughout this book.

ACKNOWLEDGEMENTS

Many people helped me, in one way or another, in the process of writing this book. I'm grateful to all of them. Therefore, I would like to thank my parents and grandparents, my wife Graziela Forte, my sister Patrícia Murtinho Pericás, Osvaldo Coggiola, Werner Altmann, José Tabares del Real, Michael Löwy, Antonio Melis, Fabrizio Rigout, Bernardo Ricupero, Alexandre de Freitas Barbosa, Rafael Soler, Paulo Barsotti, Esther Lobaina, Jorge Grespan, Marco Fernandes Brige, Paulo Martinez, Wilson Barbosa, Antônio Rodriguez Ibarra, Massimo Di Felice, Arlene Clemesha, Jacob Gorender, José Wilson Moreira, Miriam Berrios Gonzalez, Orlando Borrego, Jorge Ferrera, Robério Paulino, Tália Bugel, Susi Dorothea, Ania Cavalcante, Gladys Rocha, Mauro Azeredo, Hugo Rodas, Herbert Amaral, Carlos Mallorquín, Colin Danby, Roberto Massari, Expedito Correia, Ivana Jinkings, Lincoln Secco, Luiz Alberto Moniz Bandeira, and Wolfgang Schirmacher.

LIST OF ABBREVIATIONS

AEA – Rice Stabilization Administration

AFL – American Federation of Labor

BANDES – *Banco de Desarrollo Económico y Social* (Economic and Social Development Bank)

BANFAIC – *Banco de Fomento Agrícola y Industrial de Cuba* (Agricultural and Industrial Incitement Bank of Cuba)

CC – Central Committee

CCE – Compañia Cubana de Electricidad

CEMA – Council for Mutual Economic Assistance

CIA – Central Intelligence Agency

CILOS – *Comités de Industrias Locales* (Councils of Local Industries)

CIOSL – International Confederation of Free Trade Union Organizations

CNOC – *Confederación Nacional Obrera Cubana* (Cuban National Workers' Confederation)

COB – *Central Obrera Boliviana*

CODEP – *Consejo Democrático del Pueblo* (People's Democratic Council)

CODIAD – *Comisión Disciplinar Administrativa* (Administrative Disciplinary Commission)

CON – *Comisión Obrera Nacional*

COPA – Pan-American Confederation of Labor

CP – Communist Party

CPSU – Communist Party of the Soviet Union

CTA – Technical Advisory Committee

CTAL – *Confederación de los Trabajadores de América Latina*

CTC – *Confederación de Trabajadores Cubanos*

CTC-R – *Confederación de Trabajadores Cubanos-Revolucionaria*

ECLA – Economic Commission for Latin America (later ECLAC; also known as CEPAL)

ELN – *Ejército de Liberación Nacional* (National Liberation Army)

FAR – *Fuerzas Armadas Revolucionarias* (Revolutionary Armed Forces)

FCT – *Federación Cubana de Trabajo* (Cuban Federation of Labor)

FOHC – Cuban Humanist Workers' Front

FONU – *Frente Obrero Nacional de Unidad* (United National Labor Front)

FTC – *Federación de Trabajadores Cubanos* (Cuban Workers' Federation)

GATT – General Agreement on Tariffs and Trade

GDP – Gross Domestic Product

GDR – German Democratic Republic

GOELRO – *Gosudarstvennaya Komissiya po Elektrifikatsii Rossii* (State Commission for the Electrification of Russia)

GOSPLAN – *Gosudarstvennaya Planovaya Komissiya* (State Planning Commission)

GOSSNAB – State Commission for the Material and Technical Supply

IADB – Inter-American Development Bank

IADTL – American Institute for the Development of Free Labor

IBM – International Business Machines

IBRD – International Bank for Reconstruction and Development (World Bank)

IC – International Committee

ICDIQ – Cuban Institute for the Development of the Chemical Industry

ICDM – Cuban Institute for the Development of Machinery

ICIDCA – Cuban Institute for the Research of Sugarcane By-Products

ICIMM – Cuban Institute for the Research of Mining and Metallurgy

ICIT – Cuban Institute for Technological Researches

ICRM – Cuban Institute for Mineral Resources

IMF – International Monetary Fund

INRA – *Instituto Nacional de Reforma Agraria* (National Agrarian Reform Institute)

JOC – *Juventud Obrera Catolica* (Catholic Workers' Youth)

JUCEI – Committees for Coordination, Execution and Inspection

JUCEPLAN – *Junta Central de Planificación* (Central Planning Commission)

KGB – *Komitet Gosudarstvennoy Bezopssnosti* (State Security Committee)

MINCEX – Ministry of Foreign Trade

MINCIN – Ministry of Domestic Trade

MININD – Ministry of Industry

MINTRAB – Ministry of Labor

MNR – *Movimiento Nacionalista Revolucionario* (Revolutionary Nationalist Movement)

M 26-7 – *Movimiento 26 de Julio* (July 26th Movement)

NCNA – New China News Agency

OAS – Organization of the American States

ORI – *Organizaciones Revolucionarias Integradas* (Integrated Revolutionary Organizations)

ORIT – Inter-American Regional Organization of Workers

PC-ml – *Partido Comunista Marxista-Leninista* (Marxist-Leninist Communist Party, maoist)

PGT – *Partido Guatemalteco del Trabajo*

POR – *Partido Obrero Revolucionario*

PRC – *Partido Revolucionario Cubano* (Cuban Revolutionary Party)

PRIN – *Partido Revolucionario de Izquierda Nacional* (National Leftist Revolutionary Party)

PSOB – *Partido Socialista Obrero Boliviano*

PSP – *Partido Socialista Popular* (Popular Socialist Party)

PURS – *Partido Unificado de la Revolución Socialista* (Unified Party of the Socialist Revolution)

SLL – Socialist Labour League

SNOIA – National Workers' Trade Union of the Sugar Industry

SWP – Socialist Workers Party

TASS – *Telegrafnoie Aghentsvo Sovietskogo Soiuza* (Soviet Press Agency)

UJC – *Unión de la Juventude Comunista* (Union of Young Communists)

UNAM – *Universidad Nacional Autónoma de México* (National Autonomous University of Mexico)

UPWP – United Polish Workers Party

US-IV International – Unified Secretariat of the Fourth International

ZDA – *Zonas de Desarrollo Agrario* (Agrarian Development Zones)

INTRODUCTION

The "dependent" nature of Cuban capitalism in relation to the interests of the American monopolies during the first half of the 20th Century constituted a serious obstacle to the full development of the island's production forces. It is clearly demonstrated by the inherent difficulties faced by that period's different governments in creating real possibilities for allocating resources to projects that could, *de facto,* foster a wide agricultural and industrial diversification in the country. Even when they present relatively favorable variations, the economic indicators exemplify Cuba's chronic state of delay and the complex maze of the bilateral relations with the United States. That in turn, made it more difficult for an "autonomous" solution to oxygenate the intrinsic demands of that society for greater freedom of action on the level of State decisions.

One can't talk about economic matters without relating them to the political sphere. Domestic factors, such as the social situation, the party context, the technical-administrative policies, and other external factors, in the broader sphere of international relations (mainly in the commercial realm) are interrelated and overlapping. These aspects are important to clearly understanding any country's political and economic dynamics. Cuba had a favorable environment for the accumulation and the extension of American capital, by means of agreements signed by local dignitaries, often related to Washington or to US enterprises. This only contributed to keeping the general state of the "nation" static. Thus, for decades one can note the deterioration of several social strata, mainly in the rural areas, and moderate, if not undermost, global economic efficiency.

From 1934 onwards, there were frustrated attempts at industrial development. This situation began with the commercial reciprocity treaty signed, in that year, with the United States, reinforcing Cuba's position as a consumer of manufactured goods and an exporter of sugar. While making some concessions under the guise of democracy, the regime — the current Cuban government — had the perfect cover to continue repressing those who opposed them. It was the beginning of a new era of the Cuban economy, since the United States, propelled by Roosevelt's *New Deal,* along with the national oligarchy, interrupted the 1933 revolutionary process and began a policy of increasing exports of finished goods to the island. Thus, preventing further industrialization, and encouraging the continuation of sugar production, by granting preferential commercial advantages to Cuba.

The introduction of the Costigan-Jones Law formalized this tradition of inter-dependence between the two countries. It gave Washington the power to control, not only the American sugar industry, but also that of its possessions, authorizing the American government to establish import quotas on the countries exporting sugar to the US market. Thus, Cuba had a quota of 1.9 million tons per year, which froze Cuban sugar exports at levels below its capacity. The total export quota for refined sugar was reduced by 22%, which harmed the national refiners. The new "commercial treaty", in turn, granted preferential import taxes to 550 American products, with a tax reduction between 25% and 60%, in exchange for the reduction of the export taxes on more than 20 Cuban products, including sugar, with a reduction from US$1.50 to US$0.90 per pound; rum, from US$4 to US$2.50 per gallon; and tobacco, from US$1.90 to US$1.50 per pound. This ensured a greater influx of American materials to Cuba, while at the same time giving them a cost advantage. From that point on, Cuba had to reduce taxes on American products in the domestic market, couldn't increase its domestic taxes on US products, and couldn't impose any quantitative restriction on the items mentioned in the treaty. (LOPEZ SEGRERA, 1972, p.284)

On the other hand, the high taxes on specific products led some American companies to transfer their branches to the United States; at the same time, there was no local industrial development in the processing and finishing of products related to other sectors, such as mining, that were controlled by foreign entities, who had no interest in the country's economic progress, which maintained the island's status as primarily an agricultural country. (O'CONNOR, 1972, p.54) Since sugar was the most profitable product in the short and medium terms, significant investments weren't made in industry overall. On the other hand, with the United States' import quota on that item, there started to be, paradoxically, not only industrialization difficulties but also those related to greater trade and profits coming from sugar itself. It's true that some American capitalists began to invest in other sectors, such as electricity and mining (sometimes in partnership with the local government), in large stores, like Sears (ensuring the introduction of foreign products to Cuba), and in cattle. However, those "new" investments, which reached US$700 million between 1946 and 1956, were almost entirely reverted to the banks of the country of origin. Only US$100 million were actually reinvested in the Cuban production sector. (LE RIVEREND, 1967, p.250) The relative increase of the wage-earner layer in the sectors of service, commerce and government, was due, in part, to the growth of the State bureaucracy apparatus and of its increasing interference in economic issues. These were always related to the United States, which believed it was important to maintain Cuba's political stability in order to protect its investments there, to ensure that the country was a profitable market for its exports, and a source of unrefined sugar to supply its domestic market.

After World War II, "industrialist" sectors of the few Cuban economic elite who were dissatisfied with the corruption and irresponsibility of their leaders, and worried about potential political instability, placed their confidence in Eduardo Chibás, candidate of the Orthodox Party, who proposed "developmentalist" paths for Cuba. With the gap left in the political sphere after that populist leader's suicide, the industrialist sector of the Cuban bourgeoisie began supporting Batista, which ensured a favorable environment for the influx of American investments in the country. The bureaucratized middle class and the local bourgeoisie were ideologically and economically tied to the United States, and the idea of "development" was always linked to a position close to that country. Since the weak industrialist sector of the Cuban bourgeoisie was not able to establish itself, it became possible for the interests related to agriculture and mining to remain intact.

Some authors even characterized the Cuban State, in the years just before the revolution, as being administrative, redistributive and bureaucratic. (O'CONNOR, 1972, p.61) Such trends increased as the years went by, to the extent that, in 1950, around 80% of the national budget was used to pay the wages of bureaucrats, rather than invested in the production sector. In that year, approximately 186,000 people, or 11% of the work force, were employed by the government. (LOPEZ SEGRERA, 1972, p.340)

A readjustment of the General Agreement on Tariffs and Trade (GATT), replacing the 1934 commercial treaty, occurred in 1948, ensuring that a sugar purchase quota would be determined by the US Congress, which maintained, therefore, the privileges of the American enterprises in the Cuban domestic market. The agreement with the GATT and the law of sugar quotas (of the same year) resulted, between 1948 and 1958, in a deficit in Cuba's trade balance, in relation to the United States, of US$603.4 million, as well as having been relatively compensated in the same period with a credit in relation to other countries. (LOPEZ SEGRERA, 1972, p.294)

In the late 1950's, Cuba's dependence on the US was explicit in several economic indicators. In 1958, for example, Americans owned 40% of sugar production, 90% of electric and telephone services, 50% of the railways and 23% of the non-sugar industries. At the same time, the banking capital in Cuban hands, which reached the level of 60%, was basically used to favor the foreign monopolist corporations. (LOPEZ SEGRERA, 1972, p.277) In that year, the volume of American investments in Cuba reached US$1 billion, lower only than the investments made in Venezuela and in Brazil. However, the US companies built and equipped the production units, the headquarters of which were located in the country of origin, and established all the rules and instructions of the Cuban branch.

Therefore, the typical unit in the monopolist capitalist society wasn't represented by the small firm, responsible for the production of a specific article in reduced scale, with a homogeneous production, but by the company that produced in large scale, which controlled a substantial part of the production of a certain industry — or of many industries, the price control capacity of its products, the volume of its production and the efficient planning of its investments (BARAN; SWEEZY, 1974, p.15-16). That model was consolidated in Cuba, even with the existence of thousands of *chinchales* (small craft industries) and served as a basis, after the 1959 revolution, for the positions defended by some leaders and intellectuals, such as Che Guevara and his group. As a consequence, many enterprises had emerged in Cuba during Batista's government, from dairy industries to those of soft drinks. International Telephone and Telegraph, Esso, Texaco, Sinclair Oil, Lone Star Cement, U. S. Rubber, Firestone, American Agricultural Chemicals, Procter and Gamble, among others, were installed on the island. As can be verified, the capital invested in the industries left Cuba, as profits, and ended up back in the country of origin. It's important to recall that those enterprises emerged "large". There wasn't a process of concentration and centralization as a result of the expropriation, fusion and substitution of small enterprises through time in some sectors of the Cuban economy. In other words, the American enterprises entered Cuba already consolidated. (LOPEZ SEGRERA, 1972, p.351)

Rubber and tire production was monopolized by U. S. Rubber and by Firestone; approximately 80% of soap production was controlled by Palmolive and Procter and Gamble; around 80% of the machines for sugar mills were produced by a single company in Sagua la Grande; two paper plants from Havana supplied the entire country; American Agricultural Chemicals produced almost all of the fertilizer used on the island; all rayon production was controlled by Rayonera de Matanzas; almost all textile production was controlled by Textilera Ariguanabo. Those monopolies controlled several branches of production and established prices, with the connivance and support of the local government. (LOPEZ SEGRERA, 1972, p.357)

More politically conservative analyses indicate a different interpretation of the years just before the revolution. In 1952, Cuba ranked third in per capita income in Latin America. It was the second country in terms of per capita meat consumption on the continent, the second in miles of paved roads per thousand square miles of territory, the second in terms of the ratio of doctors to people and the third in the level of wages paid to 500,000 workers in the sugar industry. It supposedly surpassed all the Central American republics put together in terms of export volume; and at the time, there was still parity between the peso and the dollar. (VARONA apud RIVERO, 1963, p.57) A report made by the International Bank for Reconstruction and Development (IBRD), published in 1951, stated that "the general impression of the Mission members, derived from observations and travels all around Cuba, is that the living standard of the farmers and of the peasants, of the workers in the industries, in the warehouses and other places, is higher, in all senses, than that of similar groups of other tropical countries". (VARONA apud RIVERO, 1963, p.58) A World Bank document, on the other hand, suggested that Cuba should try to become less dependent on sugar and to diversify into other enterprises; to expand and create new industries of derived products, or those that used sugar as a raw material; to promote exports of other products, to reduce the country's status as a single producer, thus helping to increase the total national income and the number of jobs in distinct sectors, such as mining and food processing; and to increase production for domestic consumption. (HUBERMAN; SWEEZY, 1960, p.108) In turn, in 1956, the United States Department of Commerce reported that Cuba had a national income that provided its people with one of the highest living standards on the continent. (RIVERO, 1963) But it also noted that their only important development in the first half of that decade was the mechanization of the export cigar industry — with a rise in foreign sales — and the export of sugarcane wax, the country's traditional product. (HUBERMAN; SWEEZY, 1960, p.109)

The Cuban working class was relatively large compared to the rest of its population. According to the 1953 census, there were approximately 327,208 workers in the industries, 395,904 in the service sector, 232,323 in commerce and 104,003 in transportation, for a total of 1,059,438 workers. While in the agricultural sector the number of workers was 818,906, which was greater than any other individual sector, but less in relation to the whole. (DRAPER, 1966b, p.77-78) The Cuban population was approximately 6 million at that time, while the trade unions claimed that they had 1 million associates. By the end of the decade, the country had one automobile for every 39 people, and one radio for every 5. Around 57% of the population was urban, over lived in cities with more than 25,000 people, and one-third in four cities with more than 100,000 people each.

One-sixth of the population lived in Havana, and one-third of the entire national population was considered middle class. The dwellings of the middle urban layers, in turn, were relatively comfortable, even though the low-income dwellings, mainly in the countryside, were of poor quality. Thus, some authors — such as Theodore Draper, Harry Oshima, Felipe Pazos and Eugene Stanley — rejected the term "underdevelopment" to describe Cuba, since they believed that the social and economic differences among the Third World countries were so varied that the designation couldn't encompass every situation equally, including that of the island, which presented some favorable figures. Felipe Pazos even said that Cuba should be classified as a "semi-developed" country. According to Theodore Draper, in 1958, the country's per capita income was US$356, which was greater, for example, than that of Mexico, which was US$263 in that same period. The scholar considered this to be a positive sign for the economy. The country supposedly had the third highest per capita income in Latin America, behind only Argentina and Venezuela. Life expectancy, in turn, was 58.8 years. Around 70 newspapers were published in Cuba, 18 of them only in Havana. The most important newspapers published 580,000 copies per day. The figures from 1957 show that there was one doctor for every group of 998 people; one dentist for every group of 3,052 people; 24 telephones for every group of 1,000 individuals; and 176 radios for the same number of people. (DRAPER, 1966b, p.98)

The most conservative authors also disagreed with the label of "single producer" for the island. Workers in the sugar, nickel and tobacco industries earned wages that were equal to American workers. Those industries, as well as the sugar-cane plantations, supposedly represented a diversification in production, along with other minor ones that also paid "high" wages, such as synthetic fibers, detergents, glass, oil refining, soft drinks, rum and beer. Cuba still produced textiles, shoes and minerals, with a lower wage base. (SELUCKY apud DRAPER, 1966b, p.99) Therefore, critics admitted the possibility of the island having a "single export" model, but not "single producer". In 1954, for example, the sugar industry as a whole, contributed 25% of the national income, even though that product represented about 80.2% of the volume of national exports. (DRAPER, 1966b, p.100) On the other hand, Cuban scholars observe that Cuba's favorable per capita figures before the revolution didn't accurately represent the country, since they redistributed to the entire population, supposed benefits from a specific group that owned more than others related to the middle class, dependent on the large enterprises, or on the state bureaucratic sector, which didn't correspond to what was actually going on in the rest of the island. (LE RIVEREND, 1967, p.249)

In practice, the situation proved to be very complex. Unemployment was a chronic problem for the island's economic health. Around 25% of the work force was unemployed in the beginning of the 1950, while 75% of the workers had annual jobs. This showed that a significant part of the population depended on seasonal or temporary employment. Sugar represented more than 75% of all the country's exports, but the workers were only necessary for three or four months of the year. Between 1956 and 1957, there was a 9% unemployment rate during the harvest and 20% after it. (LE RIVEREND, 1967, p.103)

One group, labeled "the badly paid", worked forty hours per week. In 1958, within a work force of 2.204 million, on average, 549,000, were unemployed. (LOPEZ SEGRERA, 1972, p.342) In a US$650 million panel of global investments, approximately US$300 million came directly from American enterprises, which controlled at least 30 of the 161 sugar mills on the island. (RIVERO, 1963, p.62-63) The average per capita income of Cuban workers between 1950 and 1954, according to figures presented by Leo Huberman and Paul Sweezy (1960, p.3), was approximately US$312, the equivalent to around US$6 per week. In turn, Cuba's average annual economic growth was close to 1.5%, one of the lowest on the planet. (RIVERO, 1963, p.63) The 1957 report of the Economic Commission for Latin America (ECLA) stated that, from a total of US$58.5 million in direct investments made on the island the previous year, US$41.4 million had been transferred abroad again; meanwhile, the foreign debt reached US$788 million in the same period. (LOPEZ SEGRERA, 1972, p.310) The short and medium term foreign loans obtained by the official banks, which had reached US$90.9 million in 1955, were reduced to US$23 million in 1956 and reached US$27.1 million in 1957, demonstrating the degree of dissatisfaction of the foreign creditors with the country's government. (LOPEZ SEGRERA, 1972, p.311) In turn, international reserves fell from US$500 million in 1952 to US$100 million by the end of the decade. (LOPEZ SEGRERA, 1972, p.342) Meanwhile, the main American monopolistic groups invested in much of the Cuban production sector and controlled it. The Rockefeller group was the most important stockholder of Moa Bay Mining, Freeport Sulphur Co., Nickel Processing Corp., Goodyear Tire and Rubber, Standard Oil and Chase Manhattan Bank; Morgan, of Sun Oil, Coca-Cola, Cuban Tobacco, B. F. Goodrich and Procter and Gamble; Sullivan & Cromwell, of King Ranch, Pepsi-Cola, Sears, Woolworth; the First National Bank, of the First National Bank, Grace and Co., Owens Illinois Glass, Phelps Dodge and Compañia Cuban de Teléfonos; the Chicago Group, of Swift and Co., Armour and Co., as well as of Liquid Carbonic of Cuba; the Manufacturers Hanover Trust, of the Compañia Cuban de Electricidad, Colgate and Palmolive; among others. (PINO-SANTOS, 1972, p.210) All those enterprises also had capital invested in sugar production. The new industries established in Cuba during Batista's term used, in general, 74% of imported raw materials. That corresponded, between 1948 and 1958, to an increase from 32% to 35% in the use of those materials. (RODRÍGUEZ GARCÍA et al., 1985, p.20) At the same time, there was no policy for the rational location of the island's industrial park. One year before the revolution, the province of Havana, which had 25% of the population, concentrated 75% of all the non-sugar industrial production of the country. (RODRÍGUEZ GARCÍA et al., 1985, p.21)

The need for real diversification and for the creation of a broad domestic market was clear and was made explicit in several documents produced by different international organs. It could be argued, however, if those measures actually took place, with the current state of that country, and without excessive interference by the United States in the Cuban domestic affairs, the island would hardly be able to have relatively independent development without a real change in the power structures and their relationships with the Americans. Only a revolution could *profoundly* change the agrarian and industrial structures, affecting the interests of the foreign monopolies, as well as directing the investments to strategic areas, both in the social and in the production sector. That would bring about a change in the relationship among social classes domestically, and among countries in the foreign policy realm. It was a delicate undertaking and hard to do any other way.

The revolution that triumphed on January 1st, 1959 provided the possibility of change, which wouldn't be easy. At that time, between 75% and 80% of Cuban foreign trade took place with the United States, which controlled more than 75% of the island's exports. (LEÓN COTAYO, 1983, p.27) Even making statements in several public arenas, during the first few months of the revolution, about the agrarian reform and the industrialization of the country, Fidel Castro still tried to get closer to the United States. Until then, his speeches didn't worry the American monopolies too much.[1] During his visit to Washington, Castro talked about the Cuban economy — mainly about the trade of such products as tobacco and sugar — with Secretary of State Christian Herter, without, however, delving deeply into the discussions. (LEÓN COTAYO, 1983, p.34) In general, United States government didn't give due importance to the visit of the *jefe máximo* of the revolution. President Eisenhower didn't meet with Fidel because he was supposedly playing golf while the Cuban leader was in the country. The Vice-President at the time, Richard Nixon, who had already, on that occasion, indicated that Castro was "dangerous" and a "Communist", was assigned to escort him during his stay, which implicitly demonstrated a certain degree of suspicion of the island's new government. (SZULC, 1987, p.536-537) Anyway, in that trip Castro talked to Ambassador Mikhail Menshikov, which was his first meeting with a Soviet authority after the revolution. (SZULC, 1987, p.537)

The interests of the US monopolies were eventually affected by a series of laws on the expropriation and nationalization of lands and enterprises. As was stated before, only a revolution could deeply change the relationship among the classes and the ownership of the means of production in the country. Since sugar was Cuba's main product, and since much of the population was made up of landless peasants or unemployed rural proletarians, it was crucial to change the agrarian structure. Only 114 large landowners occupied 20% of all the cultivable areas of Cuba, and 30% of the people devoted to agriculture were landowners. (LEÓN COTAYO, 1983, p.38) Approximately 100,000 Cubans were in such categories as tenants, subtenants and loaners. Cuba had around 159,000 farms, in a total area of 676,000 *caballerías,*[2] with 20% of these — that is, 32,000 properties — occupying only 6,410 *caballerías:* less than 1% of the total nationwide. There were 30,000 other farms — around 19% of the total — occupying 15,700 *caballerías,* or 2.32% of the land. In other words, 39% of the Cuban farms occupied only 3.27% of all the country's agricultural area. More generally, 157,000 farms occupied 359,000 *caballerías,* or 53% of the total area. The farms between 75 and 372 *caballerías* were controlled by 780 owners, approximately 0.5%, which concentrated 107,000 *caballerías,* or 16% of the total. (LEÓN COTAYO, 1983, p.38) The Law of agrarian reform eventually changed that situation. The first Law of agrarian reform, of May 17, 1959, prohibited the large landed estate, indicating as the "vital minimum" per person two *caballerías* — the equivalent to 27 hectares, and a maximum area of 30 *caballerías,* or 402.6 hectares. An estate that was over this limit would be expropriated and distributed to the landless peasants. The estates up to 30 *caballerías,* on the other hand, wouldn't be subject to expropriation, except for the parts used by tenants or renters.

The Law also considered a limit of 100 *caballerías,* or 1,342 ha, for estates that produced rice and sugar cane, since the yield of those areas reached 50% more than the national average; it prohibited partnership contracts; it divided the country into 28 Agrarian Development Zones (ZDA), which became an intermediate administrative unit between the municipality and the province; it provided state credits for cooperatives; and it compensated the owners of expropriated large landed estates in a period of up to twenty years, with interests of 4.5 % per year, with the so-called "Agrarian reform bonds". The first Law of agrarian reform eliminated the large landed estate and redistributed approximately 67% of the lands to the small producers and to the revolutionary government. It also exempted the peasants from paying rent and ended exploitation by intermediates and usurers. It made the creation of a domestic market possible by enforcing more equitable income distribution in the country and, in the short term, it helped reduce chronic unemployment in the countryside. That process also created the National Agrarian Reform Institute (INRA), a powerful institution that worked almost as a parallel government; it established "land courts"; it expropriated estates that were idle for two years; it allowed the transference of land bonds only by inheritance; and sales could only be made to the government or with the permission of INRA. According to the new legislation, only Cubans could acquire land, but foreign owners were allowed to keep their estates, provided that they were within the established limits. All land divisions, subdivisions and sales that took place after the revolution were considered void.

The expropriations started slowly and, ten months after the Law was enacted, only around 850,000 hectares had been confiscated, and 40,200 hectares distributed to 6,000 beneficiaries. (GUTELMAN, 1972, p.242) Beginning in January 1960, however, the pace of land expropriations and distribution increased. Until June 1961, 3.8 million hectares of land had already been expropriated. (GUTELMAN, 1972) According to figures released by the Cuban government at the time, those actions benefited 55,785 farmers (89.55% of the total), 74,415 cattle raisers (82.74%), 50,000 coffee growers, rice growers and fruit producers, as well as 50,000 peasants and rural proletarians. (RODRÍGUEZ GARCÍA et al., 1985, p.154) The agrarian reform enabled 85% of the farmers to stop paying rent for land and increased by 60% the purchasing power of peasants in general. (RODRÍGUEZ GARCÍA et al., 1985, p.155) Even though the agricultural diversification was not so profound as to radically change the economic picture of the country, it was relatively significant compared to previous years, since, between 1958 and 1960, rice production grew 28%, that of corn grew 26%, cotton, 400%, beans, 39%, potatoes, 21%, and tomatoes, 108%. (RODRÍGUEZ GARCÍA et al., 1985, p.220) It's worth recalling that, before the revolution, the yield of the land per *caballería* was lower than its real capacity. The sub-utilization of the land by the monopolies implied that these enterprises eventually acquired estates as value reserve and for future agricultural expansions, almost always sugar production. A better use of the land could make greater productivity per hectare possible and, consequently, the liberation of the rest of the land to the production of other cultures.

The creation of a Law of agrarian reform and other nationalizing measures were sufficient to worry the American investors, which considered these measures much more "drastic" than they expected, since they could harm not only the US enterprises but also the Cuban economy itself, by discouraging new foreign inversions. (LEÓN COTAYO, 1983, p.39) This could lead the Congress in Washington to review the sugar Law and lower the import quota of the product. On May 21st, 1959, in a regular meeting of the ECLA taking place in Panama, the Cuban delegation, chaired by the Minister of Economy at the time, Regino Boti, recommended that the commission consider the recent agrarian reform as one of the main means to improve and to increase agricultural production, to raise the living standards of the peasants and to pave the way for industrialization; the proposal was approved unanimously, except by the United States, which suggested the inclusion of the expression "whenever appropriate" in the part of the document referring to the agrarian reform as one of the adequate instruments for the economic development of the countries of the continent. (LEÓN COTAYO, 1983, p.40) A diplomatic note signed by the Secretary of State, Christian Herter, and sent to the Cuban authorities expressed worry about the Cuban agrarian Law in relation to the compensation of the American citizens whose lands were expropriated, and disappointment that the rulers of the island hadn't heard the criterion of the affected investors. (LEÓN COTAYO, 1983, p.41-42) In a letter to the secretary, the Minister of Foreign Relations of Cuba at the time, Raúl Roa, replied that the destruction of the large landed estate, and the land redistribution, were crucial in order to prevent Cuba from continuing to be economically stalled and to slow the pace of unemployment. Roa recalled the huge funds taken from the country and deposited into foreign banks but made no suggestion or proposal that could make the national sovereignty fragile. (LEÓN COTAYO, 1983, p.42-43)

With Washington's increasing pressure on Havana, at the end of August 1959 the American and Foreign Power Company, a subsidiary of the Electric Bond and Share and head office of the Compañia Cubana de Electricidad (CCE), cancelled a US$15 million funding, since the Cuban government had reduced electricity tariffs by 30% in the country, representing a 20% loss of its profits. Al Powell, director of the Caribbean zone of the Office of Foreign Trade of the United States, reported in the beginning of September that the interests of American rice producers were jeopardized — since they exported US$37.5 million per year to Cuba — and also the interests of investors in the textile sector, who were worried about the economic direction the new government was taking. In the beginning of January 1960, a group of legal aides for the American government recommended reducing the price that Washington paid for Cuban sugar — which would represent an immediate loss to them, of US$150 million — as well as the freezing Cuban funds in that country and prohibiting American tourists from traveling to the Caribbean nation.

Some observers, however, were more cautious. An article published by *The New York Times* on January 8 of that year warned that such measures could make Castro stronger and potentially indicated the failure of the traditional "Good Neighbor Policy". Despite that, Senator Kenneth Keating suggested that the United States buy less sugar from Cuba as a reprisal for the confiscation of American estates, while another Congressman, Representative Keith Thompson, proposed a bill that suggested depriving Cuba of any participation in the occasional increase in the consumption of his country's product. (LEÓN COTAYO, 1983, p.69-

70) In that same month, while visiting Ecuador, Senator George Smathers talked to President Ponce about potentially increasing the sugar quota for export to the United States.

The American government was preparing several measures against the island. Their objective was to influence other American administrations to contain the "impulses" of Fidel Castro and his group; to write a new sugar Law, giving the United States the power to reduce or to eliminate subsidies; to establish a tariff of US$1.25 for sugar; to use all its earnings to compensate its national investors; and to create a radio advertisement against the new government. (LEÓN COTAYO, 1983, p.75) These impending regulations made Cuba look at alternatives for its foreign trade. One option was the Soviet Union.

The Soviets had acknowledged the revolutionary government on January 10th, 1959 and bought around 500 tons of sugar in that year, approximately the same as in 1955, a small amount in general terms. In addition, a delegation of Soviet workers was invited to Havana for the First of May, but was not able to obtain visas in time to attend. Even though some trade unionists from the USSR had visited the island and an important employee of the Soviet intelligence service traveled there twice, the relationship between both governments was tentative. It wasn't until October 1959 that they made some more solid attempts at cooperation. This was marked by a meeting between Fidel Castro and Alexandr Alexeiev, an agent of the KGB and a correspondent of TASS news agency, sent by the Communist Party of the Soviet Union (CPSU) as a negotiator. In that meeting the ties between both countries were strengthened and the talks that eventually led to important commercial agreements commenced. On that occasion, the notion of bringing Anastas Mikoyan (first Vice-President of the Council of Ministers of the USSR at the time) to Cuba was introduced — to open an industrial exhibition, scheduled to start in Mexico in November, and later taken to Havana. This led Alexeiev to travel to Mexico so he could speak to Mikoyan in person. Mikoyan accepted the proposal and arrived in Cuba on February 4th, 1960, for a nine-day visit. During that trip, he inaugurated the Soviet exhibition of science, technology and culture in the Fine Arts Museum of Havana — scheduled to last twenty-one days — visited cooperatives in Pinar del Río, Camagüey and Oriente, and was in Ciénega de Zapata and Isla de Pinos. Just before leaving, he signed a joint notice with Cuban authorities, stating the intention to increase and strengthen ties between both countries in the fields of economic cooperation, technical assistance and cultural exchange. At the same time, they signed a commercial treaty formalizing the purchase of 5 million tons of sugar, by the Soviet Union, at international prices between 1960 and 1964, the equivalent of 325 million pesos, with an average of 65 million pesos per year. Among other products that would be sold to the USSR, there were several types of fruits, juices, canned goods, leather and pepper, which eventually resulted in a net balance of US$36.5 million in 1960, and as much as US$ 15million annually in subsequent years. On the other hand, Moscow granted a US$100 million loan to Cuba, at an interest rate of 2.5% per year, over twelve years.

These deals with the Kremlin caused speculation in the Western press and in the American government, which believed that the USSR was "maneuvering" to increase its sugar stock, either for resale to other countries, or to increase living standards of its citizens. In fact, the Soviet Union was the largest sugar producer in the world — over 6 million tons per year. Domestic consumption of the product, however, was low, only 21 kilos (kg) per person. According to their seven-year plan, in 1965 the Soviet Union wanted to increase the per capita consumption to 44 kg, at that point they expected to be producing 10 million tons of sugar, which wouldn't fully supply their domestic market with the elimination of the imports from the island. Among the developed countries at the time, only the United States, England and Canada had a per capita consumption above 40 kg. Nations such as Italy, with 19 kg, Germany, with 30 kg, and France, with 31 kg, kept their consumption rates at lower levels than those mentioned before. Thus, for the USSR to equal the consumption levels of the United States, it would have to continue to import the product. (CEPERO BONILLA, 1989b, p.327) That meant that the Soviet Union would not only keep its Cuban import but could even increase its quota to 3 million tons per year after the agreement was over. Anyway, the agreement with the Soviets would ensure, prior to 1964, the sale of 1 million tons per year, the equivalent to half of all Cuban exports of that product to the world market in 1959.

In turn, foreign criticism concerning the agreement itself was unfounded, considering the character of the negotiations was demonstrated explicitly in several clauses. The terms of the document stated that all sugar bought by the USSR would be directed at the domestic market and wouldn't be re-exported, thus it wouldn't be deflected to other markets that were usual importers of that Cuban item. (CEPERO BONILLA, 1989b, p.329)

Between 1955 and 1959, the Soviet Union bought US$165 million worth of crude Cuban sugar, while Cuba didn't purchase anything from Moscow. For that reason, the Cubans decided to open their market to the Soviets, with a commitment to spend 80% of sugar revenue on products from that country and pay the other 20% in dollars. (CEPERO BONILLA, 1989b, p.332) In turn, the US$100 million credit was familiar to the Soviets, who, not long before, had negotiated a credit of the same value with Argentina, to finance oil production and repairs to the railway system. As far as amortization and interest were concerned, they would be paid, not in relation to the entire credit, but only to a portion of it. That payment would be made with Cuban products rather than foreign currency. Since Cuba wasn't able to obtain credit from the IBRD or from other international institutions and previously had received loans only from American enterprises with interests in the country — which, according to the revolutionary government, was an excessive reliance on foreign capital — it decided to accept the Soviets' offer. (CEPERO BONILLA, 1989b, p.337)

It's interesting to note that between 1948 and 1960, the USSR provided more than 28,800 technical documents for the production of several machines, equipment and devices to socialist block countries. In 1955, the total sum of credit and other financial obligations that the Soviet Union provided as economic and technical assistance to developing countries reached some tens of million rubles. In the beginning of the 1960's, it reached over 10 billion rubles in foreign currency, all with an interest rate of 2.5% per year. (RIMALOV, [1961 or 1962], p.43-54)[3] At that time, the USSR had 206,000 existing industrial enterprises and another 100,000 being built. The USSR had approximately 200 million consumers and US$120 billion per year in operations in their domestic market. By the end of the 1950's the Soviet Union's budget was around US$140 billion — almost twice that of the United States. It was reinvesting 50% of its capital into industrial expansion. (GUNTHER, 1959, p.380-381)

The fact is that, even though the USSR was supposedly an "economic and military" superpower, most of the country's population still lived in extremely difficult conditions. If we consider that there was a lack of many different types of consumer goods, and that what the people were able to procure was of questionable quality, we can imagine that, rather than loan or invest this capital in other countries, it could have been used domestically to elevate the overall standard of living. This demonstrates, to a certain extent, the political interest Soviet rulers had in guaranteeing close and friendly relations with several socialist and developing countries.

To some Western critics, the Kremlin's interest seemed like a means to exercise greater political influence within the island's government. Even so, the Cuban government still tried to maintain "normal" relations with the United States, which was increasingly tightening its position. The gradual deterioration of relations between Cuba and the American government can be traced through several letters between high-level authorities of both countries. All of the Cuban leaders' request for economic assistance were harshly received or completely ignored by the Americans. Beginning in the first few months of 1960, the requests to purchase helicopters for agricultural use and even those for humanitarian aide were systematically rejected by the United States.

Meanwhile, Cuba's intense process of nationalization was already taking place. Ownership of several industries was taken over by the government, with a total production of US$2.933 million. These included such companies as Textilera Ariguanabo, with 3,049 workers and production equivalent to US$1.5 million, Betroma, with 679 workers, Concordia Textil, with 635 employees, Fábrica Cubana de Tecidos, with 589, among others. Additional enterprises taken over by the government included Cubanitro, with 270 workers, Rayonera de Matanzas, with 1,308, as well as Antillana de Acero, Fábrica Cubana de Acero and Aceros Unidos de Cuba. By the mid 1960's, the government already controlled 40% of the land, 37.6% of the non-sugar industry and much of the industrial production. (RODRÍGUEZ, 1978, p.123) From the beginning of 1959, there were interventions in CCE and the subsequent reduction in the electricity tariffs; a 50% cut in rent; a 25% tax on the export of minerals to be paid by the monopolies; Law n.851, of July 6th, 1960, confiscated and nationalized all the American enterprises;[4] and, by the end of that year, the promulgation of the urban reform Law and the complete nationalization of all banks and almost all foreign monopolist enterprises. Industrial growth, which had been 17% in 1959, reached 25% in the following year. As for the GDP, it reached 10.5% per year in the first two years of the revolution. (NOYOLA, 1978a, p.121, 124)

The increase of domestic tensions, with the combination of counter-revolutionary elements using propaganda and sabotage within the country, the "implicit" support of American government agencies of such activity, as well as the tightening of the trade embargo and increasing economic pressures on the island, contributed to the breaking of diplomatic relations between both countries, on January 3rd, 1961, and to the beginning of the embargo, on September 4th of the same year.[5] It must be recalled that under Batista's government the credit and payment system was standardized, but after the revolution the United States demanded that the country immediately pay all its pending debts, which was unfeasible in those circumstances, leading the Castro regime to state that during 1960 it wouldn't pay its creditors. This displeased Washington and the groups with interests on the island.

Starting in 1959, because of several external pressures, and to promote economic efficiency domestically, the Cuban rulers had already begun to discuss the possibility of establishing a planned economic system for the country. According to the patterns of this new structure, it was already pointed, in a certain way, in the direction of socialism, at least for the groups that would control the apparatus. From the beginning of the revolution the Popular Socialist Party (PSP), which was increasingly influential both ideologically and politically, insisted on establishing the plan for the island. According to statements made in the first year of the revolution, by Blas Roca, the party's main leader:

> It's necessary that all production and economic development take place according to a plan designed to satisfy the needs of the society, to increase the wealth and to elevate the productivity of the social effort. This plan is vital for the development of socialism, since without it the economic forces can't be dominated; on the contrary, it's the economic forces that dominate society. Without the plan, the anarchy of production and the disorder of social forces and resources impose themselves. Only the planned economy can, on the one hand, avoid or combat the scarcity of one or several products and, on the other hand, avoid the excess production of others, without the hardships and the crises generated by production without plan or concert of the private capitalists. (ROCA, 1961, p.220-221)

In January 1960, Aníbal Escalante, another important PSP leader, also suggested that economic planning should be established. Escalante said, "Cuba must now work on the great task of formulating a plan for the development of its economy, with a view to rationalize the gigantic transformation project on which it has embarked." (ESCALANTE apud MESA-LAGO, [197-], p.28) It must be recalled, however, at first most of the members of the Cuban Cabinet, and later, of the Integrated Revolutionary Organizations (ORI) and the Unified Party of the Socialist Revolution (PURS), belonged to the M-26-7. That is, even though the PSP suggested making the plan, the elements of the Movement were most important for the subsequent establishment of that modality in the country.[6]

Thus, according to a resolution on February 19th, 1960, by the Council of Ministers, the Central Planning Board (JUCEPLAN) was created — to a certain extent shaped according to the Soviet Planning State Commission (GOSPLAN). It took effect on March 11th of the same year and its sole function, at that time, was coordinating the government's economic policy. (BORREGO, 2001b) It was the first planning organ formally established by the revolutionary government. The National

Economy Council, which preceded this new institution, made some plans, often independently, at the time of the constitution of INRA. But the large scale planning started with JUCEPLAN, whose first technical secretary was Regino Boti, the Minister of Economy. According to Law n.757, of March 11th, 1960, it is "necessary to establish a Central Organ in charge of establishing the general goals of the State action as far as the economy is concerned, formulating development plans, centralizing economic, statistical and technological research, providing assistance to the organs that execute the plans and keeping and an eye on its proper realization, supervising the technical assistance provided by international organs and coordinating the activities of the different organs in charge of the economic policy". (RODRÍGUEZ GARCÍA et al., 1985, p.251)

Thus, the function of JUCEPLAN was to establish, to guide, to supervise and to coordinate the economic policy of the several governmental organs and autonomous entities. It was also in charge of creating the general rules guiding the private sector. The creation of JUCEPLAN enabled a greater cohesion of criteria and action among the several economic institutions of the revolutionary government. (RODRÍGUEZ GARCÍA et al., 1985, p.251) The committee, which met once a week in sessions lasting up to 12 straight hours, was made up of the Prime-Minister, Fidel Castro, a Vice-Director, his brother Raúl, the Ministers of Finance, Trade, Public Works and Labor and of the President of the National Bank, as well as a representative of INRA and the Minister of Economy, who was the institution's technical secretary. These personalities participated in JUCEPLAN because of their political importance, their authority, and their ability to execute the plan in Cuba.

The committee was made up of a technical office, subdivided into the National Administration for Planning, Statistics and Economic Organization, and a central services office, which would provide assistance to the new government's institution. (RODRÍGUEZ, 1983c, p.123-125) The National Administration for Statistics was in charge of developing a reliable statistical apparatus, since Cuba was considered the country with the worst statistical information on the continent. Thus, it should be able to collect and elaborate economic information and make it available in an efficient manner to further the plan. Sergio Beltrán, director of the Electronic Calculation Center of the Autonomous National University of Mexico (UNAM), was invited as an expert to help organize that system. The National Administration for Economic Organization was in charge of controlling and observing the execution of the plans, and the National Administration for Planning was in charge of studying the issues pertaining to the development of the country's economy and of making suggestions to the committee about projects, resource allocation, export plans and plans for investments by sectors. According to Juan Noyola, the planning should be ambitious but realistic. Thus, one should be very careful to define the goals, to establish the means to reach them, with great precision, as well as the necessary resources, methods and instruments. It would only be possible to reach the approximate goals of the long-term plan if the every specific detail of the economy was mapped out. (NOYOLA, 1978c, p.197-198) But he believed that:

> ... while the planning had an absolutely necessary central direction (because, among other things, in order to plan information must be centralized to provide a view of the economy as a whole, to provide a general view of how the productive resources are distributed among the different sectors, how the working people are distributed among the different sectors, how the equipment and machinery are distributed among the different sectors, and how the production is geographically distributed. Therefore, it's imperative that the general policies come from above, from a global perspective) it didn't mean that the really effective, really popular and democratic planning, doesn't require and doesn't assume the participation of everyone. (NOYOLA, 1978c, p.204)

In other words, even if in the planning process the central organ, the executive organs and the enterprises had the decisive role, the workers would also play an important role. It would be equally important to subdivide the planning into global, sector and regional, with the goal of creating greater possibilities for detail, and at the same time creating an interconnection between the different sectors.

It's interesting to note that, when JUCEPLAN was created, Cuba still wasn't socialist. For many Cuban economists of that time — or for those who stood out later — it was crucial for the plan to be developed within socialism. This reinforces the idea of a natural transition to that system due to the very structuring of the economic management apparatus of the country. In other words, the island was already preparing itself both ideologically and institutionally to later assume its responsibilities in the socialist sphere, even though that horizon couldn't be seen so clearly at that time. According to José Luis Rodríguez:

> Planning in its full sense is only possible under socialism. In capitalism there can be partial planning processes, when a company plans, and there can be an indicative planning by the government, but not obligatory as in the case of a socialist economy. In other words, great parameters can be established of how the economy must develop for the private sector to take its strategies into account. [...] It's impossible to develop socialism without planning, and that's the simplest and the most complete definition of what planning means. (RODRÍGUEZ, 2000)

According to that author, even if the plan had several technical aspects, it was primarily a crucial political measure. It can be noted that during this period the revolutionary government became gradually more radical and implemented measures that could actually change the economic structure of the island. The transition to Socialism was outlined, therefore, almost as a necessity. Relations with the United States and objective domestic needs, as well as the strong ideological influence of the communists, made it natural for the government to consider the plan, and shortly after that, the socialist system — with all its domestic and external implications — the most feasible and practical solution at that time of extreme hardship for the country.

---

[1] We refer to the moment immediately after the triumph of the revolution.

[2] One *caballería* is equivalent to 33.2 acres or 13.4 hectares.

[3] The Soviet Union's policy of loans to the developing countries supposedly forced the United States, in the 1960's and 1970's, to reduce the interests and to increase the terms for payment.

[4] According to Article b, paragraph 5 of Law n.851, there would be an indemnity payment, by means of an indemnity fund that would be created by the Cuban government and opened in the country's National Bank.

[5] On September 4th, 1961, the US Congress passed the Foreign Assistance Act, which prohibited help to Cuba and authorized the President to establish and maintain a "total embargo on all trade between Cuba and the United States"; on February 7th, 1962, President Kennedy declared a trade embargo against Cuba, which prohibited any import of Cuban products and the re-export of American products to Cuba by other countries; on August 1st, 1962, the Congress made an amendment to the Foreign Assistance Act which prohibited the United States from providing help to any country that gave assistance to Cuba; on October 2nd, 1962, the United States closed its ports to any ship that took weapons to the island; ships that had stopped in ports of socialist countries were prohibited from docking in the United States during the trip and ships belonging to enterprises that traded with Cuba were prohibited from taking American products; on February 8th, 1963, the American government prohibited its citizens from traveling to Cuba and doing business with the revolutionary government; on May 14th of the same year, the Department of Commerce of the United States began to require specific approvals for food and medicine sent to Cuba; in December of the same year, the Congress made an amendment to the Foreign Assistance Act that prohibited any help from the United States to countries that didn't prohibit airplanes or ships from their national enterprises to trade with Cuba.

[6] The ORI were created in 1961 from the merging of the M 26-7, of the *Directorio Revolucionario* and of the PSP. In 1962, there was a "purification" process of the staff and the

creation of the *Partido Unido de la Revolución Socialista* (PURS), which, in 1965, eventually became the country's new Communist Party.

1

ECONOMIC DEVELOPMENT AND INDUSTRIALIZATION

Although the decision to appoint Che Guevara President of the National Bank of Cuba, and later Minister of Industry, was much more political than technical, the fact is that he played a crucial role in the economic management of the island and in the debates concerning the transition to socialism in that country. It is known that Guevara was far from having a profound knowledge of economics, but for him to feel that he was up to the post that had been entrusted to him, he made an effort to overcome his deficiencies, and before long he had the necessary tools to lead these institutions. However, his lack of a formal economic training eventually became one of the reasons for criticism by Cuban government officials in later years.

A statement made by the Argentine revolutionary's father, after his appointment as president of the National Bank on November 26[t] 1959, is widely known. He supposedly said, with surprise, that Fidel was probably crazy to do that. According to him, "each time a Guevara opens a business, it goes bankrupt". (TAIBO II, 1997, p.351) The joke told by Che himself about his appointment is also famous:

> During the meeting to constitute the first revolutionary government, shortly after the entrance of the Rebel Army in Havana, Fidel was making the distribution of the Ministries to the Commanders, more or less according to the professions each one had practiced before the war:
> "So-and-so, who's an agronomist, will be the Minister of Agriculture. So-and-so, who's an engineer, will be the Minister of Public Works. So-and-so, who's a lawyer, will be the Minister of Justice."

> Thus, Fidel constituted the government, without any problem. Then came the moment to choose the President of the National Bank of Cuba. Fidel was hesitant; he looked at everyone present and finally asked:
> "Who's an economist here?"
> I immediately answered:
> "I am!"
> Fidel stared at me, surprised. He blushed, lowered his head, seemed annoyed, and said:
> "The President of the National Bank of Cuba will be Che."
> I was very surprised by the appointment. And the others were also surprised. I thought about declining. But I didn't. That historical moment didn't allow us to decline any task imposed by the revolution. I remained silent.
> After the distribution of the government positions, Fidel ended the meeting, but asked me not to leave because he wanted to talk to me.
> When the others left, Fidel exclaimed:
> "Che, I have always known that you're a physician! How come you're also an economist? I didn't know that nor did the others!"
> "Economist? But Fidel, I heard you ask who was a communist!"
> And that's how I became the President of the National Bank of Cuba. (CASTRO, P., 1994, p.5)

That anecdote became famous in the years after Che's term, but, in fact, the appointment of Guevara as the President of the National Bank, far from having such an extravagant reason, was a clear message by Fidel Castro to both his domestic and his foreign political enemies. The bank, which was previously run by "conservatives", by "moderate" experts, such as Felipe Pazos and Just Carrillo, didn't implement the necessary revolutionary measures to lever the process that was taking place throughout Cuba in all the government institutions once and for all. It's worth recalling that in 1957, according to a suggestion by Frank País, such personalities as Castro, Raúl Chibás and Pazos had joined to elaborate the path for the island during the revolutionary struggle and in the future. After the triumph of the Rebel Army, a new government arrangement started to be constituted, including the economic sector. Raul Cepero Bonilla, who had received the positions of Minister of Commerce and temporary Minister of Finance, argued that he was overloaded, leaving the Ministry of Finance in the hands of Rufo López-Fresquet, who was considered an expert in finances, but also a defender of the interests of the old Cuban ruling class. Pazos, in turn, became the President of the National Bank. Even though the appointments were seemingly odd, their goal was to "calm down" potential problems with the country's elites. The fact is that they were prominent figures, who still maintained some institutional prestige and who could be important in a transition period.[1]

However, with a gradual restructuring of the government, starting from a radicalization of the paths of the revolution, the presence of men who Fidel trusted in the main political positions was crucial. Thus, Raúl Castro eventually became Minister of Defense; Augusto Martínez Sanchez, Minister of Labor; Ramiro Váldes, Minister of the Interior; José Abrahantes Fernández, Vice-Minister of the Interior and National Chief of the Security Department of the State; Manuel Piñero Losada, also Vice-Minister of the Interior and National Chief of the General Intelligence Management; Osmany Cienfuegos, Minister of Public Works; Rolando Díaz Astarain, Minister for the Recovery of Stolen Property, among others. Guevara's intellectual background (he was thirty-one years old at the time), and his closeness to Fidel were important reasons why he was chosen for such an important position in the government. He had been one of the main leaders during the revolutionary war and Commander of La Cabaña, and he also already had some experience with the State affairs, considering that he had been, though briefly, the Director of the Industrialization Department of INRA, starting on October 8th, 1959.

The Industrialization Department, officially encoded in Resolution n.94, on November 21st, 1959, was created as a direct response to the need for industrial development that was emerging due to the agrarian reform. Its initial goal was to manage several industries which had suffered the intervention of the government, both because their owners were tied to the old regime and became rich on public money and because many enterprises were abandoned by their owners who had gone abroad because they disagreed with the revolution. At the time, Fidel Castro, who was the President of INRA, and Antonio Nuñez Jiménez, its executive director, agreed that Che would be the ideal man to occupy such a position, even though many people thought that it had limited importance to someone of his political stature.[2]

Besides Che himself, the Industrialization Department's staff was made up of Orlando Borrego, Aleida March, José Manresa, César Rodríguez and Francisco García Vals. According to Borrego, (2001a, p.11) the Department started to work very quickly and depended almost exclusively on the new ideas that Guevara gradually developed. An organizational structure was elaborated, with the creation of the administration, accounting, purchasing, sales, juridical, personnel, supervisory and invention and innovation sections. On that occasion, Guevara said, in a letter to his parents, "the Industrialization Department was my own creation. I almost expelled it, with the suffering of an exhausted father, to plunge into my calling, apparently provided by God, for finances". (ANDERSON, 1997, p.516)

Shortly thereafter, interventions were made in Cuban factories. These factories, many of which were private, did not receive investments from the national or foreign capitalists, who disagreed with the revolution. The interventions were made based on Law n.647, which placed all kinds of interference, under the jurisdiction of the Ministry of Labor, to avert "any activity that might alter, either directly or indirectly, the economic balance of the country, ensuring the necessary production to the citizenship, to the labor sources and to the peak and development of the economy". (RODRÍGUEZ GARCÍA et al., 1985, p.62) In the beginning of that process, MINTRAB sent an employee to the company, who made an inventory, froze its bank account and appointed a workers commission, along with a mediator, to manage the works. If the plant's owner voluntarily admitted that he was "mistaken" and that he had jeopardized the national economy, the Ministry allowed him to remain working as an employee of the company, but earning only a monthly wage. In most cases, the owners were even prohibited from working in their old enterprises and left the country.

With the backing of the Ministry of Labor, Guevara was allowed to act as he deemed necessary. He was to intervene and manage the industrial sector of the country. (ANDERSON, 1997, p.521-522) This meant that the Ministry could interfere with any company, taking charge of its management, without necessarily replacing its owners. The main objectives, in that case, were to avoid decapitalization, sabotage and possible abuses by their owners. Even so, in some cases the owners still had the right to receive the enterprises' profits. That policy remained until the end of 1960, when most of the Cuban industries reverted to government ownership. By the end of 1959, however, the Ministry already controlled forty-one small and medium enterprises.

When he took his position at the National Bank of Cuba, Guevara still formally maintained his post at INRA. In practice, however, his friend and collaborator Orlando Borrego led the department, together with César Rodríguez, Juan Borroto and Valdés Gravalosa. During that period, the Department grew and by the middle of 1960, it managed more than 60% of all Cuban industries. Its main function was to complement the agrarian reform and to reduce the pressure on the balance of payments. Because the growth of the Department and the quantity of industries overloaded the institution, the Ministry of Industries was created to oversee them. The Industrialization Department controlled, until the end of 1960, the General Administration of Sugar Mills, with one hundred and sixty-one sugar mills in the entire country, the Cuban Oil Institute, which managed the four existing refineries, and the Mining Institute, which managed the main, recently nationalized, mines in Cuba. (GUEVARA, 1988b, p.96)

The National Bank of Cuba, created in December, 1948, but not operational until April, 1950 — was made up of an Auditing Department and one for Economic Surveys. It had possibly the most prestigious staff inside the government. When Guevara took over the institution, he changed its character, creating stimuli to mobilize credits for activities that the new government was interested in, as well as to issue currency to cover the budget deficits. According to the organic Law of the National Bank, enacted in February, 1961, "the National Bank of Cuba, with a State Bank character, and its own legal personality and patrimony, will exercise the monetary sovereignty of the Nation and the monopoly of the issuing; it will centralize the monetary resources, temporarily free of the organs, the enterprises and the population; it will exercise credit in the short and the long terms and the financing of capital investments; it will undertake the operations and adjustments with foreign countries; it will keep custody of the monetary reserves and those of foreign currency and it will be the only center for the adjustments of payments in the country." (RODRÍGUEZ GARCÍA et al., 1985, p.238)

Therefore, the Bank became the inspector of the economic activity of the government organs, as well as of the State-owned enterprises, developing, on the other hand, a credit policy for the private sector. Within the state sector, it oversaw the fulfillment of the enterprises' plans, demanded the rational utilization of resources and kept up with the productivity increases. (RODRÍGUEZ GARCÍA et al., 1985, p.239) Like the National Bank, many other credit and investment policy institutions were changed by the new government.

During Prío Socarrás' term, he created the Agricultural and Industrial Incitement Bank of Cuba (BANFAIC). The Bank had a capital of US$26 million, and later Che incorporated one of its sections into the Industrialization Department. The Agricultural division of BANFAIC, led by Justo Carrillo, supposedly stimulated rural credit associations, tried to improve the storage and refrigeration facilities, financed the mechanization of rice production, as well as that of other sectors, and encouraged research on several agricultural products. The main task of the Industrial Department of the same institution, in turn, was to foster new industries, direct loans and encourage foreign enterprises to establish themselves in Cuba. BANFAIC dealt mainly with the industrial sector, as opposed to most of the private banks, who invested in the agricultural area, mainly sugar. There was a documented increase, from 1950 to 1958, in loans to non-sugar industries from 28.6% to 55.6%. A large investment was made in the Cuban Hydro-electrical Plant, in the province of Las Villas. After the revolution, the new regime granted financial resources of 10 million pesos to promote its goals. The Rice Stabilization Administration (AEA) also started to cooperate with BANFAIC, granting credits to that institution to be transferred to rice producers in the Oriente province in order to increase their production. Later, that organ was incorporated to INRA, with the intention of providing it with more cohesion and efficiency.

The Economic and Social Development Bank (BANDES) was created in Cuba during Batista's presidency. Established by Decree n.1.947, in January 1955, its main function was distribution of resources to already existent credit entities, to facilitate short, medium and long term credit operations for economic development and diversification of production. This institution was abolished in February 1960; the government decided that the National Bank and INRA could take over its functions and responsibilities. Between eight and ten enterprises previously financed by BANDES, and which showed a loss or lack of profits, began showing favorable numbers after they were nationalized. These were enterprises such as Tecnica Cubana (of paper), Rayonera de Matanzas and Antillana de Acero. Often, the capital invested in those industries during the 1950's was embezzled rather than used for the growth and modernization of those plants. (GUEVARA, 1988b, p.97-98) In other words, BANDES was a prime example of misuse of public money and of an organ full of corruption. Other enterprises, not necessarily tied to BANDES' funds, such as Gravi Laboratories — which belonged to the Consolidated of the Chemical Industry — increased their production by 38.58% three months after its intervention, compared to the three previous months. The glass plant Owens Illinois, in turn, showed a 6.5% increase in just the first month after becoming state-owned, while Firestone had an 18% growth in productivity and Reinaldo Márquez Laboratories grew 19.6%. (GUEVARA, 1988b, p.96)

In the 1950's, there was also the emergence of the Financiera Nacional de Cuba, which helped finance the tunnel built by the Societé des Grands Travaux de Marseille under the port of Havana, for US$30 million and the Cuban Foreign Trade Bank. In 1956, it is documented that there was an influx of foreign capital in the approximate amount of US$35.3 million to the island, while, two years later, industries appraised at US$15 million began operating in the country. In 1958, authorization was granted for the installation of industries worth US$42 million — including the a plant for producing anhydrous ammoniac for US$18 million, as well as one to produce sulfuric acid for US$7.2 million — and the Havana Hilton hotel was built, at a cost of US$24 million and later nationalized by the revolutionary government. (RIVERO, 1963, p.91-93) In fact, until the end of 1960, all the Cuban and foreign banks were nationalized, according to Law n.891, with the goal of ensuring the government's power to control the foreign currency credit policies. That measure had the strategic importance of resource distribution, since the Bank's restructuring would have to be adapted to the government's new economic requirements. (BEKARÉVICH; MANCILLA, 1980, p.37)

Guevara "revolutionized" the style of the National Bank leaving its older employees worried, since they weren't used to the Commander's behavior. During the fourteen months in which Che remained at the National Bank, he demonstrated his unorthodox methods. From mid-morning to the break of dawn he was making decisions, chatting, discussing and studying, always with his characteristic olive-green uniform, often receiving his guests and visitors with a cigar in his teeth and his feet on the desk. (CASTAÑEDA, 1997, p.201) Meanwhile, he surrounded himself with aides and bodyguards, often boys from the heartland, also with long hair and wearing military uniforms. In addition to these responsibilities, he retained his military rank and duties. He was in charge of the cultural formation of the Army, worked as director of the Industrialization Department of INRA, and was the President of the National Bank but he insisted upon earning only 440 pesos per month, his wage as Commander. He also showed his disdain for money, when he started to sign the bills issued by the institution under his charge only as "Che".

At the time, the bank still had many employees of the former Felipe Pazos presidency, who didn't adapt to the new Cuban economic policy. After many of them were fired and went to the United States, Guevara had to find aides who could help him outside Cuba. Gradually, a new staff was consolidated. It was made up of Latin American professors and economists, all of whom were Marxists, who taught the revolutionary leader and helped him with issues pertinent to the National Bank. Even before taking over his position, Guevara had already attended lectures about Marx's *Capital,* by Anastasio Mancilla (PhD in Economic Science and professor of the Institute of Social Science of Moscow), and had taken advanced math classes with Salvador Villaseca, as well as classes on economics with one of the most important aides of the ECLA, the Mexican Juan Noyola[3].

According to Noyola, head of the ECLA mission in the country, a development policy should satisfy several requirements, such as the full use of the Cuban production resources. That meant eliminating unemployment, the causes of underutilization of land and improving the industrial sector, in the areas of power generation, transportation, etc. It would also be important to increase the capital formation rate, the volume of economic surplus, the quantity of resources for investment, as well as directing those inversions more properly. In other words: an agrarian reform, a more protectionist tax policy and a State policy that strove to unravel the financial strangulation points, increasing the productive base of the economy. (RODRÍGUEZ GARCÍA et al., 1985, p.207) In that sense, the uses for the sugar industry should be increased, using sugar as a by-product; development of the steel industry and some areas of the mechanical industry; in the following ten years the entire population, employed and unemployed, should be absorbed by the industrial and services sectors; and agricultural production should grow without increasing the number of people involved in that activity. (RODRÍGUEZ GARCÍA et al., 1985, p.207-208) The need for Cuban universities to turn out more economists was clear to Che:

> When we only have Chileans, Mexicans, Argentineans, Venezuelans, Peruvians or any fellow countryman of America, as economic aides, sent either by the ECLA or by INRA, and when even our Minister of Economy has graduated from foreign universities, simply the question of whether a School of

> Economics is needed is obvious: it's very needed, and with qualified professors, and besides with professors who are able to interpret the pace and the development path of our Revolution. (GUEVARA, 1982, p.161)

At that time, however, foreign aides were still crucial for supporting Guevara and his staff. Visitors who provided some assistance in the debates about the economic paths of the island were also a significant presence. Among them were intellectuals such as Leo Huberman, Paul Sweezy and the other Marxists of *Monthly Review,* as well as René Dumont, Michal Kalecki, Jacques Chonchol and Sartre, who discussed several themes with the country's rulers. Important Cuban economists, such as Raul Cepero Bonilla and Regino Boti were also extremely influential in the Cuban economic paths at the beginning of the revolution. A political line was slowly consolidated within the National Bank and the government in general, which would later influence Che's opinions during the economic debate and in discussions with other members of the government.

Even though the available reserve fund had increased, between 1959 and 1960, from US$100 million to US$200 million, it was still very low, which led the government to try to accelerate the import substitution process in order to ensure a lasting stability in the balance of payments, with fewer foreign currency expenses, by means of the favorable trade balance in the country. It would be necessary to begin an industrialization process, in the first five years, only in the area of imported materials and regardless of human labor and of domestic materials, specifically in the chemical sector at around US$150 million. Investment in the domestic manufacture of paper, with pulp produced totally in Cuba, would be around US$90 million. (GUEVARA, 1988b, p.98) For that to happen, the government encouraged the creation of a national savings fund. Among several measures, there was the promulgation of Law n.447 that dealt with tax reform, the objective of which was to create a fiscal policy that served to accelerate economic development, by overtaxing superfluous products and encouraging the production of social interests. Thus, the law taxed cars and watches at a rate of 20%, as well as beer and other items at 15%. The taxes were 3% of annual wages for those earning up to US$4 thousand per year, and 60% for those who earned more than US$500 thousand per year. (RODRÍGUEZ GARCÍA et al., 1985, p.69-70) Another measure requested that workers voluntarily donate 4% of their monthly wages to a government fund. Even though the burden might be heavy in the beginning, the Cuban rulers thought that this was the correct path for the economic development of the country.

The influence of the ECLA concepts could be seen in those first moments of the revolution. According to main theoreticians of the ECLA, it was necessary to embark on a structural reconditioning of trade relations with the centers, combining in a rational manner, the industrial exports with their substitute. (PREBISCH, 1981, p.9) Raúl Prebisch remarked that his objective was to transform the system by means of concrete solutions, starting from the socialization of economic surplus, correcting, as a consequence, the huge social inequalities and accelerating the pace of the growth. (PREBISCH, 1981, p.11)[4] In the 1950s Octavio Rodríguez, another theoretician of the ECLA, expressed the committee's main ideas about economic development as exemplified in the improvement of the material well-being of the population, which in turn was a reflection of the increase in the real per capita income and the growth of average labor productivity. (RODRÍGUEZ, 1981, p.36) In the international sphere, the relation between center and periphery was consolidated in a scheme in which the underdeveloped countries served to produce and export raw materials and unfinished products, while the advanced capitalist nations were in charge of producing manufactured articles for the entire system.

That scenario should be modified for real development to take place in some economically underdeveloped regions, with domestic policies that ensured accumulation, technical progress and a significant increase in employment. If the picture of technical-industrial development of the center and the traditional role of the periphery as producer and exporter of primary products remained static in the same historical patterns, the real development of the "underdeveloped" economies wouldn't be possible. The only way to overcome that inversion would be, necessarily, starting from a certain point of relative domestic accumulation, general aspects of the international economy and difficulty in allocating the labor force in the domestic labor market, investing in industrialization projects, which was the "compulsory path" for those countries. Therefore, industrialization would be the "main" and "necessary" path for the economic growth of developing countries. (RODRÍGUEZ, 1981, p.45)

But there would certainly be many difficulties in this new "development period", considering, among other factors, that the labor surplus of technically backward sectors displaced to new production units with modern technologies would create an adaptation phase that could result in an initial reduction of production. At this first stage, therefore, unemployment, though reduced, would still exist, as well as imbalances between sectors within the production sector. The expansion of the industrial sector would be important to enabling the periphery to grow at a faster pace than the center. At the same time, due to a possible external imbalance, policies that restrict imports would be necessary, limiting the entrance of certain articles and encouraging their production domestically, impeding the entrance of superfluous items, changing the characteristic of imported goods in general — gradually encouraging and deepening the imports substitution process.

In the sphere of State policy, economic planning should be implemented, that is, a conscious action and one backed by the government to ensure that resources are allocated correctly. According to the ECLA, therefore, the leaders of developing countries would have to promote initiatives that increased national savings, create effective fiscal policy mechanisms, control and allocate credit resources, have the capacity to attract foreign capital, invest in important sectors of the economy — both in infrastructure and in direct production — gradually relocate labor from agriculture to the industrial sector and invest in technology.

Although Guevara (1982, p.100) stated that "Dr. Prebisch" was "clearly on the side of the wretched", the stance of the Argentinean revolutionary was always more tied to Leninist concepts than to those of the ECLA. It should also be noted that many of his aides were members of the Chilean and Soviet CPs, and that the ideas of the ECLA were initially influential because, at the time, they constituted an interesting theoretical outline that couldn't be dismissed. But Che was aware that "autonomous" development could take place with the compliance of foreign powers, with interests on the island. Development according to new patterns would be very difficult, including those proposed by the ECLA, within the broader picture of monopolist capitalism.[5] Since Guevara was flexible and heterodox in economic terms, he was open to suggestions and to the application of ideas that were most efficient for the Cuban economy - but only in strictly technical terms - conceptually speaking, he couldn't admit that it was possible to implement profound measures according to the monopolist capitalist system of that time.

Even before the revolution, some conservative personalities linked to the Batista government, as well as progressive critics, already pointed out the need for industrialization and the conceptual differences of the term "development" in the Cuban case. Trade union leader Eusébio Mujal, for example, suggested, on May 1958, in his work *National Plan for the Strengthening and Development of the Cuban Economy*: an agrarian reform; the implementation of limits on the prices of products; the development of an aggressive trade policy to promote the diversification of exports; encouraging import substitution; increasing the income tax; ending indirect taxes; the creation of new protectionist tariffs — mainly on food and finished consumer goods from the United States — and the development of a broad popular housing project for the peasants and the urban workers. (O'CONNOR, 1972, p.76)

Carlos Rafael Rodríguez, a member of the PSP, attacked those who thought that "development" would be equivalent to growth of export activities or the ongoing process of domestic and foreign investments which, supposedly (with the increase of the amount of per capita capital of the production sector) would raise the productivity of the worker, the savings capability and consumption. He believed that the idea of "development" related to the rise in sugar production would also mean a detour from the path and ultimately moving away from development. (RODRÍGUEZ, 1983b, p.41) According to that author, the several definitions of the term don't tackle its main problem, that is, the structural form of the economy, since it would be impossible to develop a country that lacked advanced production forces. The Cuban economy could have "grown" in the years before the revolution, but it hadn't actually "developed". Rodríguez said that there couldn't be development without a certain level of industrialization, with simultaneous growth in several spheres of the production sector. (RODRÍGUEZ, 1983b, p.42) He also believed that, among the "bourgeois theoreticians" of economic development, Raúl Prebisch had the most accurate theoretical picture of that process. The member of the PSP claimed that he agreed "unreservedly" with Prebisch on the development process. In the Cuban case, however, development should go beyond merely technical improvement in agriculture, or industrialization limited to agricultural products. (RODRÍGUEZ, 1983b, p.57) According to him:

> But we go somewhat further than Wallich, further than Pazos and further than Prebisch and the ECLA technicians. The latter, in their most recent contribution, called *Analysis and Projections of Economic Development,* assign a double role to the government: to use the fiscal and credit monetary instruments, to create a proper environment for the private enterprise and to execute those basic undertakings that the private enterprise couldn't execute, for one reason or another. Considering the historical conditions of our development, we believe that the government must take a step further, not only in the realm of investment, but also in that of the regulatory policy. […]
>
> We must go further. Some industrial sectors that have a great strategic importance for the development of the country might only be able to operate with net losses at first. And, due to their importance to the economic process itself, they might have to be, despite that, developed. In that sense, as has already been noticed by several economists, one can't take as an index what is decisive for the private businessman, that is, the marginal productivity of the business, but the social productivity. A development plan will have to take the necessary measures to transfer the profits of the profitable state-owned enterprises to others that are not, or to use state funds obtained by loan to support, temporarily, while those sectors consolidate themselves. (RODRÍGUEZ, 1983b, p.59-61)

Before the revolution, Rodríguez already defended the nationalization of the foreign banks and the public services. He also supported control of foreign trade and of the exchange rates. He believed that the using fiscal, contingency or multiple exchange rate measures would be crucial to inhibiting or prohibiting the consumption of certain luxury products, establishing new bases for foreign trade, stimulating national industry, increasing domestic consumption and encouraging the diversification of production. (RODRÍGUEZ, 1983b, p.65) He believed that the lack of a domestic market was one of the reasons for the country's limited economic development. In practice, there couldn't be a prosperous economy if almost half the population wasn't a part of the consumer market system. The production capacity of the shoe industry in the 1950's, for example, was approximately 24 to 32 million pairs of shoes, while their consumption in Cuba never surpassed, at best, 10 to 12 million pairs. (RODRÍGUEZ, 1983b, p.141) The country, which had around six million inhabitants, only had a global production capacity for three million people. Most of the Cuban industries were small and, among the 14 largest, with more than 500 workers each, were Textilera Ariguanabo, Cervecera Nacional Hatuey, Nickaro Nickel Company, the Compañia Nacional de Alimentos, Crusellas y Compañia, Polar and Tropical. These enterprises, with the exception of Nickaro Nickel Company, produced articles for personal consumption, often superfluous or at least non-essential, and that didn't represent a real base for the development of an industrial structure in the country *de facto.* (RODRÍGUEZ, 1983b, p.147) It would also be necessary for the population to increase, since Cuba needed more labor and it needed to increase its consumer market. According to Rodríguez, for a significant increase in production to take place it would take at least US$500 million per year to invest in machinery, and another US$200 million to maintain the country's existing industrial apparatus. (RODRÍGUEZ, 1983b, p.171)

Regino Boti and Felipe Pazos, on the other hand, outlined an analysis of the amount of domestic savings necessary to finance the investments over ten years which, theoretically, would eliminate the problem of unemployment, thus using ideal models based on estimates of existent capital in the government funds, labor figures in agriculture and industry, existent idle capacity and the low productivity of social capital. The economists believed that it would require US$200 million per year, the equivalent of the total of funds of the National Bank at the time. (O'CONNOR, 1972, p.78-79)

The post-revolution economic project was largely influenced by ECLA — many of its ideas were being discussed in Cuba in the 1950's — as well as by a more "radical" course of action advocated by the communists. In practice, the proposals were very similar; the main difference, in the beginning of the process, was the emphasis on deepening the measures, not necessarily on their content. But, as has already been stated, Guevara's background, as well as that of many of his aides, led the Argentinean revolutionary to become increasingly politically radical, and to propose more original projects for the economic sector.

Guevara believed that there were many reasons for the stagnation of underdeveloped countries, intrinsic to the very "nature" of the advanced capitalist system, which expanded, among other factors, by means of the control of production and trade of the raw materials, and by means of the penetration of capital as a crucial condition for economic dependence to be established. This would present itself in "open" forms, such as loans, investments, control of foreign trade by international monopolies and the use of force as economic power. It would also occur in more "subtle" forms, such as the use of international organs, both financial and credit, among many others, to interfere with and control national economies and foreign trade in the developing countries. (ARIET, 1988, p.139) According to Guevara:

> The International Monetary Fund is the Cerberus of the dollar in the capitalist sphere. The International Bank for Reconstruction and Development is the penetration instrument of American capital in the underdeveloped world, and the Inter-American Development Bank fulfills that sad function within the American Continent. All those organs are guided by rules and principles that are intended to be presented as safeguards of the equity and reciprocity in the international economic relations,

> when, in truth, they are nothing more than fetishes behind which the more subtle instruments for the perpetuation of the backwardness and exploitation hide. The International Monetary Fund, supposedly watching over the stability of the kinds of exchange, and over the liberalization of the international subsidies and profits, only hinders the minimum defense measures of the underdeveloped countries before the competition and the penetration of the foreign monopolies. (GUEVARA, 1981a, p.64)

Between 1951 and 1954, for example, the revenues of the foreign monopolies in Latin America reached US$3.276 million, while the introduction of capital to those countries was US$662 million. In turn, the global total of American investments between 1957 and 1960 in all the developing countries increased by US$1.83 billion, while profits were US$6 billion in the same period. The profits transferred from Latin America to the United States in 1962 were US$761 million, in 1963 they were US$801 million and in 1964 they were US$965 million. (VAKHRUCHEV, 1975, p.63-64)

It is documented that the profits received by the United States were significantly greater than the capital exported to Latin American countries, the combined foreign debt of which was US$10.5 billion in 1964. (VAKHRUCHEV, 1975, p.73) By practicing dumping, the United States, backed by Law n.480, undermined the Latin American economies, since sending their production surpluses — with the funding of exports by means of its own budget and by means of "aide" and "reciprocity" agreements — only made it more difficult to develop national production. In turn, the monopolies controlled several spheres of industrial production and established products and prices. Thus, the development of those countries was linked to the monopolies while ensuring production would trickle into other markets with favorable prices. With protectionist policies, the American government established limits and imposed tariffs on certain products to safeguard domestic sectors. If the full operation of the monopolist structure and of privileged relations among governments wasn't guaranteed, such countries as the United States claimed they had the right to intervene militarily or to support opposition groups in order to restore the *status quo* and support for their interests.

The international credit mechanisms were also used to maintain an ongoing domination of the underdeveloped countries. The IBRD, which had its outlines sketched in Bretton Woods, in 1944, and was officially created in 1945, had an initial subscription sum of US$9.1 billion. Of this, US$ 3.175 billion were supplied by the United States, US$1.3 billion by England, US$450 million by France, US$325 million by Canada, US$225 million by Belgium, US$275 million by the Netherlands and US$200 million by Australia. Each member would have 250 votes plus 1 vote for each "fraction" of US$100,000 of its initial deposit, which enabled the United States to control the organization. (VAKHRUCHEV, 1975, p.186-187) In 1963, the subscription shares of the member countries reached US$20.7 billion, while the sum of the United States' subscription capital reached US$5.715 billion. (VAKHRUCHEV, 1975, p.188-189) In turn, the net profit of the bank was US$558 million in 1963, distributed among all the participants. The loans to needy countries were made at an interest rate between 5% and 7% per year. Between 1960 and 1965, only the payments considered as reimbursement to the underdeveloped countries reached US$627 million. (VAKHRUCHEV, 1975, p.191) Analyses of the domestic economic situation and the possible solutions to the underdevelopment problems, explained and sent by the governments of the indebted countries, should necessarily be made according to the models set by the IBRD and approved by them, for the credits to be granted, providing guarantees that those countries would pay back the loan. Cuba wasn't linked to that institution after 1960.

The Inter-American Development Bank (IADB), in turn, was established in 1959 as a regional version analogous to the IBRD, with clauses that coincided with those of the previous organization. Article 1 of the IADB Charter assigned to the institution the role of encouraging private investments in the continent. With an initial fund of US$800 million, IADB was also structured to favor American control, since each member country was entitled to 135 votes plus 1 vote per share, and the United States had 35 thousand shares, the equivalent to 40% of all the organization's shares. (VAKHRUCHEV, 1975, p.241-242) Among the other members, only Brazil and Argentina had a quota of just over 10,000 shares. Although a council of managers met once a year, the effective power was concentrated in the Board of Directors and their assistants, who were appointed by the government and were able to vote on their behalf. The IADB, which actually began to operate in 1961, used capital loaned at annual interest rates of up to 8%, from other banks in countries with advanced capitalism. (VAKHRUCHEV, 1975, p.245)

Finally, the International Monetary Fund (IMF), outlined during the Bretton Woods Conference, in 1944, took effect on December 27th, 1945, and began its actual activities on March 1st, 1947, with an original capital of US$8.8 billion. With a US$2.75 billion share in the institution — far above the other members — the United States ensured 27,750 votes, or 37.9% of the votes of the founding members. In 1959, the year that the Cuban Revolution triumphed, the founding members of the IMF increased their shares, which rose from US$9.228 billion to US$14.261 billion by 1963. The American share, in this case, reached US$4.125 billion. In 1965, there was a new increase of shares belonging to developed countries, which reached approximately US$3 billion, while the shares of 74 "underdeveloped" countries reached only US$1 billion at the time. (VAKHRUCHEV, 1975, p.274-276)

Between 1947 and 1965, the total of IMF loans reached US$10.8 billion. With a foreign debt of US$36.4 billion in 1965, Latin America had to pay US$1.7 billion. (VAKHRUCHEV, 1975, p.295) Between 1953 and 1963, the trade volume of raw materials and semi-finished products increased by 5.3%, with a 4% reduction in prices, while the trade of industrialized products grew by 6.8%, with an 8% increase in prices, that is, a balance that clearly favored the industrialized countries. (VAKHRUCHEV, 1975,299) To solve the problems in the balance of payments, the developing nations were forced to increase their loan requests. Thus, in 1964 the IMF granted the equivalent of US$180 million in loans to those countries. (VAKHRUCHEV, 1975, p.304-305) Among the preliminary measures that the IMF took to grant credits there were, among other factors: monetary reforms (such as the devaluation of the local currency), freezing of wages, destruction of the "artificial industries" — those industries that in general didn't use national raw materials — liberation of the economy from governmental control, balancing the State budget, and elimination of the bureaucracy. All those measures were oppressive, forcing the local governments to greatly restrict their activities and to act according to the interests of the developed countries.

Guevara believed that underdevelopment was the result of the unequal trade between the countries producing raw materials and the developed ones. The advanced capitalist nations could control markets and create obstacles to the improvement of economic conditions in other regions of the world. Several measures should be implemented for the full development of the "underdeveloped" countries and to resolve the critical inequity of trade and poverty in the Third World. In the continental realm this could establish defense and trade union mechanisms counter to US interests, and in the international realm, redefine foreign trade by means of a "new world economic order". Initially this would involve elimination of all commercial discrimination; equitable trade; a new international division of labor — with the full use of all of the countries' natural resources — reaching "advanced" technical development; reinstatement of the traditional markets; and concrete uses for surplus production. (ARIET, 1988, p.139-140) Many people thought that those propositions were somewhat idealistic. On January 18th, 1965, however, in an interview with the magazine *Prensa Latina* and with the newspaper *L'Etincel,* he clarified his position and denied that he wanted to create a "common market" in Latin America:

> I didn't say that. In fact, Latin America is dominated by the United States and, under those conditions, it's impossible to make a progressive Latin American market. The Latin American countries might unite in a production zone when they free themselves and reach socialism. That's an inevitable reality, but it belongs to the future of the unit of the revolutionary movements of Latin America, and it wouldn't make sense to predict the nature of that trade union (if by means of a central Latin American government or some other form). First we must reach that stage. The problems are remote. It would be risky to talk about the conception of a central Latin American government today. (GUEVARA, 1982, p.272)[6]

Guevara insisted that in order to quickly develop a certain economy, it wasn't crucial for the government to take control of all means of production, but he believed that "such measure would solve the serious problems being discussed, faster and with greater efficiency". (GUEVARA, 1981a, p.73) About the specific case of industrialization in Cuba, he said:

> Even today, despite the effort made — which, I believe, has been very big and very well managed — it can't be said that there's an industry fully designed and built by the National Agrarian Reform Institute within the sphere of its Industrialization Department; since those are, as I have said before, long-term tasks. There's a textile industry that will

> commence operation in about four or five months; a pencil plant that will be starting in two or three months … But, as you can see, the effort yields much less than in agriculture. Besides, the investments are large, and the number of employed workers is comparatively much smaller than what is possible in agriculture or fishing, for example. Also, we must completely destroy that cancer of the Cuban economy, which is unemployment. That is, it is imperative that we give much emphasis to agriculture, to fishing, to all kinds of activities — still within industry — that may ensure a high employment rate with a relatively low investment level.
> Therefore, even knowing that the basis of the industrialization is heavy industry, we have taken slower steps as far as the heavy industry is concerned and we have devoted ourselves more to developing the small industry, manufacturing, the one that employs more workers than this other industry, which is very heavy, very technical, very productive in terms of capital and of product in itself, but that employs few people. Besides, since those industries are highly technical, we would also have to rely on skilled foreign workers. (GUEVARA, 1988b, p.92)

During the entire period that he was in charge of the National Bank, Guevara maintained an intense schedule of appointments, culminating with his trip, beginning on October 21st, 1960, to several countries of the socialist block, where he led a commercial delegation.[7] His trip lasted more than two months and included Czechoslovakia, the Soviet Union, East Germany, Hungary, North Korea and China. He was escorted by his bodyguard, Leonardo Tamayo, the sub secretary of Foreign Relations, Héctor Rodríguez Llompart, and was aided by some Latin American Marxist economists. His performance as head of the delegation at that particular moment was of great importance.

In Prague, Guevara visited a tractor plant and obtained a US$20 million credit to install an assembly plant for making tractors, trucks and engines in Cuba, extending the agreement that had already been established by the Czech Minister of Foreign Trade on the island. Agreements were also signed for the installation of small workshops, such as one to produce screws, built in Santiago de Cuba.

Later, he went to the Soviet Union, where he stayed from October 29th to November 14th, 1960. Moscow promised to buy 2.7 million tons of Cuban sugar. An agreement was made with the Soviets, who would undertake geological probes on the island to locate mineral riches such as copper, nickel and manganese. The USSR also promised to build a rasp plant and another for spare parts, which, according to Che, would be "strategically crucial" for the country, this in addition to a complete sugar refinery, with a capacity of 1 million tons per year. (GUEVARA, 1982, p.103-105) The President of the National Bank also wanted to negotiate a steel mill with a production capacity of 1 million tons of steel, and to obtain financing to increase steel production from 70,000 tons to approximately 1.5 million tons in the short term. Che believed that, in ten years, Cuba could be one of the largest steel producers on the continent. (BANDEIRA, 1998, p.298)

On November 17th of that year, the Cuban delegation arrived in China, where it obtained a US$60 million credit with no interest, to be paid off in fifteen years. Guevara was impressed by the Chinese government's political attitude, he stated:

> We had a discussion with Prime-Minister Chou En-lai, when a joint communiqué was signed, in which the Cuban delegation wrote in a paragraph: "The disinterested help of the socialist countries". That generated a long philosophical debate, because they absolutely refused to admit the word "disinterested". They said that they would provide no help, but an interested help. And it was actually an interested help, without monetary interest, because Cuba was one of the countries in the frontline of the struggle against imperialism at that moment, and imperialism is the common enemy of all people. Helping Cuba was in the interest of all socialist countries. Thus, the expression "disinterested help" was changed to just "help". (GUEVARA, 1982, p.108)

Guevara went to Pyongyang on December 3rd, describing North Korea as one of the most "extraordinary" countries he had visited with his delegation. Guevara's interest seems to have been, on that occasion, moral rather than economic. His attention was captured primarily by the population's ability to rebuild their nation after many years of war. When he spoke on Cuban television on January 6th, 1961, Guevara tried to demonstrate that even though Korea had a relatively small territory — approximately 110,000 kilometers — and with only 10 million people, it was able to overcome huge adversities, as a result of the "spirit" of the North Korean people, who fought against foreign domination of their political system, and of "extraordinary" rulers, such as Marshall Kim Il-sung, who transformed North Korea into an industrialized country.

Guevara returned to Moscow on the 8th of the same month and shortly thereafter continued on to East Germany, where he obtained loans equivalent to 10 million pesos. Che considered this a very significant gesture, since the GDR was undergoing financial difficulties. The attitude of the East Germans was supposedly an example of socialist "solidarity".

The Cuban delegation went back to Czechoslovakia and obtained an increase of the credit extended in the first visit. From there, he went to Hungary and then returned to Cuba. Later, Guevara said that, if Antonio Nuñez Jimenez — who had been to the socialist block before him — was nicknamed "Alice in Wonderland", for having praised those nations so much, then Che, himself, after returning from his journey, had been even more impressed and should be nicknamed "Alice in Wonder Continent". (GUEVARA, 1982, p.107) As it is known, some time later he changed his mind drastically. But, at that specific moment, Guevara believed that the agreements had provided conditions for Cuba not to remain an exclusively agrarian country and to become, at least, an agrarian and industrial nation by 1965. (GUEVARA, 1982, p.111) Even though the agreements were not profound, in practice, to the extent of radically changing the Cuban industrial structure, they were extremely important in tightening commercial ties with the socialist countries and for the future development of the country.

---

[1]For further information on the backstage of the new revolutionary government formation, see Buch Rodríguez (1999).

---

[2]It must be recalled that during the revolutionary war Guevara stood out as an innovator and entrepreneur, since he had encouraged the creation of small industries in the peasant villages, such as bakeries, workshops, shoe making and plants for the production of rough bombs.

---

[3]About Noyola, Celso Furtado said: "[...] he had studied economy at the Autonomous University of Mexico and he was a legitimate representative of the generation that graduated with the enthusiasm of the revolutionary journeys of Lázaro Cárdenas's phase. [...] The awareness that his country had made a forward leap in History was clear to Noyola. In its spirit, History only advances on the wings of a revolution and all the revolutions of a certain period result from the same historical mutation. And Mexico was in the center of the revolutionary process of the 20th Century. [...] At the time Noyola studied, a Marxism that was fundamentally a mix between agrarianism and anti-imperialism was predominant in Mexico's Economics tradition. The roots of the oppression that victimized the people were probably located in the large landed estate structures and in the international domination. [...] Noyola imagined himself as a Marxist when he thought in political terms, but he was the first one to resort to the instruments of conventional economic analysis when specifically economic problems were addressed. He had a full background as an economist and the two years that he spent in the IMF had vaccinated him against monetarism". (FURTADO, 1985, p.125-126)

---

[4]For further information on the ECLA and the ideas of Raúl Prebisch, see Prebisch (1962, 1964). For details of Raúl Prebisch's thought, see Grespan (2001).

[5]For a criticism to the ideas of the ECLA, see Losada Aldana (1968).

[6]Noyola, however, believed that a common market on the continent was possible: "It is said that the Latin American countries are not complementary economies, but rather quite competitive ones. In other words, [...] they are more or less specialized in the same kinds of products for export outside the Latin American area, and almost all their imports are obtained in other supply centers outside Latin America. [...] That can't be a decisive argument or a reason to discard the possibilities of increasing trade within Latin America, since the complementary nature or the competitive position of the economies doesn't result from natural laws. [...] But most of the world trade doesn't take place between tropical and industrial countries; it takes place [among] industrial countries [...], and the factors that determine the specialization in commerce between the industrial countries are not exclusively geographical or differences in natural resources. [...] The relations between colonies and the countries that have them are more intense than they would be if those colonies were independent, due to the investments made in them, the existence of paid agreements, several factors of an institutional or historical kind or of relative prices that are not directly related to the endowment of resources. As a consequence, the complementary nature or the competitiveness of the economies are not vague, they are liable to historical change, especially as it influences economic policy more, in that sense". (NOYOLA, 1978a, p.88-90) On the other hand, Noyola acknowledged that "of course a common market can only make sense when the Latin American countries actually achieve their economic independence, that is, when they enact profound agrarian reform, when they destroy the power of the imperialist monopolies and when they are able to industrialize themselves according to the interests of their own people and through the use of their natural resources". (NOYOLA, 1978a, p.139)

[7]In 1959, Guevara had already led a diplomatic mission to several countries. On that occasion, he visited Egypt, India, Indonesia, Ceylon, Burma, Japan, Sudan, Morocco, Pakistan and Yugoslavia. The objective of that trip was to strengthen the commercial and diplomatic ties with those nations.

2

ADMINISTRATION, PLANNING AND PRODUCTIVITY

Che Guevara left the post of President of the National Bank shortly after his trip to the socialist countries and, on February 23rd, 1961, he became Cuba's Minister of Industry. That was the position he wanted: he had never hidden his desire to manage the industrial sector, and the choice was almost natural for him under those circumstances. Once again, his domestic prestige and his experience in the Industrialization Department of INRA and in the National Bank helped with the decision. Besides, he was always worried about issues concerning Cuban development, and his performance as head of the commercial delegation became very significant when he took up his new post.

His first task was to appoint a Board of Directors, which included well-known people such as Orlando Borrego, Gustavo Machín, Juan Valdés Gravalosa, Júlio Cáceres, José Manresa, Enrique Oltuski and Alberto Mora. With that staff, he would try to manage the enterprises inherited from the old department, as well as many others that had recently been nationalized. All of the agricultural industries were outside of his sphere, they were under INRA, and the construction sector was under the Ministry of Public Works. But Guevara had to worry about managing the *chinchales* — small craft industries, such as the shoe plants and the tobacco industry — which was not easy. The mechanization and rationalization of these industries would leave thousands of workers unemployed. Thus, between 5,000 and 6,000 workers connected to the shoe sector would have to be transferred to larger plants or to other areas. This took place until 1964, with the increase of the industrial sector. Many *chinchales* were eliminated and others were modernized. That is to say, those small production units were consolidated and received new technology, even though many workers had still not adapted to this new arrangement within the Cuban economy.

In 1954, there were 830 "industries" with no more than five workers each, 45.1% of the total of the country; approximately 333 small plants with six to ten employees, which represented 18.2% of the total; others, employing between eleven and twenty-five men, were 320, or 17.3% of the total; around 250 industries had between twenty-six and one hundred workers, the equivalent to 13.6% of the plants; 67 of them had between one hundred and one and two hundred and fifty workers, 3.6% of the total; only 26 had between two hundred and fifty-one and five hundred workers on staff, or 1.4%; and only 14 had more than five hundred, which represented 0.8% of the total (LOPEZ SEGRERA, 1972, p.352). From this industrial reorganization on, the number of workers in the plants grew from 112,000 to 155,000 between 1962 and 1963, a 38% increase of workers in the country's industries (GUEVARA, 1982, p.120). Thus, in 1962, for example, there were already only 97 plants with no more than five workers each, which represented 8% of the total; there were 102 with six to ten workers, or 8.5% of the Cuban industrial picture; around 259 plants had between eleven and twenty-five employees, the equivalent to 21.7% of the total; 532 had between twenty-six and one hundred employees, or 44.4% of the total; those between one hundred and one and two hundred and fifty workers raised to 140, that is, 11.7% of that picture; there was also an increase in those between two hundred and fifty-one and five hundred workers, which reached 43 in that year, or 3.6%; and, finally, a significant growth in those with five hundred or more employees, which reached 25, or 2.4% of the total of the island (LOPEZ SEGRERA, 1972, p.352).

Once again, Guevara acknowledged, and repeated many times, that he wasn't an "expert" in the area; but he felt it was his duty to act (since he was part of the revolutionary government) and he was moved by the enthusiasm to build Cuba's industrial sector. About the recently created Ministry he said:

> Cuba's Ministry of Industry is constituted according to the dynamics of our economic development, to the youth of our institutions and to the changing nature of the panorama, in such a way that it isn't, absolutely, strict or schematic. It changes completely and constantly, and the flow chart that I will present now might change in a few months, because we're constantly advancing in our needs, which impose on us the difficult task of industrialization. It's even more challenging because we, the heads of this Ministry, the directors of this Ministry and most of the Cuban workers, are learning as we go. Of course, the learning process includes mistakes, and those mistakes must be corrected. (GUEVARA,.1982, p.27)

Some time after becoming Minister, Che talked to the Russian writer Boris Polevoi in Havana:

> I'm a physician by profession, but now, fulfilling my revolutionary duty, I'm the Minister of Industry. [...] I believe that this might not be a surprise to you, since Vladimir Lenin was a lawyer by profession, and among his ministers there were physicians, jurists and famous engineers [...] The revolution is the revolution, and the revolutionary need distributes men in its own way. If when I was in Fidel's —whom I'm proud to call an old friend — detachment (and I acted specifically as a physician in that detachment) and we boarded the yacht *Granma*, someone had said that I would become one of the organizers of the economy, I would have laughed. (LAVRETSKI, 1975, p.175)

The creation of the Ministry led by Che was part of a broader change within the institutions of the Cuban government. In 1961, a few state-owned organs were restructured, a crucial factor in advancing the plan of the island's economy. Thus, organic laws of the National Bank and of the Ministry of Foreign Trade were promulgated (so that they would adapt to the new conditions of the Cuban economic policy) and the Ministry of Industry was created. The main strategies of that last measure were to try to eliminate the monoculture and to provide an agricultural diversification as a basis for a development of the national industry. At that point, a few outlines to further this goal were established, such as: energy and fuels; steel industry and metal products in general; sugar industry and its by-products; chemical industry; development of the mining sector; and agricultural industry. (PÉREZ-ROLO, 1989, p.261)

This economic restructuring gave JUCEPLAN more powers. It would still have prominence in the national plan, but would be aided by the Coordination, Execution and Inspection Committees (JUCEI), which were put in charge of inspection and information tasks at the local level. The first JUCEI was established in the province of Oriente, in the middle of 1961, by Raúl Castro, who was the Minister of the Revolutionary Armed Forces at the time. JUCEI's main task was to see that each locality and institution was properly informed of the decisions made by the government and the Ministries, as well as ensuring the enactment of the plans in the provinces. It coordinated the activities of other governmental organs, and ensured the plan's execution and efficacy in the provinces; in addition, it made sure worker efficiency was maximized and the people and the authorities maintained a good rapport. (MESA-LAGO, [197-], p 28-31)

The first Cuban plan[1] was scheduled for implementation in 1961, but due to difficulties with production organization, it was postponed. Thus, given its late start in 1962, what was initially a five-year plan became a four-year plan. Annual plans were also outlined for 1963 and 1964, showing that they could vary depending on the geographical location and on the terms of their fulfillment. These strategies were meant to regulate several aspects of production, from quantity and quality of the products to the productivity of workers, wages, production cost and volume of investments. (MESA-LAGO, [197-], p.35) According to some critics, the first plan was developed with the help of several technicians, five Soviet, two Czech, one Polish and one East German. Even the Ambassador of the Soviet Union, Sergei Mikhailovich Kuzmin, apparently participated in the debates as well. During this planning period, the revolutionary government already had an industrial sector worth US$2.6 billion, forty-three banks, thirty insurance companies, fishing, mining, housing and transportation systems, as well as 95% of the country's agricultural sector. (RIVERO, 1963, p.90)

Shortly after this governmental restructuring Guevara decided to implement the so-called "budgetary finance system" more vigorously. At the end of 1960, INRA's Industrialization Department already managed several nationalized enterprises using that system. They had an overall lack of qualified technical staff and scant resources, often belonging to the same production chain. To circumvent these problems, a centralized bank fund was created — according to the Department's assessment —to make up for what the plants, as a whole, lacked. Capital was directed and distributed to where it was needed at the time, in order to generate greater production efficiency. From this, the "consolidated enterprises" emerged, that is, production units that worked as a part of a larger, governmentally controlled company.

Guevara believed that, in the budgetary finance system, a company was a conglomerate of plants or units with a similar technological basis, a common destination to its production or a limited geographical location. In practice, that was equivalent to saying that the private monopoly would be replaced by the state monopoly and that the planning and management of the enterprises would be centralized. As a result, they wouldn't have bank credit, since money would be made available by means of the central organs. In 1964, in a conversation with members of the government, Guevara stated:

> To face our problems, the path is, on the contrary, the improvement of our budgetary system, which is unified financing; and deepening the causes, the internal motor effects, the specific relations that exist in socialism between the individual and society, to use new economic development instruments and use them to their full extent, which has not occurred until now [...] My opinion is that the budgetary system means, in all its aspects, a step forward; it allows us to intervene in due time in the system where it's necessary, avoiding imbalances, and according to an advanced form of management, such as the monopoly. This might seem a contradictory statement, but it's correct. (GUEVARA, 1982, p.58)

Such overvaluation of the budgetary finance system was controversial and, later, reason for the accusation that Guevara was one of the main culprits responsible for the Cuban economic problems.

To manage the "consolidated enterprises" more effectively, Guevara divided the Ministry — according to the model previously implemented in the Department — into a Board of Directors, which met every week, and four sub secretariats: heavy industry, light industry, economy and industrial construction. The sub secretaries — which were later called Vice-Ministers — were also responsible for directly managing the enterprises, worrying about the maximum use of the installed capacity in the country and the coordination of the means of production. Later, three main Boards of Directors were established: that of General Inspection (the function of which was to inspect and audit the accounting operations of the Ministry and other government areas), Personnel (which selected and hired the Ministry's employees and oversaw work conditions, trained personnel, evaluated human resources and ranked posts) and Internal Services (which provided legal services, took care of the Central Library and of vigilance and internal security). In addition, there were other complementary Boards, which will be discussed briefly later. An advertising agency was created, which was extremely important for disseminating the institution's measures to the people and in gaining popular support.

The consolidated enterprises consisted of sugar, electricity, cement, ceramics, medicine, mining in general, paper, oil, fertilizers, synthetic fibers and basic chemistry, among others. Although the Ministry initially encouraged the project of centralizing the Cuban economy, it encountered several difficulties along the way, including a lack of technicians and expert staff. Of course, when Che advocated the centralization he didn't leave the lower levels out of the decision process. The amount of centralization could have some flexibility and vary according to the kind of production or service; emphasizing that encouraging individual participation in the plants was crucial. He had no desire to "mechanize" the people. An interesting anecdote about Guevara's relationship with the employees and technicians of the Cuban industries was an exchange he had with Francisco Hernández, a technician in a soft drink plant:

> The first thing he asked me was if I was the technician of that department. When I answered that I was, he continued to question me, to find out what we were doing to substitute imports. We were struggling to find a syrup that would match the flavor of Coca-Cola. I showed him some of the vats holding the test syrups. With a movement of his hand, he indicated that things were not going well.
> "What are you doing to solve the problem?" he asked.
> I explained to him that I hadn't slept for many nights trying to find that blessed substitute, but we didn't have the basic ingredients.
> "They must be found, right?" he said.
> I told him we would find them. [...]
> One day, when Che was speaking on television, he said that the soft drink tasted like cough syrup. That hurt me a lot; I was

> offended because I was doing all I could. At the first opportunity, I expressed my feelings to him. He responded:
> "We must be honest and always tell the truth. We should not only speak about what's good, but also criticize what's bad".
> "But if we improved the taste, Commander…"
> "That's not enough. We must provide the best to the people, and you shouldn't feel offended, because you belong to the people; I'm certain that you will continue your efforts to achieve a product of maximum quality."
> Time went by, and we continued experimenting. One day, I was surprised to hear his voice calling me. He had recognized me in the middle of the street and he simply said:
> "Congratulations, Pancho. The flavor has improved one hundred percent". (CABRERA, 1987, p.143-144)

Centralized management in a national sphere proved to be necessary because of the greater potential for efficiency. When he developed a management system for the national economy, Che Guevara wanted to establish certain principles as a starting point, adapting their application, all the way from the base to the highest levels of the government.[2] As basic principles that directed his project, he encouraged the unity of political and economic directions; democratic centralism; collective debate; individual responsibility; the planned nature of management; the participation of the workers in management; and control in the lower and higher levels.

Once a month, Che called a meeting to analyze the total production of the ministry. In these meetings, which usually lasted from 2pm to midnight, the discussion ranged from administrative issues to specific product features. (CABRERA, 1987, p.144) Che would analyze each company individually, listen to what the administrative council had to say, and reach his conclusions later. Thus, by combining the smallest details of every action with a broad vision of the technical-economic development of a certain sphere of production, he would generate forecasts for the next twenty years. (CABRERA, 1987, p.144-145)[3] All the plants were visited personally every two months. Due to the strict technical need and to the high level of planning, finances played a crucial role. The purpose of finance, in the budgetary finance system, was control and training measurement, distribution and redistribution of funds, accounting of social work expenses in production and service, analysis and cost reduction in order to increase economic efficiency and financial discipline. (TABLADA PÉREZ, 1989, p.229)

When Guevara became Minister of Industry, the Ministry was divided into several different departments. The Supply and Sale Department[4] was in charge of the supply of raw materials and of sales to the various Cuban industries and the Ministry of Domestic Trade. The Labor and Wages Department analyzed the cost of production and pricing. The Finance Department was in charge of establishing financial control over each company's production plan. The Technical-Economic Cooperation Department, according to Che, was to receive the technical-economic "help" from the socialist block countries. The Relations with Private Industries Department was limited in practice, due to the reduction of the country's private sector. The Organization Department was in charge of optimizing the entire structure as well as it could. (GUEVARA, 1982, p.31)

The Organization Department decided how and where to build a factory. Then it transmitted the information to the Sub secretary for Industrial Construction, which, by means of its Investments Department decided how and where the necessary investments would be directed. Then the Projects Department developed the plans for the plant, which could be discussed with technicians of other socialist countries and with the Technological Research Department. At the end of this process, the Projects Execution Department executed the plans.

According to Orlando Borrego, Guevara demanded strict discipline in managing the boards. If a member arrived ten minutes late he couldn't participate in the meeting, which lasted no more than four hours. In those meetings, topics of discussion were carefully chosen and prepared by the department boards ahead of time; this included organizing all necessary documents. Collective participation was extremely important, because of the interconnection of the several sectors of the ministry. Directors of other organs were also invited to the Board if the discussion was related to other government areas. Once decisions were made, it was expected that they be strictly obeyed. It was important to avoid the centralization of issues in the Board of Directors of the Ministry because in some cases those responsibilities fell to other management levels. Another worry, mainly Guevara's, had to do with the quality of the record of proceedings. And, finally, a polite and calm environment was encouraged in the meetings. (BORREGO, 1989, p.326-327)

The Councils of Local Industries (CILOS) were created in an attempt to conciliate social interests with individual ones within Cuba's industrial sector. Their objective was to instill closer cooperation among industries in the same region. That system encouraged the exchange of goods and raw materials when one plant needed items that another could supply, according to their inventories and production cycle; exchanges of common use means of production; exchange of technical knowledge; mutual technical assistance; and collective debate, between the managers, over the laws and governmental regulations of production, to ensure that they had a unified interpretation. (BORREGO, 1989, p.329-330) Plant managers were required to attend the CILOS meetings to learn about better production techniques in other industries, as well as to share experiences concerning the management of socialist enterprises. (BORREGO, 2001a, p.288-289)

Within the budgetary finance system, Guevara developed subsystems for providing greater agility in the management of the plants, such as the subsystem of "organization" which was in charge of outlining specific goals for the several consolidated enterprises, and establishing flow charts and regulations for specific plants and workshops. Even though he was aware of the differences among the production units and their particular features, he established general courses of action that should be obeyed in all of them. The unique needs of the plants were dealt with by means of specific internal organic regulations developed by all of the workers and fulfilled by the company directors.

The main action techniques were also conveyed to the rulers, starting from the preparation, execution and control of the work. Each management level, therefore, was in charge of establishing some tasks according to the existent conditions, using simple "mottos" to explain to the workers what should be done. The directors, in turn, had to act according to the idea of "global management", that is, devote their attention to all phases and tasks of the plant as a whole, leaving the detailed execution of activity to lower management. Therefore, the heads of the Economic, Production and Exchange Departments, together with the director, made up the executive tier of a company.

According to the company management handbook developed by the Ministry of Industry, the economic management system should be tied to a system of maximum control. That meant suggesting control measures based on efficient information channels that allowed variations to be detected in the different levels of administration and that provided sufficient informative elements for the rulers to be able to make accurate assessments so they could act at the right time. In other words, a system of general accounting and cost analysis for the rational use and optimization of material resources, as well as for issues related to the labor and financial resources of the company should be prepared. The cost analysis should be done based on the comparison between the real costs and those of the plan, with the contribution of all levels of the company.

Control of inventory and accounting was also crucial. The handbook advised that, for operational control, the directors make periodical and systematic visits to the plants and that the workers themselves participate more in company matters. Each company should render yearly detailed accounts to the ministry, which next appointed a commission of experts to audit the management. After the commission had analyzed all company documents, it would make the necessary recommendations to the minister. On the other hand, costs and production of all enterprises would be controlled on a monthly basis, with inspections sometimes taking place every ten days. Approximately 60% of all industrial production would be mechanized, always taking into account the plan, the cost and the quality of the products. In general, the ministry commission was accompanied at the inspections by the Norms, Metrology and Quality Control Department, as well as by members of the Product Studies Department, which was in charge of industrial design and developing new products. Within the ministry, the Supervision and Audit Department became, as time went on, one of the government's most powerful control organs. After receiving the audits, the Vice-Minister transmitted the information to the Minister.

For stricter control to take place, the Administrative Disciplinary Commission (CODIAD) was created. This was a tribunal made up of personalities of "acknowledged prestige", which analyzed the cases to decide between punishment and acquittal. The punishments could vary from a warning and wage reduction to transfer to another sector and compulsory physical labor in Guanahacabibes, in the far west of the island. (BORREGO, 2001a, p.68-69)

When a company had to deliver materials to another government organ, such as the Ministry of Interior Trade (MINCIN), for example, there were meetings with the employees of that institution and with all those responsible for delivering the products to the client. That is, there was a close relationship between the Ministry of Industry and other organs of the government. (BORREGO, 1989, p.333-336) On the other hand, Che was aware that there were problems in the ministry, such as poor administration and a lack of communication among parallel, horizontal levels, so sectors and plants of the same kind sometimes operated differently and couldn't exchange experiences.

Guevara also took advantage of some aspects of the organizational structure of American enterprises on the island, aiming to execute industrial management more efficiently based on methods already proven to have positive results by the US enterprises. Because Cuba was small, with a limited industrial panorama, not much diversity in production and relatively quick means of transportation and communication between the plants, he believed that his system could work. The previous techniques would serve as the basis for developing both capitalism and socialism.

In Cuba's case, the "imperialist monopolies" that settled in the country, came before the budgetary finance system. (GUEVARA, 1982, p.188) Standard Oil, for example, distributed procedural handbooks to its employees with instructions to simplify accounting and prognoses in its production units. Reports indicated that the objective of the "plans" were to promote information. Estimates of net profits reflecting the changes as predicted in the results of operations, prices, costs and other factors; and also the reach that each affiliated unit would have to cover current operations and other input sources; their needs for capital expenses; the situation of the company's operation capital; and other figures for the company's administration. (KUCZYNKI, 1973, p.56)

As a method for predicting prices and sale volumes, Esso's Trade Department included in its accounting, the costs of maritime freight; insurance; the 2% currency redemption taxes; bank commission; customs rights; taxes on sales; and unloading expenses. (KUCZYNKI, 1973, p.58)

Even though the company's estimates were not extremely precise, they were relatively detailed. The 1958 prognosis indicated that there would be a 17.5% increase in the production of refined oils, 22.6% in that of gasoline and 37.8% in distilled fuel oils. In practice, there was a 3.8% increase in the production of refined oil, 12% in gasoline and 8.3% in the distilled fuel oils. In the beginning of 1959, the company had already made estimates for the following year, with fuel consumption forecasts until 1966, using the quantity of cars, trucks and buses that circulated in the country to reach an approximate figure. For the remaining uses of oil, Standard Oil analyzed the real number of consumers and consumption, as well as the growth of other sectors that would need the fuel. Even so, the prognoses for 1959 were incorrect.

The Compañia Cubana de Electricidad (CCE) also had an organizational structure directed towards maximizing its profits by means of plans. Between 1956 and 1960, the CCE elaborated a development and expansion strategy. The company's directors believed that a detailed plan, using scientific methods, could reduce costs, optimize and increase the production of electricity. To that end, the company put together a planning department to come up with both annual and long-term strategies. Finally, it received the assistance of the Ebasco International Corporation, created in 1942 by the American and Foreign Power Co. to study the financial position of enterprises, making prognoses and production and market surveys.

When the American monopolists left, they took their superior and intermediate technical staff with them. At the same time, a kind of prejudice developed among the revolutionaries in relation to certain procedures, simply because they were directly associated with the United States and with the bourgeoisie.[5] Thus, the proposed new system couldn't develop as fully as the foreign monopolies.

To a certain extent, Che Guevara agreed with the assumptions made by economists such as Oskar Lange, from Poland, whom he read and greatly admired. He claimed that:

> ...to manage a socialist economy, we must investigate what the bourgeois economy achieved in the area of the capitalist company's problems administrating (the fact, however, that such achievements are derived directly from the experience of a kind of bourgeois economy limits its applicability to a socialist system), the econometric method of market analysis, that is, the analysis of the flow among sectors, the methodology of the national economy balance, the linear planning and finally the most modern application of cybernetics to economic problems. (LANGE, 1966, p.73)

Guevara's project was very similar to the ideal proposed by the Soviet theoreticians Bukharin and Preobrazhensky[6] in the beginning of the Russian Revolution. It's hard to know if he had access to the texts by those scholars, but the outlines of his economic ideas were, to a certain extent, very similar.[7]They said:

> Society will be transformed into a huge cooperative organization. Thus, there won't be disintegration or production anarchy. In that social order, production will be ordered. One company will no longer compete with the other: the plants, workshops, mines and other production institutions will all be subdivisions, so to speak, of a huge company of the people, which will encompass the entire national production economy. It's obvious that such a broad organization presupposes a general production strategy. If all the plants and workshops together with the entire agricultural sector are combined to constitute a huge cooperative, of course everything must be precisely calculated. We must acknowledge, in advance, the volume of work necessary for the various industry spheres; what goods are required and how much of each will be necessary for production; as well as how and where the machines must be placed. Those details and other similar ones must be forecasted, with, at least approximate, precision; and the work must be guided according to our calculations. That's

> how the organization of communist production will be constructed. Without a general plan, without an overall system, and without careful calculation and detailed records, organization is impossible. But in the communist social order, that plan exists. (BUKHARIN; PREOBRAZHENSKY apud ELLMAN, 1980, p.32-33)

At that time, the Ministry of Industry owned 70% of the country's industrial production — light, basic, mechanical, and pharmaceutical industries, among others — with approximately 260,000 workers, 48 consolidated enterprises and 1,500 businesses across the nation. (TABLADA PÉREZ, 1989) But there were several problems for the new Minister to deal with in his administration. One of them was the country's infrastructure — the port of Havana, for example. Before the revolution, when an American company located in Cuba had a problem, such as the lack of spare parts, it received resources quickly by means of an efficient system of barges, which could reach the island in a short period of time. But the port of the Cuban capital wasn't adapted to the new businesses: it was small and couldn't hold the huge Soviet cargo ships that had to cross the entire Atlantic Ocean to deliver materials and equipment[8]. Cuba also lacked modern ships so the development of a national naval industry was crucial. This led Cuba to sign agreements with Poland for the construction of shipyards. However, for that to happen, an interaction between several spheres of the industrial sector was necessary — metallurgical, engines, cables, electric equipment and carpentry, for example. Since Cuba didn't have all of the necessary manufacturers at that time, the country would have to transport approximately 8 million tons of parts, raw materials, equipment and merchandise in 1965 alone, when the "birth" of that industry was scheduled. The volume of products, the transportation difficulties and the distance led some critics to suggest continuing to import certain products instead of rushing to create, possibly with insufficient resources, so many industrial spheres at the same time.

It must be recalled that, since the middle of 1960, the Americans had proclaimed their intention to stop sending oil to Cuba, and to prohibit the use of their refineries to process the product coming from the Soviet Union. On June 28th of the same year, Fidel Castro signed Resolution n.188, forcing Texaco to refine the crude oil that the government bought from the USSR; if that didn't occur, the company would suffer government intervention. Shortly after the document was signed, the ship *Marie* arrived at the installations of Texaco, in Santiago de Cuba, with the equivalent of 5,000 barrels of Soviet oil. Employees of the Cuban government were on board, and communicated to Robert T. Carter, superintendent of the company, that the *Cristina* would arrive immediately behind them, carrying 21,000 more barrels. It was crucial that the oil be refined. Otherwise, the industries in Santiago could run out of fuel. The American company, however, refused to receive the oil so there was the promised intervention. On July 1st, the ship *Irene* left the port of Havana, with more than 5,000 barrels of oil from Russia, for the city of Regla, where the Shell refinery was located. Since Shell's superintendent Baird Smith also refused to process the product, that refinery suffered government intervention as well. In that same month, the oil tanker *Chernovci* arrived in Havana bringing 70,000 barrels, which it unloaded quickly to go back to the USSR. That procedure started on April 17th, with the arrival of the ship *Andrei Vichinsky* in the port of Casilda. Next, another Soviet ship, the *Klide Field,* arrived with another large oil cargo. The purchase of Soviet oil, its quick delivery and the nationalization of the private refineries ensured the supply of gasoline and oil by-products to the island. But the increased traffic of large ships from the Soviet Union forced the Cubans to invest in the infrastructure of their ports. (LEÓN COTAYO, 1983, p.95-102) Anyway,

Cuba eventually purchased a new refinery from the USSR, increasing refinement capacity from four million tons to 1.5 million tons by 1965. (GUEVARA, 1982, p 45)

Because of these kinds of structural problems, it was necessary to make detailed plans for the location of the industries, the production goals, the energy distribution and the best spheres for investments. The plants, according to the leaders of the Ministry of Industry, should be built taking into consideration the labor force — where there was an idle population, political factors [9] and especially economic ones [10].

In that sense, electricity would play a crucial role, mainly because Cuba had reached the limit of its capacity to generate electricity. In the beginning of 1960, the country had approximately 620,000 kilowatts, in addition to 300,000 underused kilowatts improperly installed in some supply stations and smaller private enterprises. The ministry's goal was, in the next five years, to purchase 600,000 more kilowatts from the socialist countries and 65,000 kilowatts from western countries. In other words, to double the country's real installed capacity. (GUEVARA, 1982, p.40) By the end of 1960, the kilowatt production had already increased to 2.145 million, and one year later to 2.237 million. Until 1965, energy production increased gradually, until it reached 2.592 million kilowatts. Although growth was stable, it wasn't a terribly significant amount of growth, , particularly for a country that strove, at all costs, to accelerate the development of its industrial sector.

It's worth recalling here that, in the beginning of the revolution, General Electric demonstrated some interest in building a lamp plant on the island, while Phelps-Dodge Company, a Dutch enterprise, intended to build a copper tubing plant at a cost of US$1.8 million, half of which would come from BANFAIC and the other half from the multinational itself. Also on the agenda, was expansion of the Compañia Cubana de Electricidad, a subsidiary of the American and Foreign Power Company, with investments around US$147 million, of which US$77 million would come from overseas. From that total, US$45.5 million would be invested in power generation, US$19 million in transmission and the rest would be divided among merchandising, services, replacement and distribution. The plan was to build nine more generation plants, with a capacity of 280,000 kilowatts, in the next five years. (RIVERO, 1963, p.93-94) In other words, lower electricity generation than the revolutionary government achieved. Not only that, but the electric sector would remain closely tied to foreign capital, which could create problems for the Cuban economic plan.[11]

Mineral resources were another concern for the revolutionary government. The leaders turned to the Soviets, who believed they could find metal and non-metal minerals in the country, for a detailed exploration of the deposits in Cuba. Oil prospecting and minerals could be crucial to the development of Cuban industry. For that reason, the Cuban Institute for Mining and Metallurgy Surveys (ICIMM) was created. One of Guevara's main interests was to fully start two modern industries for nickel processing — both with advanced American technology — in Eastern Cuba, a difficult undertaking. The Nicaro plant had the capacity to obtain nickel sinter, which was taken to the United States and transformed in metal nickel, while that of Moa could produce nickel sulphuret and, on a smaller scale, the metal nickel itself. All the materials used in the production process were imported from the United States, which had no interest in the plants returning to work after the revolution. Even with the exit of old Cuban technicians, who had previously worked in both enterprises, and of Soviet experts, there were enormous obstacles to fully realizing his goal. That led Guevara to try to find out who the technicians previously responsible for the construction and management of those industries were, and to try to bring them discreetly to Cuba. In short order, one of these technicians, P.

K. Roy, from India, was invited to the island to help however he could. Even with Roy's presence, the production goal wasn't reached, although Guevara was pleased that both industries were able to turn out reasonable levels of the product.

Meanwhile, the lack of spare parts was a growing problem for the Cuban leaders. Since their reserves and inventories had been excessively spent, stoppages were occurring in some plants. In an attempt to overcome the crisis, the government organized, among other things, a promotional campaign encouraging the formation of parts committees, which in turn urged the workers to find creative and original solutions to problems in the plants. At the ministry level, the Superior Committee of Spare Parts received information solely on issues that could not be resolved by the other governmental divisions or within the enterprises. (GUEVARA, 1988b, p.168-169)

The revolutionary government prepared another campaign, called "Build your own machinery", to encourage the workers to create teams that copied all of the existing machines on the island, to reproduce them and consequently to increase the amount of industrial equipment made from available materials. To help the government, the Central Organization of Cuban Trade Unions (CTC), and its affiliates, insisted that it was crucial to conserve as much as possible, from drops and kilowatts, to materials and fuels, to take care of the machines and to strive for maximum productivity. (MIRANDA FERNÁNDEZ, 1984, p.314-315) Some scholars believe that, in fact, the main problems with the Cuban economy were not necessarily tied to the administration, but were a consequence of the embargo. That, however, was not what Guevara believed. In an interview with journalist Jean Daniel, he claimed that, "we have serious difficulties in Cuba. But they're not caused by the situation that you call blockage. First of all, there was never a full blockage. We didn't decrease our trade with Great Britain and France, for example." And he continued, "Our difficulties derive mainly from our mistakes. The greatest one, the one that caused more problems for us, as you know, is the under-exploration of sugarcane. The others involve all the inevitable hesitations that the adaptation of collectivism to a local situation implies." (DRAPER, 1966b, p.147)

In this period many economic difficulties started to emerge in Cuba. The scarcity of foreign currency made it difficult to import more goods, which the larger consumer population demanded. There began to be shortages of such items as bread, cookies, rubber, cardboard boxes, paper bags, toothpaste, soft drinks, bottles and some pharmaceutical supplies, among others. In the case of the toothpaste, for example, even if production was paralyzed for four months, there was enough inventory to sporadically supply the domestic market until a shipment of bicalcium sulphate — the raw material required to make it — arrived. However, this would lead the factories, in an attempt to accelerate production, to make a toothpaste that became "as hard as rock" if it wasn't consumed within five weeks of purchase. Distribution of goods presented an important ethical issue. For Che, it wouldn't be good if there was soap available in Havana but it wasn't available to the consumers in the countryside. In other words, if one locality lacked a particular product, the item couldn't be sold in any other place until it could be evenly distributed. (GUEVARA, 1988b, p.173) Guevara believed that many could be blamed for the supply problems, from the Ministry of Foreign Trade (MINCEX), which supposedly had the greatest degree of responsibility (since it should have analyzed the general situation in the country better, created inventory balances, predicted product shortages and gathered the existing merchandise, warning the enterprises about the imports), and the Ministry of Domestic Trade (MINCIN), which had made many mistakes in the distribution of products, to the enterprises themselves, which used their resources ineptly and didn't produce enough. (GUEVARA, 1988b, p.176-177)

Already in 1962, it was clear that the strategy of import substitution and quick industrialization didn't reach expectations, nor was it a feasible solution in the short run to resolve the problems with the balance of payment. As Guevara himself admitted:

> ...we didn't give due emphasis to the use of our own resources: we focused on import substitution of finished articles, without seeing clearly that those articles are made with raw materials which we must have in order to produce them. [...] Let's see some examples: in the next few months, a plant for the production of planes and brushes will begin operation. That plant will work with imported raw materials. A screw plant will work with imported raw materials until we have the steel industry. A pickaxe and shovel plant with imported raw materials. The welding electrodes plant will work with imported raw materials. The barbed wire plant with imported raw materials. Some others are in a similar situation. [...] Everything indicates that we lacked the basis of raw materials, and, one of the pillars of a country with our characteristics is the steel industry. We are already developing a steel industry with the help of the Soviets, and we will have to do that quickly, as quickly as possible, according to our strengths and to the real conditions, but until we have that, we won't be able to take the first step to walk on our own. (GUEVARA, 1988b, p.196)

Since December 1961, the government had increased the savings campaign based on Resolution n.933, signed by Raúl Cepero Bonilla, who was the President of the National Bank, which increased the ordinary savings accounts and the fixed term deposits from 318 million pesos to 583 million in 1962 and 718 million in 1963, an increase of more than 100% in only two years. (FERNÁNDEZ FONT, 1982, p.208) But in 1962, because of the scarcity of consumer goods on the island, a booklet of ration coupons was introduced. In fact, from 1960 to 1962, the Cuban balance of payments presented consecutive deficits. The export of agricultural products didn't increase as they had planned and import capacity didn't change. Some members of the government started discussing whether they should continue with the diversification project. And there were still other problems. While in 1962 the average wage was 2,264 pesos, in 1963 it dropped to 1,928 pesos, largely because of the influx of thousands of new workers to the labor force. In turn, the production per worker, which was 11,200 pesos, went down to 8,598 pesos in the same period. (GUEVARA, 1988b, p.228) There were also documented problems with financial discipline of the planning organs, such as the absence of payments, charges, balances and not fulfilling the state budget. In 1963, for example, the planning organs should have distributed 687 million pesos to the enterprises, but they only delivered 435 million, that is, they didn't fulfill what was projected. (GUEVARA, 1988b, p.229) We must recall, however, that in 1961 the greatest drought of the century occurred in Cuba, and in October 1963, the island suffered the effects of hurricane Flora, which swept the provinces of Oriente and Camagüey, killing 1,200 people, causing material damage in some cities and destroying much of the agricultural production of the region.

Despite all the problems, it must be noted that during that time there was actually a colossal industrialization effort. According to Michel Gutelman, between 1960 and 1963, the country invested US$850 million in the sector, approximately the same amount the Americans had invested in the island over fifty years. (GUTELMAN, 1972, p.233) Despite everything, it wasn't enough to resolve the overall technological and industrial backwardness of the country. The need to import large quantities of machines and equipment for the new Cuban industries was a part of the reason for the poor economic performance in the first few years of the revolution. The entire production sphere had to be converted to Soviet machinery or that of the other socialist countries. Those industries also depended exclusively on imported spare parts and raw materials. According to economist René Dumont (1970, p.77):

> Factories erected long before the Revolution represented a given factor, a sort of heritage. But much of the new equipment that was ordered could not be put to work for lack of buildings and qualified administrative personnel. Extremely delicate machines, therefore, piled up on the docks, and then in temporary warehouses and hangars. A special term was even jokingly applied to them: people talked of machines as being in "raw accumulation". In the warm tropical climate, with its salty fogs, these machines were threatened with rapid deterioration, for the more modern they were the more fragile they were." (DUMONT, 1970, p.77)

To give an idea, by the end of 1964, only 50% of the total capacity of the imported machinery was operating, due to the lack of maintenance, repairs and organization (DRAPER, 1966b, p.148). Still according to Dumont:

> The lack of spare parts often interfered with the proper functioning of machines; more parts could have been made domestically. These spare parts ought be the very first thing imported, for they do away with bottlenecks at less cost than other measures. The raw materials necessary to use existing equipment are a more pressing demand than building new factories, especially if there's no assurance that these can be used [...] Cuba's present difficulties have been aggravated by the absence of a clear industrial policy, drawn up by a single center having to answer to the political authorities, the Revolutionary leaders, for its decisions. (DUMONT, 1970, p.78-79)

From the beginning of his term in the Ministry of Industry, to try to solve that problem at least partially, Guevara insisted on Soviet help. In a letter to the Vice-Prime-Minister Mikoyan, dated June 30th, 1961, Che asked for "the increase of the capacity of the first cast iron unit built by the Soviet Union, from 250,000 to 500,000 tons; the increase of the capacity of the oil refinery from 1 million tons per year to 2 million[12]; enterprises of the chemical and cellulose industries worth 157 million rubles; a thermal power plant in Santiago de Cuba with power of 100,000 kilowatts; and several technicians and experts". (CASTAÑEDA, 1997, p.253)

There were several agreements made with the socialist countries. Until the middle of 1961, Cuba had been able to sign contracts with different enterprises in those nations. From the Soviet Union, the Cuban government obtained file plants, a steel industry, a plan for a mechanical industry, the reconstruction of a metallurgic, an ammoniac plant, two nitric acid plants, two urea plants, one ammoniac nitrate plant, two complex manure plants, one triple superphosphate plant, one of newsprint and other kinds of paper, a nickel industry, one of pre-pressed elements, such as poles for lines, as well as the others that have been mentioned before. The agreements with Czechoslovakia included plants for the production of padlocks and built-in locks, a plant for the production of black and precision screws, nails, axes, hammers, machetes, hoes, stainless cutlery, workshops for pressure foundries, shovels, bicycles, candles, pencils, diesel engines and compressors. East Germany would provide a kaolin plant, another one to process silex and yet another one to make shoes. For 1962, it qualified the country to produce 25,000 spindles and 500 looms; one year later, 50,000 spindles and 1,000 looms; and in 1964, 65,000 spindles and 1,500 looms. Also learning workshops for the metallurgic industry, a plant for the trefilation of thick wire and steel cables, a plant to produce white and gray cement, another one for cameras and finally a manufacturer of electric engines and assemblies of typewriters. Poland would also commit to supply manual tools and to install a steel and pig and malleable iron foundry, to extend a plane glass factory from Owens Illinois, refractory materials, dry sinks and similar products, small presses, shipyards, citric acid, butanol, radios and televisions. Meanwhile, Yugoslavia would put into operation plants for producing ketchup, tomato juice and depulping machines in Colón, Majagua, Batabanó, Bahía Honda, Jatibonico, Los Arabos and El Caney. Bulgaria would install a plant to produce calcium carbonate, silica sand, feldspar and marine products. The commercial treaties with Hungary, in turn, indicated their commitment to put plants for making security and hollow glasses, tubes and glass wools, electric siphons and fluorescent tubes plants, workshops for the repair and production of agricultural machinery spare parts, a teaching center for the production of machine-tools, of agricultural and electric machinery and of machine handling, as well as a factory for the production of heparin.[13] And from China, the Cubans would receive plants to produce chlorine, DDT, polyvinyl chloride, ferric chloride and chloral, rubber pipes for the automotive industry, conveyor belts, incandescent sealed units for vehicles, shock absorbers, accessories for motor vehicles, rings for pistons, clutches, brake linings, gas pumps, valves for industries, steam utensils, coal for goldsmith's sweepings, plants for the production of husk pulp for papers and cards, plants for the production of feather pens, textile pins, one of dynamite and a textile plant for approximately 50,000 spindles. (GUEVARA, 1988b, p.54-55) In 1960 alone, the Soviet Union had granted 100 million pesos, Romania, 15 million, Bulgaria, 5 million, and Poland, 12 million (GUEVARA, 1988b, p.194) Thus, theoretically speaking, Cuba was ensured of fast economic development, which didn't work as well as expected in practice.

The lack of technicians, administrators and specialized workers was certainly a great problem and something that made consistent productivity growth and the ability to generate better quality products difficult.[14] According to Guevara:

> ...those deficiencies must be directly attributed to the insufficient development of the employees, which is nothing

> fatal, but must be attributed to the scanty work by the ministry in that matter. We won't be able to find a system that allows us to develop the employees and, at the same time, transfer to the other levels those employees who don't have the minimum requirements for leadership tasks, but who could be well employed somewhere else. With rare exceptions, in two or three months a man shows how much he's worth. It's unusual that a comrade evolves gradually, slowly and continuously [...] And we insist on keeping them in leadership positions when they are unqualified, what is worse, without providing them the necessary help for, if they have character, to improve. Thus the director, left alone, falls into a kind of routine, of conformity, until in a certain moment it's necessary to lay him off [...] It's necessary to pay close attention to the employee, it's necessary to develop him; that requires that he's in a stable position. He can't be groomed while he continues to wander desperately like a crazy atom; our administrative employees are sent from one place to another without having time to attain serious and reasonable experience. We established that a man must remain at least six months in a post before being transferred or promoted, but this wasn't taken into consideration. (GUEVARA, 1988b, p.63-64)

To give an idea, the Ministry of Industry, for example, never had more than 473 engineers. Of the 300 agronomists that were in Cuba before the revolution, 270 left the country. Therefore, the country depended on technicians from the socialist countries. In the beginning of 1960 alone, the Soviet Union sent 53 engineers and technicians, 1 employee and 5 translators to the Cuban Mining Institute; 9 expert engineers to the thermoelectric plants; 2 experts in energy planning to the Cuban Oil Institute; as well as 1 engineer of chemical industries, 1 economist, 1 statistician, 1 labor expert and 5 translators and interpreters. Czechoslovakia sent 62 technicians, among them, mining engineers, geologists, experts in the fields of electricity, machinery production and sugar, among others. Poland sent 3 geologists, Yugoslavia, 1 agricultural technician. Hungary, in turn, contributed 1 chemist, and China sent 10 experts in industrial machinery.

Guevara believed that it was most important that Cuba qualify oil and mining fields, as soon as possible, to help with the industrial development of the country, since only foreign technicians had contributed to the government. Many young Cubans were quickly sent to the Soviet Union[15] for technical education. But the relationship between the Soviet experts and the Cuban ones was not always good, mainly due to cultural differences and work styles. That contributed to criticism of Cuban methods by some Soviet technicians, who were employed in several sectors of the Cuban economy. On June 4th, 1962, Khrushchev made a rough speech in Moscow for one thousand young Cubans who had completed one year of training as agricultural mechanics in the USSR. He believed that this training was more important than arms and heroism in solving the island's problems, that is, more emphasis should be given to increasing the awareness, discipline and technical capability of the population in general. It would also be important for concessions to be made to some social sectors, especially to the Cuban middle class, to ensure the development of the revolution. (DRAPER, 1966b, p.143) Later, Fidel himself gave public explanations for the fact that many Cubans were dissatisfied and disagreeing with the advice of the Soviet technicians. On June 29th of the same year, in the farewell ceremony to a group of technicians from the USSR, the *jefe máximo* of the revolution said:

> We're aware of our deficiencies; we know about many [Cuban] administrators who don't have any experience and who, in some cases, are not even very politicized; and who, in other cases, aren't very hospitable.
> And therefore we know that a [Soviet] technician who went to a state-owned farm managed by an experienced and hospitable comrade, aware of his obligations, would be treated very well; but we also know that there were many places where the

> administrator received them coldly or with indifference, or wasn't responsible enough to use the knowledge that they have. Thus, we have reports about the occasions in which on some state-owned farms the administrators didn't treat the technicians well, or in which the administrators didn't use the knowledge of the technicians; [...] reports such as those concerning administrators who thought that the way to treat the technicians well consisted in taking them out or offering young women to them. (DRAPER, 1966b, p.144)

Therefore, the Soviet technicians were still extremely necessary, and those at the highest level of the Cuban government were aware of this. Their presence represented more than political support by the Kremlin: in practice, they were crucial to Cuban development in that specific phase of economic restructuring, despite the substantial growth in the number of Cuban technicians and experts over the following years[16]. On the other hand, those same experts exemplified, even if indirectly, Cuba's increasing relationship with and dependence on the socialist block.

---

[1]The plans could have national, regional or local objectives, being prepared according to the region and the kind of company (agricultural, industry, groups of workers and even individual workers).

---

[2]According to René Dumont (1970, p.76-77), "his ministry didn't seem to be concentrating on its real work and it busied itself with problems that shouldn't be its concern; it was therefore snowed under by day-to-day concerns. He [Che] tried to run the factories by himself, for the lack of power and raw materials threatened to paralyze these factories at any moment".

[3]According to Alcides Bedoya (apud CABRERA, 1987, p.144-145), in the Soviet Union, Khrushchev started to make longer term plans (plans for 7, 10 and 20 years), unlike the previous tendency to develop only five-year plans. That certainly influenced some sectors of the Cuban government. With the arrival of Brezhnev and Kosygin in power, the previous system was taken up again.

[4]Later, since Guevara disagreed with the mercantile relations within the state sector, the name of that department changed to Exchange Department.

[5]According to Carlos Rafael Rodríguez, (1983b, p.477) as a result of the degree of neocolonial economic and cultural submission reached in Cuba, there were technicians who were "clearly against the process"; these were unrecoverable. Nevertheless, there was another kind of technician who, although he was not convinced by socialism, or even convinced of the need for capitalism, his national awareness allowed him to react in defense of his country. "The experience of the Cuban revolution indicates that we must work with those technicians". According to this author, the radicalism of management, mainly at the local level, was supposedly responsible for the poor integration of that kind of technician.

[6]Bukharin insisted on the need for an equivalent exchange between industry and agriculture, thinking about development of the state-owned industry depending on agriculture. Therefore, the industrialization would be slow, but it could only take place if the medium layers of the peasantry weren't alienated. Bukharin's theory of balanced development implied the need to advance very slowly, both economically and politically, towards socialism. See Bernard Jobic (1973, p.193-194). Preobrazhensky, in turn, advocated fast growth, stating that "in a stopping period, the accumulation could only be successful by means of a wage reduction or a price increase; a price reduction could only be possible to the detriment of the accumulation or of the wages [...] However, with the increase of labor productivity that triangular problem can be globally solved." (PREOBRAZHENSKY apud MIRANDA, 1980, p.172)

[7]Roberto Massari (1993, p.169-170) draws an analogy between the ideas of Guevara and those of Preobrazhensky. This intellectual believed that the fast development of industry was the key to solving all problems — including the political ones. It would be necessary to have a policy of "non-equivalent exchanges" between agriculture and industry, in favor of the latter, so that industrialization could take place. This would consist of the "primitive socialist accumulation", since it would benefit mainly the "socialist" or "state-owned" sector, by means of an accumulation based on the surplus created by the socialist economy during the transition period, used for its reproduction and extension. For some critics, this would be an example of State capitalism: the "primitive socialist accumulation" would consist of the

exploitation of a private capitalist sector by the State capitalist sector, which would ensure its power. For further information, see Bernard Jobic (1973, p.192-193).

---

[8] At that moment, the Soviet Union was selling four million tons of oil per year to Cuba and brought back, in the same ships — after cleaning them with a special detergent — 2,700,000 tons of sugar bought from the Cubans.

---

[9] The idea was that the populations of some regions, even though they weren't extremely in need of work at that moment, "deserved" compensation in the form of some kind of industrial development, as a reward for their revolutionary attitude. One example would be the peasant zone of Ciénaga, in the region of Playa Girón, where the people fought "bravely" against the counter-revolutionaries financed by the United States.

[10] According to the plans of the Ministry of Industry, with the objective of balancing the distribution of production units throughout the entire Cuban territory, not many industries would develop in Havana.

---

[11] Between 1947 and 1958, Cuba's electrical services grew significantly. In that period, the number of localities receiving power services jumped from 248 to 301. The generating capacity of the power plants also increased: in 1947, it was 138,542 kw; in 1950, it raised to 163,590 kw; in 1953, it reached 191,090 kw; and in 1958, the Cuban power plants generated around 429,900 kw. However, the amount of electricity available in the entire country was still low. During Batista's government, several obstacles were eliminated making it easier for foreign investment. Between 1947 and 1958, new power plants were built and there was an extension from 4,065 miles (6.6,000 km) of electric lines to 6,313 miles (10,000 km) by the end of the decade. Only between 1954 and 1958, CCE's profit was US$28,128,343, compared to US$14,969,245, between 1949 and 1953. The company's reserves increased from US$27.5 million in 1948 to US$57.5 million in 1959. The number of employees also grew, rising from 4,765 in 1949 to 7,464 in 1958. For most of the population, however, the electricity tariffs were high. Even though there was Cuban capital in the company, stock control of the company still belonged to Foreign Power, which owned, in the beginning of 1959, around 88% of the shares; the 1,343 Cuban stockholders owned only 4%. When the revolutionary government determined the reduction of the tariffs, on August 19th, 1959, CCE, a subsidiary of Foreign Power, tried to negotiate with the new regime, but one year later, on August 6th, 1960, the foreign enterprises were nationalized and CCE had to join the

general planning system of the revolutionary government. For further information, see: BAUDIS; GARCÍA, 1973.

---

[12]The figures mentioned apparently differ from those presented by Guevara on other occasions.

---

[13]Anticoagulating medicinal chemical product.

---

[14]For further information, see Huberman and Sweezy (1970, p.73).

---

[15]It should be observed that, even though it sent technicians to other countries and trained foreign students, the Soviet Union had a huge deficit of expert personnel internally. Between 1946 and 1950, there was a 17.9% deficit of mechanical engineers, 17% of chemical technicians, 4% of engineers in the light and textile industries, 66% of economists and 41% in other sectors. In 1962, concerning the agrarian expertise fields, there was a 36% deficit of mechanical engineers, 53% of electrician engineers and 33% of veterinarians in the country. See Coggiola and Paulino (2001, p.43)

---

[16]The number of Cuban technicians and experts supervised by the Soviet technicians grew substantially in the following years. In 1968, Cuban workers already controlled the sophisticated machines of the Moa nickel plant, one of the most advanced in the world. The Cubans welded cracks in titanium *heat exchangers*, which cost US$40,000 each and US$10,000 for repairs. Thus, it is possible to evaluate the level of development and technical knowledge they attained. In that year there were already 46,595 workers in technological institutes and 1,626 Cubans in military technological institutes. See Huberman and Sweezy (1970, p.46-48).

3

THE ECONOMIC DEBATE IN THE SOVIET UNION AND IN EASTERN EUROPE

The presence of aides from the Soviet Union in Cuba and the greater circulation of Russian economic manuals decisively influenced some members of the Cuban government in that period.[1] The tendency toward decentralization occurring in the USSR, that began in the middle of the 1950's, and the ideas of "reformist" economists such as Liberman, Kantorovich, Novozhilov and Trapeznikov didn't please Guevara, who distrusted the implementation of practices that he believed were incompatible with the Cuban reality.

Some "regionalized" decentralization attempts were fostered by Khrushchev beginning in 1956, on the suggestion of Alexei Kosygin, who proposed flexibility in the pricing system within the enterprises. One year later, an industrial rearrangement began, which didn't greatly alter the USSR's productivity in general. With the growth rate of the economy slowing every year in the Eastern European countries, including those that were the most industrially advanced, discussions concerning decentralization re-emerged in the beginning of the 1960's in the Soviet Union.[2] During the years of the Khrushchev government, the average wage of the Soviet workers rose only 2.4% per year, while the official prices of meat and milk rose between 25% and 30%. Wages had been frozen since the beginning of 1960, the enactment of legislative measures to reduce working hours and the increase of low incomes and pensions for the elderly was postponed; the housing plan was shortened and there was a reduction in the general pace of economic activity. (DEUTSCHER, 1969a, p.14-15) Industrial growth was lower than what had been predicted and the products were not of high quality.[3]

From 1962 forward, the debate concerning the path of centralized planning became more intense, until it culminated in the Soviet economic reform of 1965 and in the analogous changes in the "economic mechanism" of other countries, such as Czechoslovakia and Hungary, in the following years. The "reformists" proposed that the plan for a company should determine the total of production in very general terms, but that the implementation details of that total should be the responsibility of the unit itself, according to the concrete need of the consumers. It would also be interesting to create a "summarized list" of the company's results — to replace the multiple lists that existed then — in the form of a balance of net income or profits, as well as a single incentive fund tied to it.[4] (DOBB, 1970, p.43) Economist Yevsei Liberman, in his influential article called "The plan, the profit and the premia", published in *Pravda* on September 9th, 1962, stated that:

> It is essential [...] to construct a system of planning and judging the work of the enterprise so that they shall have a lively interest in fulfilling the plan-targets to the maximum, in introducing new techniques and high-quality products, in a word, in maximum effectiveness of production [...] the proposed system will free central planning from petty tutelage over enterprises, from costly attempts to influence production, not by economic, but by administrative measures. The enterprise itself knows best and can discover its potentialities. (apud DOBB, 1970, p.44)

As far as the company's profit is concerned, Liberman said:

> Our profit, if one starts with the fact that prices correctly express average expenses of production for the branch [of industry], is nothing but the result of an increase in the productivity of social labor concretized in money form. That's why we are able, by basing ourselves on profitability, to

> encourage real effectiveness of production. But with that said, encouragement is not enrichment.... What is of benefit to society and the State must become of benefit to every enterprise and to every worker involved in the production. (apud DOBB, 1970, p.44)

For one or two years there were instances that occurred in enterprises that were selected according to some new methods advocated by the "reformist" economists, such as the case of apparel plants, which had the freedom to establish the details of their production program according to store orders, that is, a flexibility that gradually tended toward capitalist economic policies.

In August, 1964, after renewed interest in some ideas advocated by Liberman, Vladimir Trapeznikov suggested a macroeconomic reform in the price system. Thus, around the Institute of Mathematical Economics of Leningrad, run by Vasili Nemchinov (one of the main promoters of the use of statistical models for planning) and later by Viktor Novozhilov (an economist who worried about capital allocation in the planned economy), an economic school advocating Liberman's theories was developed. At the same time as the academic debates in other sectors of the government were going on, there was a power struggle within the CPSU which culminated in Khrushchev's removal, while some elements who gradually ascended in the ranks of the Presidium showed their nonconformity with the manner in which the economic changes had been developing in the Soviet Union. Even so, after further debates, Prime-Minister Alexei Kosygin, in a speech to the Central Committee of the CPSU on September 27th, 1965 — after Khrushchev's removal from power — officially introduced the economic reform, which extended to most of the Soviet industry in the next three or four years and which was incorporated into a *Statute of the Socialist Industrial Enterprise,* approved by the council of ministers on October 4th of the same year. Its first clause stated that "the socialist industrial entreprise shall be the basic unit of the national economy in the USSR. Its operation shall be based on centralized direction combined with economic independence and initiative on the part of the enterprise. (DOBB, 1970, p.45)

The main objective of those reforms was to diversify production and to stimulate productivity without, however, giving up state control, since the measures that had been taken since the second half of the 1950's, although not excessively radical, had been able to dismantle, to a considerable extent, the old centralized system. Those economic changes had also been largely inspired by the ideas of Leonid Kantorovich and his work *Economic Accounting of the Use of Resources,* published in 1960, in which he advocated "optimum planning", recommending an economic accounting system applied to the entire economy that permitted the solution of technical problems such as the more rational division of labor related to the machines, processing raw materials with a minimum of waste and the division of the cargo between several means of transportation. He defended the assumptions of Liberman and Trapeznikov as far as the administrative decentralization and the autonomy of enterprises were concerned. The "Kantorovich model" was also endorsed by such economists as Nemchinov and Novozhilov, who had elaborated a similar model. For him, only the linear programming methods would bring about maximum profitability in the company. (FAVROD, 1978, p.120-121)

Critics of the exacerbated centralization said that, due to the very limited autonomy of the individual company, this organization impeded the broader acknowledgement of local conditions and it became too complex for the central organs. It was a fairly inflexible structure, with most of the decision-making coming from Moscow or from the capitals of the Soviet republics, it was difficult for the industries' managers to act, because they first had to obtain instructions from superior levels which, in turn, had to receive the details of the units in order to make the plan and forward it to the supervisors. Thus, many managers felt as if they were in a straitjacket, since they couldn't make independent decisions. According to I. Mironov, another advocate of the reforms:

> There must be an adequate measure of whether a plant is working well or not. It must be stable and constant, and not influenced by the management of the plant itself. The only indicator is price, and it must be the plant's profit that acts as an incentive. The price of a product is the economic lever that fosters or suppresses production growth. It must lead the plant not only to devote itself to a simple and easy process, but also to produce what the national economy needs (and what the economy needs must be a source of gain and profit for the plant). Price and methods to measure the execution of the plan must be maintained, and all other obligatory indicators must be kept to a minimum. (MIRONOV apud LANDAUER, 1966, p.482)

Other economists from several socialist countries advocated the reformist ideas. Professor Angel Milochevski, from Bulgaria, proposed the complete adoption of the Yugoslav system. Even more important was the intervention of another Bulgarian theoretician, Professor Petko Kunin, considered one of the most important economists of his country at the time. He believed that all the enterprises should be financially self-sufficient, as well as autonomous in relation to the government. Kunin proposed a new planning and accounting system that permitted real "competition" among enterprises. Forms for the more rational and economic use of fixed capital funds should be found as well as better use of the labor force, mainly using profit and the division of profit as incentive. According to Kunin, the profit should determine the remuneration of the managers and be the main source of the wage increases. Many considered this to be a return to capitalism, but Kunin insisted that these were socialist practices, and that to reach communism it would be necessary to develop and to put into practice "bold" ideas and take "daring" steps, realistically and in a competent manner. (BROWN, 1966, p.18-19) Kunin's assumptions had a great influence on the Bulgarian government, which shortly thereafter began putting them into practice[5].

Ivan Mironov himself, in an article published in May, 1964 in *Ikonomicheska Misal,* supported the self-financing and autonomy of the enterprises. Based on what had already taken place in Bulgaria with Kunin's ideas, he proposed that wages and capital accumulation were tied to the profitability level of each company alone; that each company was subject to a tax on property; and an interest rate based on fixed and circulating capital. In turn, the workers would play a new role in the system. According to him, "when the accumulations of the company, and a considerable part of wages, depend on the volume of profit, the workers can't be indifferent to administrative problems and the results of work in the company". (MIRONOV apud BROWN, 1966, p.19)

Even though some people said the opposite, the slow redirection towards capitalist practices was noticeable. The ideas of the Soviet "reformists" had many supporters in Cuba. Liberman's influence was so great in that period that the term "libermanism" was coined to refer to the practices of economic decentralization. (HALPERIN, 1967, p.47-49) We must recall that Cuba was gradually moving closer to the Soviet Union, and that her political influence was certainly an important element in leading the Cuban rulers to adopt similar measures. But the cases of Cuba and of the USSR were very different. Countries of different sizes, ethnic background, social organization and history, they should be looked at separately, regardless of how close they appeared at that moment.

From 1957 on, most of the ministries for individual industries — around twenty-seven — were broken up, and their responsibilities were delegated to several *sovnarkhozes,* or regional economic councils, sixty-eight of which were in Russia alone. Local control mechanisms by CPSU were also created. However, the regional organs tended to produce more for their own consumption or to encourage the development of industries that were more useful to the interests of the region. Due to a fear of "ideological detours" in the *sovnarkhozes,* coordination and planning councils were created in seventeen great Soviet economic regions. That meant yet another complication in the already complex control system of the production units and an increase in the bureaucratization of the state apparatus. (LANDAUER, 1966, p.482-484)

Such facts clarify the internal disputes within the CPSU, not only in the political sphere but also those relative to the theories of industrial management. Thus, from 1965 on, the *sovnarkhozes,* associated with the Khrushchev era, would be eliminated and replaced by the State Committee for Material and Technical Supply (GOSSNAB), an organ of gigantic proportions which employed approximately 600,000 people at the time. Its function was to distribute the raw materials, machines and spare parts among the several production units. GOSSNAB depended on the Council of Ministers, but was autonomous in relation to GOSPLAN and to the ministries, which had been reconstituted. That institution developed around 25,000 products, 13,000 through its 21 central departments of products — such as electrical and agricultural equipment — and around 12,000 through 56 territorial departments. This system proved to be excessively complex, since any company that needed new machinery must place its orders directly to GOSSNAB, which would then approve the purchase for the industry; the latter contacted an appointed supplier, who would receive a sales order and would later establish a detailed contract with the purchaser. In general, deadlines weren't respected.

The supply problems led to the emergence and proliferation of the *tolkachi,* official mediators, often individuals with a good relationship with the supply services who, by means of retributions, were willing to examine the dossiers and to bother those responsible until the conclusion of the business. (FAVROD, 1978, p.102-103) In other words, the rulers who came into power replacing Khrushchev dismantled the new administrative structure created by the former First-Secretary of the CPSU, but they continued to support Liberman's reforms, which were based on the market, prices, profits and initiative of the business managers. The Soviet system also began, a little later, to emphasize the commercial "advertisement" of several products on the radio, television and newspapers, specifying the differences of "brands" of the same articles and persuading consumers to buy, which could lead to consumerism and to capitalism. (SOLGANICK, 1967, p.44-45)

All of the movement during the first half of the 1960's towards decentralization, bureaucratization, valuation of profit and approximation of capitalist practices displeased Guevara very much, and he fought those ideas every way he could. But that caused him problems with some elements of the Cuban government. In discussions with their members, Che said:

> There are two extremely interesting processes in progress, in which we should delve deeper. See: when I was in Moscow, I attended several scientific debates in an institute of math applied to the economy, where serious and very well educated people worked, as the Soviets often are, with extraordinary strength and technical skill. We started to talk about prices, but we abandoned the topic, since it led us nowhere. During the successive debates, I was asked if I knew of a system that was being tested in a Soviet plant that works directly with the public. The use of products is based on public demand and the profitability of the industry is measured according to sales. I was asked: "Do you know this system?" I hesitated a bit and then I said: "I don't know this system very well in the Soviet

> Union, but I have already seen it elsewhere. In Cuba it was widely developed before the Revolution, since it's pure capitalism, since a company that works based on public demand and measures its profit and its management criterion in relation to that is not a secret nor something rare; its the process of capitalism. The only difficulty is that if this system was transferred from an enterprise to the entire social complex it would be replaced by production anarchy, which would necessarily lead to a crisis, after which socialism should be rebuilt."
>
> This has been going on in some industries in the Soviet Union; those are private enterprises and I have no intention whatsoever to prove that there is capitalism in the Soviet Union. I simply mean that we're witnessing certain phenomena because there's a theoretical crisis, and the theoretical crisis takes place because the existence of Marx has been forgotten and because these systems are based only on a part of Lenin's work. (GUEVARA, 1982, p.69)

Guevara stated that the government was responsible for many kinds of mistakes. According to him, "basically, as far as planning is concerned, we have done two opposite things that can't be harmonized. On the one hand, we copied details of the planning techniques of a brother-country, whose experts came to help us and, on the other hand, we maintained the spontaneity and the lack of analysis of many decisions, mainly political ones, but with economic implications, which must be made everyday in the government process." (GUEVARA, 1982, p.12) Concerning a debate with Soviet economists, Che commented:

> There were several Soviet comrades present. I invited the lads to go to the embassy, mainly the economists; but others who dealt with automation also joined us, there were approximately fifty people in all. I intended to engage in a great battle against the self-management finance system. Well then, I never had such an attentive and worried audience, or one that understood my arguments so quickly. Do you know why? Because it had to do with many of the things I'm saying now, and if I say them in a theoretical manner it's because I have no other experience;

> they were the ones who knew them by means of direct experience [...] It's a fact that in the "self-management" system there's no connection between the apparatus and the masses. In the self-management system, the value of the man is measured according to what he produces, which capitalism achieves perfectly, or better yet, very perfectly. I would like to say that, if here we have flaws and we want to correct them, we don't correct them by using the method of rewarding a worker more or less. That won't lead us anywhere. Some students made very interesting arguments, except for one who simply repeated the traditional point of view; but all the others interjected with some really interesting questions. Certainly, when we started to discuss a violent situation emerged; that was a "Bible", the *Manual* — since, unfortunately, the "Bible" is not Marx's *Capital,* but the *Manual* — and it was opposed in many areas, including some dangerously capitalist arguments, from which a revisionist tendency evolves. (GUEVARA, 1982, p.68)

That was certainly a rough criticism of those who advocated the new Soviet model of planning.

Even the Western scholars saw the difficulties of applying Liberman's models in the socialist world. According to Professor Ernst Halperin, the Soviets were not placing much importance on the "libermanism", by considering it only as a new organizational technique. At the same time that there was an increase in the number of decentralized enterprises, the bureaucrats who had lost their places in the old "system" were placated, by receiving posts at ministries in the Soviet capitals to avoid an intrinsic resistance within the government. According to Halperin:

> ...the Soviet leaders could still decide to give Liberman's experience a proper ideological foundation by proclaiming that it would mean a new and higher stage of the advance from socialism to communism, and by establishing something similar to "worker control" within the plants. [...] Nowadays, however, there's no indication that the Soviet leaders might be considering that path, not even remotely. On the contrary, both in industry and in agriculture, a partial rehabilitation of Stalin is making it increasingly difficult to provide ideological

> motivations for the urgent and necessary practical reforms. [...] In the absence of some ideological stimulation, Liberman's reform seems to us to be destined to failure — for the same reason that the two successive decentralization attempts, led with an equal lack of imagination, ideology and in a purely pragmatic manner, already failed in Czechoslovakia. In this case, there can be a greater decline in the productivity and in the growth rate, with harmful effects for the status of the Soviet Union as a world power, which may hardly be avoided. (HALPERIN, 1967, p.49)

That was exactly what Guevara thought at the time. Khrushchev leaving and the "triumvirate" led by Podgorny, Kosygin and Brezhnev[6], coming into power at the end of 1964, led to the gradual decline of the Soviet Union as a superpower through the 1980's. This culminated, shortly thereafter, with Gorbachev's *perestroika* and the disintegration of the country.

It's useful here to comment briefly on some of the ideas advocated by Polish economist Oskar Lange, one of the scholars of socialist planning who stands out. According to Lange, in order to establish a planned system it is crucial, in each specific case, to first closely observe the concrete historical conditions of the transition from capitalism to socialism. Those peculiarities would determine the actions of the government and the different kinds of planning procedures. The strategy would be made up of three aspects, namely: the goals (realistically prioritized on a national scale); the formulation of a consistent plan; and options for the means of its execution. In general, the plans emerge as a form of economic restructuring, with the objective of feasibly renewing and modernizing, in technical terms, the economies in question. Since most of the countries undergoing the transition to socialism were backward, this was achieved basically through industrialization and agricultural modernization. Therefore, the governments had to worry about resolving the problem of obtaining resources for capital accumulation (derived from the profits of the enterprises, a variety of contributions from the rural population and taxes) and allocation of investments. The methodology of investment was based mainly on principles of accounting and budgetary development originating from the capitalist enterprises, creating a system of balances, calculated from the country's workforce, manufacture of different items from the production sector, as well as from existent reserves and labor. At that time, the balances were organized in a chart of "product flow". Therefore, the national accounting should take into consideration the composition of production together with the total of available financial resources, in order to balance the government accounts and make its projects feasible. The general balance of the economy would have to be harmonious, coordinated with other balances and systematized in the form of tables, sources of national income and distribution.

The socialist countries had gone through the first planning phase, when the main objective was to develop the economy's production capacity. However, a second phase was necessary and, with it, a change of priorities. In other words, it was important to discuss the purpose and the direction of economic growth, using several numerical indexes, different approaches and the objective needs of the population. Lange ([198-b]) also mentioned the importance of incentives, the use of computers to formulate the plan and calculate the optimization of the economic results. Concerning the company in socialist countries, he claimed:

> Two extremes can jeopardize the socialist nature of the company. One is the absence of delegation of the public interest. In that case, the ownership of the means of production, regardless of its legal nature, is no longer socialist ownership and it becomes only group ownership deprived of any responsibility towards the society. This is called anarcho-trade unionist degeneration.

> The other extreme, which is called bureaucratic degeneration, takes place when there's a lack of effective self-government of the workers within the enterprises. In those cases, the socialist nature of the ownership of the means of production becomes fictional, because the workers have less influence on the practical use of the means of production. The influence that may eventually exist is processed by means of the channels of a centralized bureaucratic machine. Thus, the risk of "alienation" (to use a very well-known expression by Marx) emerges for the producer in relation to his product; then there's a distortion of the socialist nature of the production relations. The socialist ownership of the means of production signifies both the use of the means of production in the interests of society as a whole, and the actual democratic participation of producers and other workers in the administration of the means of production. (LANGE, [198-a], p.92)

Those statements reflect Che's theories about the socialist company. Regardless of how complicated and centralized the administration of industrial apparatus in Cuba was, Guevara always insisted that the decisions were made on several levels and that it involved the actual participation of the workers: "Of course the government couldn't impose rules, make plans, establish goals without the participation of the people, since in that case it would be a cold and bureaucratic plan. For that very reason, the company must turn to its employees and workers when discussing the plans, to incorporate the staff with the production and with the production problems, in such a way that the final result is something lively, a result of practical discussions about certain themes and that offer final conclusions." (GUEVARA, 1982, p.132)

Lange's discussions about planning, however, also extended to the developing countries that weren't necessarily socialist. But, since many of the cases that he mentioned were "popular democracies", some of his specific analyses were based mainly on the socialist plan. Guevara quoted Lange extensively in his article "The Budgetary Finance System", published in *Nuestra Indústria* magazine in 1964. In that text, the Argentinean revolutionary reiterated the importance of using the useful capitalist techniques for developing the country during the transition to socialism. (GUEVARA, 1982, p.186-187) But that was only in relation to improving the technological and administrative aspects of the country. In other words, it was possible to learn a lot from the techniques of the capitalist enterprises, but for the purpose of developing socialism more profoundly, which would necessarily include ideological and cultural components as integral and crucial to the formation of communist awareness.

According to Che, the Soviet industries were excessively backward as compared to the Western enterprises, both in terms of accounting, costs and inventory control, and in terms of machinery. For example, when a Cuban delegation visited an electronics plant in the Soviet Union, with approximately 5,000 workers, they saw that the company calculated costs using an abacus! Meanwhile, in Cuba, the old nationalized American industries, such as the Compañia Cubana de Electricidad, had IBM card perforation machines (considered the most modern of the time). (BORREGO, 2001b)

In 1965, the reforms officially reached Poland, following the tendency of other Eastern European countries. From then on, the plans were more "scientific" and less "arbitrary", with the calculation of costs and profits playing an ever-increasing role overall. This included an increase of reserves and a decentralization of decisions concerning the allocation of resources.[7] As in the other cases, the goal was to improve the quality of the products, increase productivity and discourage the systematic production of goods with little marketability. In other words, the plan should be progressively more directed to the enterprises and their workers.[8]

The Polish decentralization redirected most decision making from the ministries to the *zjednoczenia,* the industrial associations, each one of which was in charge of all the enterprises in a specific branch of the industry.[9] These associations were supposed to be autonomous, self-financed, with their own investments and incentive funds. The enterprises' objectives, as a result, also changed and were not considered the main performance criterion anymore. They were replaced by a profitability rate defined as the total of profits, before taxes, divided by the total production cost. In that sense, each company had a profitability goal, which should increase over time. The government rewards and bonuses would be paid according to the fulfillment of those goals.[10] Instead of receiving free investments directly from the government, the enterprises would receive bank credit for building new plants, to be repaid without interest providing there were no delays, by the company's profits. The decisions concerning modernization were made by the enterprises, which financed them according to their profits. In turn, price determination would continue to be centralized. Although they were less radical than those in Czechoslovakia, for example, the Polish reforms tended towards capitalism, since they adopted profitability as the main gauge of performance and introduced loans for investments with interest rates to be paid in cash. In theory, such changes were influenced by the desires of the enterprises themselves. In 1964, a survey of 354 plant administrators showed that 85% of them believed that the system of centralization of materials allocation was the greatest obstacle to operating the company efficiently. Some critics thought that the system didn't have much development potential, since many governmental institutions still used centralized practices, weren't punctual in sending the production and profit goals to the company and didn't punish the plants that weren't operating according to the system. In some cases, the annual production goals arrived six to nine months late, after the beginning of the year. In other words, the plans were still formulated according to old methods. (SMOLINSKI, 1966) Guevara was against those reforms, which had already been tested for some years in the country. As for the Polish system, the Minister of Industry of Cuba stated:

> I would like to say, now that I'm reading some analyses circulating in the socialist sphere, more exactly the Resolution of the Plan of the IV Congress of the Polish Communist Party,[11] a synthesis made by the Presidium, and also some interventions of the comrades from the *Politburo*, in which they face the same problems that afflict us.
> In Poland, where nobody suspects that there is anything other than the so-called "economic accounting system", we find similar problems to ours: those of investment, cost, the increase of unproductive staff in the plant (from the firefighters to the doormen), growing administrative staff, limited analysis of production costs, the fact that they are more worried about increasing production than with knowing how and if the products will be distributed; [...] in short, problems that also worry us and which we tend to ascribe to the budgetary system, are enumerated here, one by one, by the Polish. […]
> But, above all, the path which the economic accounting system ultimately follows when it goes deep, when it goes, as it must go, to its expression of principle, leads to a blind alley, because the logic of the facts leads it to search, step by step, for further solutions by means of the same mechanism. That is, increasing the material stimuli, guiding the people mainly to their own material interest, and through that path to the free game of the law of value and re-emergence, to a certain extent, of categories that are already strictly capitalist. That's what's going on; Poland demonstrates this and I believe that the other socialist countries do as well. (GUEVARA, 1982, p.57-58)

When Guevara attacked the new administrative forms of the socialist countries and defended his scheme, he tried to show that the occasional problems that arose were not necessarily within the budgetary finance system. The potential mistakes weren't intrinsic to the model, which couldn't be blamed for the economic difficulties of the island. According to him, the Cuban problems were a result of the very change of the structure of the country's economy and of the new administrators' lack of experience.

Yugoslavia, and its more flexible method of business management, was also widely discussed in the socialist world at the beginning of the 1960s. Even though he admired Marshall Tito, Guevara was a strong critic of the Yugoslav system. (BANDEIRA, 1998, p.178)

Yugoslavia was a small, mostly agricultural, country with few natural resources. It was made up of associated republics — Croatia, Montenegro, Slovenia, Bosnia and Herzegovina and Serbia — with two autonomous regions: Kosovo and Voivodina. While the small rural estate and the *zadruga* (patriarchal community) were consolidated forms in Serbia, the large estates prevailed in Croatia, Montenegro and Macedonia.

During World War II, when Tito freed many territories, he began implementing several social reforms in them, expropriating lands from the Germans, from the traitors, from the limited enterprises and some from the Church, restricting the rural estate to forty-five hectares and redistributing the land. In 1946, the industries, which were previously ruled by Germans, Italians and their collaborators, were nationalized. At first, forty-two crucial industrial sectors were nationalized; this was followed by a second nationalization, which deepened the measures already taken by the new government. Thus, the government took control of all industry, including mining, transportation and banking, among others.

In April 1947, the Yugoslav government laid the groundwork for a five-year plan with the objective of quintupling agricultural production and investing at least 30% of the entire GNP annually, using the traditional Soviet plans as a model. After severing relations with Moscow in 1948, Belgrade fostered a new administrative method, which was initially praised by several independent Marxists and anti-Soviets as a new example of humanist socialism. But a few years later, serious mistakes became obvious leading the country to increasingly move away from socialism. The ideas of worker "self-management", mainly inspired by Kardelj, were a reaction against the previous bureaucracy and excessive centralization. For the followers of that model, centralization was characterized by an "authoritarian collectivism", making individual action impossible, promoting excessive vertical control and lower productivity. There was also a new form of exploitation, since one social stratum monopolized management and profit distribution. The bureaucrats, acting on behalf of the workers, would be the new exploiters.

Thus, the self-management system was implemented, in 1949 in a consultative manner, and later with decision-making authority according to the law, on July 27th, 1950. Certainly, that was much more of a political than an economic measure, but it was gradually consolidated within the country. In a speech, Kardelj stated that the Soviet Union had exaggerated the role of the government, which would have taken on a very special economic stance within the system of social relations. According to him, the "evolution" to socialism in Western Europe through the existent political structure was feasible and supposedly was already taking place. The Yugoslav revolution was necessary because of the local bourgeoisie's inability to advance History and, therefore, it would be a task of the new regime to change the balance of social forces in favor of socialism through industrialization. For that reason, internal discipline was also necessary. But Yugoslavia had, unlike the Soviet Union, managed to avoid the bureaucracy when it started the gradual dissolution of the government through measures that gave more power to social ownership, that is, to the workers' councils. (BRZEZINSKI, 1965, p.189)

There was much criticism of the old system. The Yugoslavs believed that the global evaluations of quantities and quantitative objectives imposed on the enterprises made any individual action impossible. They believed that there was a lack of stimuli, coercive employment, predetermination and rationing of consumption and the tendency for the plan to extend into other areas, such as arts and sciences. Thus, the current model should be replaced by another more flexible one, with more general strategies, more consumer freedom and giving the enterprises greater internal decision-making power. From then on, the free market was re-established in the country, with the possibility of creating businesses that could choose their products and their investments, sell their products freely and establish their own prices. The Yugoslav arrangement only defined the overall objectives in monetary terms, not in quantities, and it didn't establish industrial regulations in an authoritarian manner. Its goal was to control the balance between demand and distribution, to try to ensure economic development based on crucial proportions of great masses.

The general scheme was elaborated by the Federal Office for Economic Planning, with approximately two hundred employees, debated by the Executive Council and, after completion, it would be subject to a vote of the Executive Council itself and of the Federal Council of producers.[12] Each plan would determine the development guidelines, that is, the GNP growth rate (often 9% per year) and the development of the most backward regions. The plan also established the relationship between social consumption — the fulfillment of collective needs by public services — and individual consumption, as well as the great production masses to be worked out. The Yugoslav government ended rationing, the compulsory delivery of harvests and the administrative distribution of goods and raw materials etc. In the first phase (1950-1953), the objective of the new economic scheme was to impose a minimum tax on production capacity (which varied around 5%), a corresponding wage fund, minimum wages for each category, a minimum volume of governmental investments, contribution to support the social funds of the federation, the republics and of the communes based on taxes and social security; and freedom for the enterprises to use the rest of the surplus capital as they pleased. In 1954, some of those instruments were abolished and others became more flexible. In other words, Yugoslavia tried to rebuild its economic model by means of gradual measures towards the free market.

A national investment fund was created, as well as similar instruments in the republics and communes.[13] Its goal was to control the portion of investment that was still centralized, while others fell under the domain of the enterprises.[14] Since not all of the enterprises were in the same financial condition, a special fund was created to help the poorer businesses. In turn, the banks were communal, managed by representatives of the local companies and a representative of the worker's council. Their gains weren't made through the interest payments, but through commissions on the operations. Therefore, the bank's main role was ascribing funds and overseeing their use. In turn, the National Bank's resources came from budgetary "donations", and from interest and annuities paid by the enterprises in debt. Most of the funds were used in "fast" development programs for the most backward regions, as well as in large public undertakings such as building roads, drainage and irrigation, among others. Another portion was used to enhance the investments by the enterprises and communes for executing projects that the government found worthy of supporting.

Progressive taxes were charged on the companies' net profits, and these were passed on to the funds for the federation and for the territorial units. The company's profits were subject to an additional tax when they were greater than 20% of personal profits. The prices of some basic items were fixed and others, such as those for specific industries, were frozen. Any price increase had to be approved by the government thirty days prior to taking effect. The prices of several agricultural products were controlled, as well as essential food, dwelling and transportation. Everything else, primarily consumer goods, was not regulated. Some commercial contracts were prohibited to the enterprises, if they weren't a statutory part of their business. The enterprises also couldn't use intermediaries for purchasing, create monopolies, or impose conditions upon consumers regarding the supply and sale of goods between businesses. The government controlled all foreign trade. (LASSERRE, 1966)

For the Yugoslav economists, the free market was a criterion for determining the enterprises' profitability, showing which of them were the most efficient and which were qualified to continue doing business. In other words, the free market provided an incentive to increase productivity. It indicated whether the enterprises were able to adapt their production to consumer needs. In 1962, several liberalization and decentralization measures taken in the previous year were corrected, mainly regarding the distribution of wages to the detriment of investment and the distribution of unrealized profits. In that year, the control of foreign trade was intensified, several professional departments were merged into a single economic division and a special coordination committee was established to monitor the plan's execution more closely

There was a great deal of criticism of the Yugoslav system. Some people believed that the increasing production of superfluous items was encouraging the growth of the private capitalism sector, while the private sector of agriculture still controlled 85% of the land. Self-management was a business model that would allow capitalism to develop, and a new caste, that of the "agent bureaucrat", would emerge from the industrial managers. (MCFARLANE, 1969b, p.107) That, combined with material incentives, would use profit as motivation.

After the rupture with the Soviet Union, in 1948, a greater number of economists who graduated from Western institutions and were influenced by capitalist practices gained authority within the Yugoslav government. Boris Kidric, President of the Economic Council and the Federal Planning Office, defended the continued use of the law of supply and demand, instead of centralized planning, for practical reasons. (MCFARLANE, 1969b, p.109) Those who wanted to maintain the centralized system until the economy had reached a higher level were gradually replaced. Thus, such personalities as Nikola Cobelic and Radmila Stojanovic, both aides of the Planning Committee, resigned, and were replaced by "conservative" economists who were returning to the country after finishing their graduate courses in England or in the United States. Thus, such economists as Branko Horvat and Professor R. Bicanic became influential within the government.

But Yugoslavia's economic situation was far from good. In 1963, for example, only 54% of the industrial capacity was being used, partly because the machines depended on raw materials that weren't available and partly due to the lack of power, which had not been sufficiently developed in the "rush" to decentralize. Increasing the tax on fixed capital also proved inefficient. It was established in order to compensate some "monopolistic" enterprises for their idle capacity and to increase production and reduce prices. The fact is that, since 1954, some monopolized sectors had actually emerged — although they were against the general statutes of the governmental scheme — and many industries weren't sufficiently competitive. During that period, the economic situation reached a point where the sector's idle capacity made it possible to increase production by at least 20% without any investments. (MCFARLANE, 1969b, p.113-114)

Paradoxically, there was a rise in industrial production between 1963 and 1964, because capital was redirected to projects for reorganizing and optimizing operations in the plants in some less developed regions. (MCFARLANE, 1969b, p.114) Beginning in 1964, the investment banks were abolished, and were replaced by the "economic banks", which operated with profit incentives, making high interest loans to the investment markets. This also gave businesses the right to obtain long-term credit. Under this system, bank funds were naturally directed to the strongest sectors of the economy. The central organs only controlled the investor's share percentage. (MCFARLANE, 1969b, p.115) In the first few years of the 1960's, the cost of living continued to go up; it rose from 7.5% in 1961 to 10.5% in the following year. In August 1964, the cost of living was raised 24% by decree, while the minimum wage rose 10% in the same year. Between August 1964 and March 1965, overall prices went up 33%, while wages only rose 15% in the same period. There was also an implicit fear that the enterprises' high productivity and profitability rates were a reason for greater taxation by the government. Because of this fear of taxation, many enterprises didn't invest in new machinery and technological innovations that could increase production.

In general, there was a growing resistance to the idea of centralized planning. Between 1961 and 1965, many articles were published in Yugoslavia supporting greater economic autonomy for the enterprises and communes[15]. Slovenia, for example, in 1964 refused to implement the plan advocated by the central government and instead adopted a general development strategy determined by its own Parliament. Inequities began to emerge among the businesses, the individuals and over-valued profits. There was also an increasing similarity to Western countries and capitalist practices in general. Some years later, many European and American ventures began investing in the country. An article published in *The New York Times* on August 19th, 1968 stated:

Western capital has gained an important foothold in Yugoslavia and is helping to turn what was once chiefly an agricultural country into a new industrial State.

Investments by such diverse enterprises as Fiat — the Italian auto giant, and Printing Developments, Inc., of New York City, a subsidiary of Time, Inc. — represent both the voracious demands of capital for new outlets and the conscious designs of a Communist state to accept a market economy and most of the trappings.

Conversations with Belgrade officials, specializing in economic activities, show their firm conviction that this route will be followed by other countries of Eastern Europe.

To them Yugoslavia is a pacesetter in the East as well as a show window for Western capital. Western companies operating here will have enormous competitive advantages once markets open up elsewhere in Eastern Europe.

Following reforms that shifted control of enterprises themselves and introduced the disciplines of the free market and the incentive of profits, Yugoslavia promulgated an equally revolutionary law a year ago to attract foreign capital.

The law did not come without strong opposition from those fearful that Western capital would dominate the key sectors of the economy.

To guard against this, foreign capital is barred from acquiring more than a 49% interest in a Yugoslav enterprise.

Yugoslav companies are controlled by their workers through workers' councils, which, in turn, name a board of professionals, such as accountants and production engineers, to manage their plant.

At first foreign companies were reluctant to get involved because the minority stake, they felt, would not give them any direct control over their investment.

The foreigners are permitted to transfer profits out of the country provided they keep 20% on deposit with a Yugoslav bank. They can sell their stake to other foreign companies provided they first offer to sell it back to the Yugoslav company.

The law has produced some dramatic results.

Fiat, which is supplying the technology and most of the equipment for a big Soviet auto plant, put US$ 10 million into a Yugoslav company, Crvena Zastava (Red Flag), which makes Fiat cars under license.

The American company, according to published information here, has gone into a joint venture with Beogradski Graficki Zavod (Belgrade Graphical Printing Company) to do color printing using especially fast, new processing equipment from the United States. (apud SWEEZY, 1972, p.6-7)

According to the economist Oskar Lange, the initial development phases of a socialist economy should follow a specific pattern, that is, something similar to a war economy. In other words, he believed that, if the production forces of a country were in a backward stage, political and economic centralization was crucial, trying to decrease production sources, pricing and control techniques as much as possible. Lange believed that, regardless of how tough that period was, it was a historical need. Political and economic flexibility could come about gradually, when the national economy was in a more developed and mature stage. However, advocates of the Yugoslav system claimed that what had occurred was the opposite. Yugoslavia had supposedly proven that the “socialist market” was possible in the transition period. With greater abundance of merchandise and improved living conditions, the economy could be planned based on better material conditions. (MCFARLANE, 1969b, p.127-128) Some Marxist scholars proved to be extremely critical of the economic “innovations” in

Yugoslavia during that period. Ernest Mandel even said of that country's economists:

> ...the market economy is not necessarily harmful during the transition period between capitalism and socialism; but it must be maintained after the construction of socialism is completed. Some of them still argue that the production of goods will occasionally disappear "under communism". But those arguments are actually inconsistent. The most coherent theoreticians, such as Horvat, boldly conceive a communist society with flourishing production. [...] The pragmatic and eulogistical origin of that concept is evident. What really matters to the Yugoslav scholars is explaining and to justifying what is going on in their own country. Because they're either unaware of the long-term theoretical implications or they really despise them. (MANDEL, 1967, p.22)

As has been previously stated, Che Guevara was also extremely critical concerning Yugoslavia. His initial opinions seemed to demonstrate that he still didn't know the system sufficiently to be able to discuss the topic more deeply. As the years went by, however, a clear position against that method of economic administration can be seen. By the end of 1959, when he came back from an official trip through several countries, he wrote articles for the magazine *Verde Olivo* about each one of them, even claiming that Yugoslavia might have been the most interesting place among all that he visited. Che said:

> All the collectivities of Yugoslavia, be them peasant or worker-industrial, are guided by the principle of what they call self-management. Within a general plan, well defined in terms of its scope, but not in terms of its private development, the enterprises fight among themselves within the national market as a private capitalist entity. It could be said, in general, exaggerating, that the defining characteristic of Yugoslav society is business capitalism with a socialist distribution of profits. In other words, considering each company not as a group of workers, but as a unit, this company would operate approximately within a capitalist system, according to the laws of supply and demand and undertaking a violent struggle for the prices and quality with their peers; undertaking what, in

> economy, is called free competition .... The system, hard to describe in a few words, is well coordinated and is often successful at providing small luxuries to the population, which is well dressed, well nourished and happy, even though there isn't, in my opinion, a great enough insistence on reiterating the great paths of industrialization, which should take place in a poor and underdeveloped country like Yugoslavia, based on greater sacrifice by the population, giving up all those small luxuries that I have detailed. (GUEVARA, 1988a, p.68-69)

A few years later, in 1964, Guevara's opinion was more incisive. Apparently, he already wasn't so complacent about Yugoslavia. In a meeting with members of the Cuban government, he insisted that:

> ...in Yugoslavia the law of value works, in Yugoslavia plants are closed because they aren't profitable; in Yugoslavia there are Swiss and Dutch delegations that gather idle labor and take it to their own countries to work in the conditions imposed by an imperialist country on foreign labor, considered as the last step of society. Thus, the Yugoslav comrades end up as laborers or peasants in countries where work is scarce, threatened with unemployment, to wind up in the street, like a Puerto Rican in the United States. (GUEVARA, 1982, p.70)

And he completed:

> That goes on in Yugoslavia. Poland is following along the same path, making a whole series of collectivization measures void, returning to private land ownership, stabilizing a series of exchange systems, increasing contacts with the United States. Czechoslovakia and Germany are also studying the Yugoslav system in order to implement it. In short, we're before several countries that are all changing their paths. Before what? Before a reality that can't be ignored: that the Western block advances production at a pace that's greater than the pace of the socialist path of the popular democracies. Why? Instead of going deep, to the root of this, to try to solve the problem, a superficial answer is given, there's a return to the market theory, people resort once again to the law of value, and material incentives are reinforced. (GUEVARA, 1982, p.70)

Che was extremely critical of the process taking place in the Soviet Union and in Eastern Europe, and he had very clear ideas about the development of socialism, mainly in Cuba. His criticism made him move further away, ideologically, from those experiences and made him appear to have dissonant and radical positions in relation to the concepts advocated by some theoreticians of that period.

---

[1] One example is the manual *El partido marxist-leninista*, by Kuusinen. Even though he criticized those manuals, Guevara wrote the foreword of Kuusinen's book using the same jargon and expressions as the Soviet texts (MASSARI, 1993, p.122). According to Ernst Halperin (1967, p.47), during the Khrushchev years the act of worrying about ideology was no longer a function of the main rulers, but ascribed to "second rank" personalities such as the "dogmatic" Suslov, the "bureaucratic pedantics" Pospelov and Ponomarev and the "loquacious talker" Kuusinen. Carlos Rafael Rodríguez (1983b, p.192), on the other hand, considered Otto Kuusinen a "great theoretician" and "divulger of Marxism", who supposedly wrote the "best introductory manual of Marxism-Leninism published in Spanish".

[2] For further information on the annual growth rate of the industrial production in the Soviet Union and in countries of Eastern Europe, see Dobb (1970, p.42-43).

---

[3] According to Isaac Deutscher (1969a, p.15), "the general pace of the economic activity decreased. The net national income increased only 5% in 1964, compared to the growth rate of 7 to 8% in the previous years (and a rate of 8% predicted for 1965). The growth rate in the construction and equipment of plants increased only 3.3% in 1964 — with a predicted rate of 8.2% for 1965. The scale of industrial development was still impressive: the metallurgical industry, for example, with its 85 million tons of annual production, almost reached the American level of the beginning of the 1960's". As in the Stalinist era, the growth was once again distorted and unequal, relatively mild in the traditional industry (heavy and arms industry), but slow and hesitant in the new industries (synthetic fibers and electronics). The quantity of the production was not matched by its quality; the state-owned commercial organizations presented huge surpluses of inferior quality consumer goods that couldn't be sold. For further information on the Soviet economy of the period, see Baráibar (1957, p.1-8) and Laurat (1957, p.54-57).

[4]There were also changes in other countries, such as in Bulgaria. Even with a more "cautious" project than those of East Germany, Czechoslovakia and Hungary, the Bulgarian program had profound repercussions on the country's economy. Unlike the East German and Czech economies, Bulgaria was largely underdeveloped. According to the Bulgarian leaders, the underdevelopment of the country was already enough for another model of economic management to be tried. Except for the heavy industry, all the other sectors and aspects of the economy, such as the quality of the products, profitability and pricing, for example, were performing poorly. The debates about Liberman's ideas greatly influenced the change of the country's economic path. In the VIII Congress of the Communist Party of Bulgaria, a resolution was approved which accepted the principle of the need of reform in the management and planning systems, as well as the increase of the material incentives in the entire economy. For further details, see Brown (1966, p.17-18).

---

[5]In January 1964, Kunin's ideas were tested in the textile plant Liliana Dimitrova, in Sophia, with such innovations as non-state funding and reward and prize systems based on profit. In the same month, the politburo of the party and the Council of Ministers announced similar practices in fifty other industries from April 1st, 1964 on. In 1965, the experiment was extended, with the use of 33.5% of all the workers in the country and contributing 44% of the total of the industrial production.

---

[6]Podgorny was the Head of State, since he was the President of the Presidium of Supreme Soviet of the Soviet Union; Kosygin, the Head of Government, was the President of the Presidium Commissioners Council; and Brezhnev, the First-Secretary of the Communist Party of the Soviet Union and who actually had the greatest share of political power.

---

[7]For further information on the previous Polish economic plans, see Harris (1949, p.432-453).

[8]It must be recalled that, at that moment, Lange no longer participated. As for Cuba, Guevara was also no longer participating directly with the economic matters of the island.

---

[9]Polish rulers, however, had already demonstrated some skepticism about the workers' decentralization and self-management. According to W. Gomulka, First-Secretary of the Unified Polish Workers' Party (UPWP), "if each plant became a kind of cooperative

company of workers, all the laws that rule the capitalist company would become reinvigorated and would produce all the usual results. The central planning and the administration [...] would have to disappear." Maybe that partially explains the greater "caution" of the reforms in Poland compared to other countries. Despite the criticisms, the changes continued to occur. See MCFARLANE (1969b, p.106).

[10] Lange apparently supported that measure: "We will mention one example of the Polish experience: the fact that the rewards paid to the administrative staff and to the workers in the enterprises were related to the extent that the plan was executed and generated, with the regularity of an economic law, two consequences: first, the plans were very modest, because there was the incentive of a modest plan that can be easily overcome; second, the plans tended to be overcome only slightly, in such a way that they weren't greatly extended in the following year. [...] We wish, so to speak, to abolish that kind of economic law. Instead, the rewards will be based on the relative improvements of the company in relation to the previous year". We must recall that this article was written in 1957. Therefore, the Polish had already been testing differentiated mechanisms of economic management much before they officially implemented their new economic policies. See Lange ([198-]a, p.90).

---

[11] Guevara refers to the Unified Polish Workers' Party (UPWP), which was, in practice, the country's Communist Party.

---

[12] The boards of producers were representative organs created by a Constitutional law in 1953. They existed on several levels. On the national level, they had the same rights as the National Assembly as far as economic, social and labor legislation was concerned. The boards of producers also existed in the republics and in the communes. They included only the representatives of agriculture, crafts and industry, elected by the producers proportionally to the share of each sector in the national income. The function of the boards of producers was to acknowledge the situation of several sectors and economic organs, of the plans, budget and distribution of funds, and they were a powerful means to fight against some possible tendencies of the local power organs.

---

[13] The communes were the only organs on which the enterprises really depended. It was they, not the central administration, who represented the collectivity before the enterprises. There

were 708 communes in Yugoslavia, with around 5,000 to 20,000 inhabitants. The commune created most of the enterprises, appointed their directors, received part of the profits and sometimes granted loans to them.

[14]In December 1963, the National Investments Fund was all but abolished. It was an important instrument for unifying the branches of the economy as a whole, based on the distribution of funds to the sectors and industries that needed to develop, and according to their importance within the plan.

---

[15]For example, the article by V. Bakaric, in the magazine *Economska Politika*, of November 10th, 1964, for whom "today we're getting close to changes in the economic system from the point of view of the centralization *versus* decentralization. Making things even simpler — I, alone, have the power or it's shared by five people. In that specific matter, the ideological base, the base of economic or social relations, in that achievement, doesn't change. We must turn to the sphere of freer economic relations." See McFarlane (1969b, p.119).

4

THE CUBAN ECONOMIC DEBATE

The economic discussions in the Soviet Union and in Eastern Europe had repercussions in other parts of the world and they certainly influenced several members of the Cuban government. What was commonly called the "economic debate" in Cuba was characterized by several articles that were published in magazines and journals of official institutions of that country. The debate began with the article "Considerations About Production Costs as a Basis for the Economic Analysis of the Enterprises Subject to the Budgetary System", written by Che Guevara and published in *Nuestra Indústria, Revista Econômica,* in June, 1963, and it ended with "The Socialist Planning and Its Meaning", by the same author, which was published in *Cuba Socialista* (the most influential "theoretical" government publication) in June, 1964. Its main topics were the strategy, industrial management, the budgetary finance system, the economic accounting system, the incentive system, the role of the banks, the theory of value, the socialist emulation and voluntary work as a way to increase the awareness and productivity of the workers.[1]

Therefore, the economic debate was included more broadly as a reflex and continuation of the discussions that were going on in the socialist world, and also demonstrated the concern about discussing topics specifically related to the Cuban economic development in that period. Members of the government, such as Alberto Mora and Carlos Rafael

Rodríguez, and foreign intellectuals, such as Charles Bettelheim and Ernest Mandel all participated in the debate. According to Mandel:

> Therefore, the unity of revolutionary theory and practice is constantly threatened by the parallel risks of pragmatism on one side, and of dogmatism, on the other. A great series of effective socialist practices are essential before the theory can ultimately encode the "economic laws" for constructing socialism, which we can't find out, in the current phase of the experience, except by means of multiple touches and of multiple mistakes, according to the method of successive approximation. As a consequence, the unity between theory and practice at the time of the transition must necessarily include a certain degree of theoretical autonomy, without which the practice itself runs the risk of being unclear and disoriented, and the risks of detours and mistakes are multiplied. [...]
> Not all the participants in the economic debate of 1963-1964 were aware of those reciprocal dialectic relations between the revolutionary theory and practice. But it can be stated, without hesitation, that they tried instinctively to conciliate the imperative of the relative autonomy of the theory and that of the immediate effectiveness of the practice. That's what gives a tone of sincerity and seriousness worth praising, even though in certain contributions the babbling of an idea being formed can be recognized, more than the mature expression of a theory that has already reached full awareness of the social reality from which it emerged. (MANDEL, 1982b, p.166)

During the entire debate, Guevara defended the notion that Cuba should consolidate the budgetary finance system, which has already been discussed. According to him, the principle that rules capitalism would be the law of value, which expresses itself in the market. In Cuba, however, despite the scarcity of goods, which could have led to a logical rise in prices and to the return of the supply-demand relationship, the government had imposed a price freeze and increased rationing, impeding the expression of the value of the goods through the market. Thus, the prices were defined according to several inter-related factors, from raw materials to all kinds of expenses in the production process and the distribution of goods.[2] If the products acted according to "inter-related" prices —different from what takes place in the capitalist market — a new price relationship would emerge, different from what exists in the world market.

For prices to coincide with value, the law governing them should be intentionally written to maintain the balance of the mercantile fund and at the same time reflect real prices. That is a hard task, but, with greater centralization and less bureaucracy, that process could commence.

The Argentinean revolutionary believed that it would be possible to gradually develop new and more efficient control techniques, taking advantage of the advances in general accounting made by the capitalist enterprises. Besides, a product would only be considered as such when it had already gone through a "long process" of internal flow, and it would only become a good when there was ownership transference, that is, when it was in the hands of the consumer. Therefore, while the item was circulating within the state-owned production sector it would not be a good.

The cost analysis would be crucial in that case, since a "coincidence" is needed, of an intimate relationship between production cost and price within socialism. The prices of the international market would be different from those proposed for the internal realm of the island, which in practice would represent an ideal measurement form.

To avoid distortions between internal and international prices, a system could be established, based on a certain "historical measure" of prices used in the capitalist world market. Thus, prices would be established and would be kept for a certain period of time, without changes. Guevara believed that, if the prices of the basic items of the economy were set and if prices of the other products were based on the former, according to approximate calculations, it would be possible to reach the "historical level" of the world market prices. According to him, the price of goods to the population could be different from the price in the enterprises. In turn, the most important thing for the enterprises would be the cost analysis, the main industrial management rate.[3] For that to happen, government technicians would be forced to develop an entire system for cost analysis, rules for the consumption of raw materials, of indirect costs, of products being produced, inventories and finished goods, as well as the systematization of the inventory control and elaboration of the exact economic works concerning those rates.

New technologies to avoid waste, conserve electricity and fuel consumption, greater administrative control, qualified rulers, greater economic analysis and, above all, greater productivity on the job are all important elements for controlling and reducing production costs and the final prices to the consumer. All these factors should be included in a centralized scheme for the economy, which, in turn, should make it possible for decisions to be made on different levels and with the broad participation of the workers. (GUEVARA, 1982, p.172-177)

Therefore, the budgetary finance system was crucial to managing the Cuban economy efficiently and to keep it moving towards socialism. As has been shown before, in that system a company is a conglomerate of plants and production units with the same technological base, a common destination for the production and a similar geographic location. In the economic accounting system, the enterprises are production units with their own legal identity. In the budgetary finance system, money is used only as an arithmetic measure, as a reflex of the enterprises' management of prices, from which the analysis of the central organs is made to establish controls in the operation of such enterprises. In the financial self-management system, it is used not only for the same purposes, but also as an indirect control instrument. Therefore, a greater individual relationship among the enterprises exists. In the system proposed by Guevara, the enterprises don't have their own funds, receiving investments according to removal quotas of the deposits from the accounts created for each one of them, but according to the decisions of the central organs and of the budget. All the enterprises' deposits, in turn, go directly into a general government fund, which later redistributes the money to the accounts as it sees fit. In the economic accounting system, on the other hand, the enterprises have their own funds and receive credit from the banks, which would make loans in return for the payment of interest.

A Soviet economy "dictionary", broadly circulated in Cuba, claimed that economic accounting was a planned management method for attaining maximum effectiveness in production, using economic laws from socialism and monetary-mercantile relations, and in which the company or the consolidated enterprises must be profitable. (SAVIN; FONTE; JORSOV, 1981, p.11) The text went further, implying that, in general, this system was the most efficient. It said that the enterprises have the right to make economic agreements with other businesses, suppliers or consumers, to have charge and payment accounts in the bank, to obtain bank credit, to organize the functions of their labor force and, from the production plan on, they had the autonomy to acquire materials, fuels and to manufacture their products. The better the company worked, the greater its profit, which would increase stimulation funds to the company. Therefore, the rates created for them by the central organs would be reduced. Profit, credit, economic independence, interest and greater material stimuli would play a greater role. In other words, it resembled something very similar to capitalism.

According to that same manual, the profit in socialism would be characterized only by the economic effectiveness of the company and by the economic stimulation instrument. (SAVIN; FONTE; JORSOV, 1981, p.55) In turn, Che thought that, to stabilize the mercantile fund and demand, it would be a function of the Ministry of Internal Trade (MINCIN) to level the purchase power of the population with the price of goods, giving special emphasis to the essential products ensuring, therefore, a low price. In other words, in certain cases the ministry should ignore the law of value and set the prices for each specific case. (GUEVARA, 1982, p.195) According to Guevara:

> All the import raw materials will have a fixed and stable price, based on a measure of the international market, plus some more points due to the cost of transportation and of the foreign trade apparatus. The real production cost of all Cuban raw materials will be priced in monetary terms. Both would take into account the added expense of planned work plus the wear and tear of the basic means to elaborate them. That would be the price of the products distributed to foreign trade and among enterprises, but they would be constantly affected by rates reflecting the price of that good in the world market, plus the costs of transportation and of foreign trade. The enterprises that operate by means of the budgetary finance regime would operate according to the base of their planned costs and wouldn't have profits; those would be carried to the MINCIN (naturally, this refers to that part of the social product that takes place as a good, is the fundamental as consumption fund); the rates would tell us (the state-owned apparatus and the company) continuously what is really effective and would prevent mistakes. The population wouldn't suffer with all those changes, since the price of goods would be independently fixed, meeting the demand and the vital need of each product. (GUEVARA, 1982, p.196)

Based on an intricate system, the central organs would make the calculations relevant to the entire production sphere, from imported machinery, raw materials, wages, and equipment expenses, resulting in the real costs of each undertaking, in its idealized cost and in the cost compared to the international market. This provides more of a basis for choosing materials, with the goal of keeping costs as low as possible, not worrying so much at this moment about mathematical optimization — since other factors could be considered, such as politics and the foreign market. The use of this technique gives a basic idea of the real production costs and trade. (GUEVARA, 1982, p.196) If this technique were adopted in other socialist countries, it would be possible to create, according to the conception of the Argentinean guerrilla leader, a "global socialist market" of prices better than the one currently used.

In practice, however, the budgetary finance system had many problems. Guevara himself admitted that the enterprises didn't operate as they should: plants weren't supplied in the manner or on the schedule determined by the plan. They received raw materials for technological processes different from theirs, which forced changes that led to an increase in the company's expenses and in the cost of the products, and there was still the difficulty of investments and modifications to the plan. There weren't any "automatic devices" to identify those problems and solve them immediately, they were reported to the ministry, which served only to collect information. Since there was still a bureaucracy and the plans were complicated, the entire process was eventually delayed. Depending on the situation, the employees had to solve the problems themselves, while in other cases matters were resolved by phone or by CILOS, which analyzed the immediate problems and then made relevant administrative decisions.

According to Che, the system "lacked maturity", in addition to a scarcity of specialized staff, mistakes in the supply of materials and transportation and in the quality control. There was also a need for greater dispersal of the system throughout the country, to develop a more efficient central apparatus and to improve relations among the governmental distribution organs and with the organs that supplied materials. (GUEVARA, 1982, p.199) On the other hand, he believed that the system had advantages, since, the fact that it was extremely centralized, made a more rational use of the national funds possible, as well as the apparatus of the industrial administration itself, conserving the work force, increasing productivity and making the control of investments easier. As time went on, it would be possible to create plants that are more productive and to develop socialism in the country.

Luís Álvarez Rom, who was the Minister of Finance at the time, Mario Rodríguez Escalona, Miguel Cosío and Alexis Codena who had similar ideas, developed in a similar manner to Che's, participated in the debate. The articles advocated the same issues presented by Guevara but, in some cases, they attacked the individuals who promoted ideas that opposed those of the Argentinean revolutionary more directly. Also participating in the debate were Juan Infante, a high-ranking employee of INRA, who wrote an article in which he advocated the economic accounting, and Miguel Figueras, who discussed whether or not it would be advisable to reprioritize agriculture as fundamental for economic development.

One of Guevara's main critics at that time, who defended the economic accounting system, was the important French economist Charles Bettelheim. He underwent a theoretical transition that culminated, a few years later, in changing his position. In a Conference at the University of Havana in 1963, Bettelheim exposed several themes that he later advocated in his article "Forms and Methods of Socialist Planning and Development Level of the Production Forces", published in the magazine *Cuba Socialist* in April, 1964, dealing with topics related to planning and industrial management in the transition period to socialism. Bettelheim believed that in all of the socialist countries, regardless of their development level, mercantile categories would continue to exist. In other words, they would have the calculation of value, currency, and credit and financial systems. Therefore, the mercantile categories would be consciously used. This would occur because, at that time, there were different forms of socialist ownership coexisting in the same economic environment.

The French economist said that the idea of having no mercantile categories within the socialist sector of production or, according to him, to consider that sector as a "single State monopoly", with products circulating, but not necessarily being traded, thus constituting a "pseudo market", was a mistaken and an "unrealistic" way to analyze the situation. "I believe that this is exactly the way to reach the crucial issue: in the current phase of the socialization of production forces, the socially necessary working time (in all the senses of that term) is still not fully measurable directly; and that's why the mercantile categories are objectively imposed as the only means of measurement, and of indirect measurement, of the socially necessary working time." (BETTELHEIM, 1976b, p.23)

It would be difficult for a central organ to determine the allocation of all the financial resources for the harmonious development of the industrial sector and of distribution. In practice, an ideal system would be one in which a general centralized management, in the realm of the national planning, could coexist with a flexibility in the economic sector, making decentralized management possible on some occasions, since, within socialism, differentiated production centers which could be independent from one another would exist. (BETTELHEIM, 1976b, p.24)

Even knowing that the "superior" form of socialist ownership was supposedly State ownership, "inferior" forms, associated with a specific historical moment and related to the development level of the production forces of a specific country would still be necessary. Government decisions should be made towards recognizing the most efficient kinds of collectivity for certain production processes. The development of the production forces and of production relations would gradually take part in transforming the structure of the socialist sector. (BETTELHEIM, 1976b, p.27) According to him, the connection and interdependence of that sector were growing in several countries, and that "integration process" would lead to greater planning. The dynamic of that process should be respected. Before the integration occurs, the production units should be kept relatively autonomous in financial terms. That interdependence would represent, in practice, the beginning of the integration, and would be responsible for creating the need for real planning within socialism. (BETTELHEIM, 1976b, p.28)

The prices would represent the decisions (which could vary according to each enterprise) about the managing the resources and the elaboration of methods that allowed for a concurrence between the production optimization of each enterprise and the concrete social situation, based on what had been worked out in the plan. The economic accounting, anyway, could not be consolidated if it only took into account the current prices, but the probable future prices must be considered, to give a more objective idea of the enterprise's development. Therefore, the planning and the calculations of working time would be crucial to greater economic efficiency in the particular way that he advocated, always indicating, however, the need for greater freedom of the socialist enterprises to act. Bettelheim advocated some of Stalin's concepts present in the *Economic Problems of Socialism in the Soviet Union* (STALIN, 1953), primarily the validity of the law of value in the transition period to socialism.[4] According to Stalin:

> Some comrades deny the objective character of scientific laws, specifically of the economic laws in socialism. They deny that the laws of political economy reflect the regularity of processes that take place regardless of the desire of men. They consider that, due to the peculiar role reserved to the Soviet State by History, the Soviet State and her rulers can abolish the existent laws of the political economy, can "form" new laws, "create" new laws.
>
> Those comrades are deeply mistaken. As can be seen, they confuse the scientific laws, which reflect objective processes of nature or of the society, and take place regardless of the desire

> of men, with the laws that are promulgated by governments, created according to the desire of men and that only have legal force. However, there's no way they can ever be confused. [...] One of the peculiarities of the political economy is the fact that its laws, unlike the laws of the natural sciences, are not permanent. At least most of them act within a certain historical period, after which new laws replace them. But those laws are not destroyed, though they do lose their validity as a consequence of new economic conditions, and step down to be replaced by new laws which are not created according to the desire of men, since they emerge based on new human conditions. (STALIN, 1953, p.3-6)

According to Stalin's elaborations, a law dealing with the harmonious development of the national economy would make it possible for the central organs of the government to better plan social production, which doesn't mean that that law of value could be abolished or transformed. The ruler rejected the criticisms that mercantile production would necessarily lead to capitalism, since, according to him, "mercantile production" and "capitalist production" are different things. Stalin said that:

> ...capitalist production is the superior form of mercantile production. Mercantile production leads to capitalism only in this case: *if* there is private ownership of the means of production, *if* the labor force presents the product to the market as a good that can be bought and exploited by the capitalist in the production process; *if,* as a consequence, there is a system of exploitation of the wage earners by the capitalist within the country. Capitalist production begins where the means of production are concentrated in private hands and the workers, deprived of the means of production, are forced to sell their labor force, as a good. Without this, there's no capitalist production." (STALIN, 1953, p.14-15)

Thus, the law of value would exist and would act, considering the fact that there would be mercantile production. That law wouldn't be so important as a regulator of socialist production, but it would influence production.

This would make the leaders calculate all of the production sector's potential by analyzing the concrete reality. It would improve production methods to reduce costs, it would generate "financial autonomy", it would increase the enterprises' profitability and it would better prepare the new leaders. (STALIN, 1953, p.20) Meanwhile, it would act in a parallel manner to the "law of harmonious development" of the economy, which would take the place of competition and anarchy of production, together with the five-year plans which, as a whole, would limit the action of the law of value. As a historical category, it would only disappear when the mercantile production was over. According to Stalin, in capitalism the law of value could only regulate production. (STALIN, 1953, p.24) It must be recalled that from 1928, with the publication of *Political Economy,* by Lapidus and Ostrovityanov — who felt that the law of value was in the process of disappearing in the Soviet Union — until the beginning of the 1950's the concept of objective economic laws in socialism didn't exist in the Soviet Union as they weren't analyzed until a later period. In 1952, with Stalin's book, the conception changed radically. Thus, for example, the director of the Institute of Economy of the Socialist World of the Academy of Sciences of the Soviet Union, G. Sorokin, even said:

> In the transition period from capitalism to socialism and in an established socialist society, planning is a kind of economic administration by the government, based on the knowledge and the use of objective socialist economic laws, regardless of personal wishes or desires. If the necessary material requirements are given to the planned economic development, the efficiency of any planning depends on how accurately the government organs apply the basic economic laws (apud MAGDOFF, 1985, p.118-119)

In other words, the interpretation of the economy also started to be directed — although people said the opposite — in favor of the Stalinist theses, showing a much more political than economic trend in the discussions. As Harry Magdoff (1985) showed, what the Soviet "theoreticians" called economic laws were no more than tendencies and lines of action. According to Magdoff:

> ...the law of value rules the distribution of the social work and its replication when the means of production are private ownership, and the interconnection of the social work is obtained by means of the private exchange of the work products. Most importantly, above all: the law operates as an objective tendency not because it's a law of nature, but because of market discipline. From the moment when the latter loses control, the law of value loses its relevance. For example, if commodities continue to be traded according to the necessary social work incorporated in them (a crucial attribute of the law), how can it be known how much work is socially necessary and how much is unnecessary? Under capitalism, this decision is made by market competition. But there's no mechanism or significant substitute for it in a planned society. (MAGDOFF, 1985, p.125)

Those propositions were certainly opposite to the thinking of many economists who advocated the Stalinist ideas on the planned economies of the socialist world.

It's interesting to observe that much of Bettelheim's ideas are basically in accord with Stalin's assumptions, even though the French economist criticized and rejected the ruler's theory about the origins of the survival of the mercantile categories in the Soviet economy.[5] Bettelheim believed that knowing who actually owned the means of production in a socialist country was more important than discussing "legal subjects". According to him, in the Soviet Union the agents weren't the workers, but the government sector, through the managers of the enterprises who were appointed by the government. That is, it was the managers of the enterprises who actually disposed of the means of production and of their products, created by the workers. In other words, the idea that the government would impose itself on the ownership of the means of production put limits on the enterprises themselves. Therefore, the degree of the enterprises' autonomy depended exclusively on the decisions made by the bureaucrats. Thus, according to him, the power the government to dispose of the means of production and their products would only be an effect of the socialist production relations, to the extent that those powers could really ensure the domination of the workers on the production conditions.[6]

According to Bettelheim, the most "advanced" form would be to establish "popular communes", if they were inserted in economic relations that were an organic part of a social formation controlled by the workers. For him, what would distinguish the popular commune from the cooperative is that the former would be only an economic unit, while the latter would be both an economic and a political unit, in which the social and political demands would overcome the economic ones.

The self-management of the enterprises could have a capitalist nature without socialist planning, since it would be dominated by capitalist production relations working to extend capital. Even so, that variety can be useful for the workers during a transition phase, since, as capitalist "apparatus" *per se,* it would be an environment where the capitalist social relations would articulate and reproduce themselves, leading to an alternative to "revolutionization" of the "enterprise", the only way to replace them by a new kind of apparatus, with socialist social relations. But that revolutionization couldn't take place by decree, but must happen gradually, according to the demands of the objective reality and through practice. (BETTELHEIM, 1972, p.104-108) According to the economist:

> On the one hand, "economic" and "legal" illusions that consider as "given", once and for all, the "social" nature of State

> ownership, which identify it as a perpetually active production relation and which *tend, therefore, to reduce the role that corresponds to the political level* under the pretext that its interference with the economic level would be "arbitrary".
> On the other hand, the "subjectivist" and "voluntarist" illusions tend to identify the *dominant* role of the political level as a kind of *determinant* role ultimately. Voluntarism and subjectivism mainly characterize economic plans that are not elaborated based on a rigorous social and economic analysis. (BETTELHEIM, 1972, p.185-186)

This was an implicit criticism of the kind of industrial planning and management advocated by several leaders of the socialist world, including Guevara and his group.[7] Even though those ideas were expressed a few years after the Cuban "economic debate", they represent, to a considerable extent, Bettelheim's opinions throughout the 1960's.[8] According to Roberto Massari, "in the years of the debate he took a coldly academic stance, but he was actually an advocate of the Soviet system and mainly of its planning criteria. Then he changed, and became a Maoist and an advocate of the Chinese economic system. Finally, he critiqued himself (in his volumes about the Russian Revolution), but this time he didn't persuade anyone." (MASSARI, 2001a) At the time of the debate, it was possible that Bettelheim believed that Che wanted to overcome objective reality and impose a model that was not in tune with the historical moment and with the concrete reality of the country. These conceptual differences between the two Marxist theoreticians were clear. In the 1970's, Bettelheim critiqued himself and, when he talked about Cuba, he advocated the same ideas as Guevara, without, however, supporting him in a even a nominal manner (MASSARI, 2001a). The disagreements between Bettelheim and Guevara in the 1960's, however, certainly influenced other members of the Cuban government.

At that time, perhaps the most important government official and Marxist theoretician on the island to debate the Minister of Industry, was Carlos Rafael Rodríguez, then President of INRA and a well-known Cuban intellectual. In his article "The New Path of Cuban Agriculture", published in *Cuba Socialista,* in November, 1963, Rodríguez also advocated the economic accounting system, without, however, quoting or criticizing Guevara directly, maybe to avoid possible problems and divisions within the government. A few years later, Rodríguez said he felt for Che a "deep affection, permanent controversy and essential identity". (RODRÍGUEZ, 1984, p.133) In his article, he claimed that:

> ...centralization originates serious vices and dangers. Bureaucratic centralism is the worst of them. The method of establishing general directives without taking into consideration the specific peculiarities of each place leads agriculture to make serious mistakes. If this generality is accompanied by the centralist inflexibility that requires each decision by the local managers to be made according to rules of the national center, without allowing the managers to take responsibility for their domain, it results in the systematic formation of "strangling points", it leads to the staunching of problems and to the despair of the workers at the base. Rather than creating energetic workers who are capable of making decisions and developing as a group, this system generates administrative puppets who are incapable of solving problems and who lack all momentum other than what is produced by the administrative threads linking them to the central apparatus [...] No regulation can replace the conscious and technical initiative that derives from local analysis and experience. For that reason, this year spent studying the developmental conditions of our agriculture leads us to the leaders of INRA, to the conclusion that it is crucial to eliminate the general administrations that rule the group of farms from Havana, regardless of whether they are village farms or irrigation farms, and to replace them with a decentralized system in which the farms are grouped regionally. (RODRÍGUEZ apud GUEVARA, 1982, p.276)

The fact is that, for some time, both the economic accounting system and the budgetary finance system co-existed in Cuba. Even though he was a strong advocate of the economic accounting system, many years later Rodríguez said that "with the distance of time, the budgetary system now seems to be a contribution of exceptional value". (RODRÍGUEZ, 1988, p.3) According to him:

> Much was written abroad, and there are books that deal with the contradictions between Che and some comrades, specifically pointing to me. I'm proud to be able to say, even though there were some contradictions, in what was fundamental, in what was essential when the economic problem was approached, we always deeply identified and worked together, with other comrades, to impose some order on the Cuban economy, to obtain the maximum efficiency of the Cuban economy and to establish what is essential to us: economic control regardless of the starting point. And the budgetary system was based, first and foremost, on the use of more advanced accounting techniques and on a very modern — and I would say anticipated — conception of the use of electronic computation. In that realm, Che, being ahead of his time, with the long-term vision that he always had, understood that the use of computers, which had just begun, could provide valuable economic control over all aspects of the economy. And a strong accounting, together with the computation used worldwide, were the basis of the budgetary system that he advocated. (RODRÍGUEZ, 1988, p.3-4)

In order to discuss the banking system in Cuba, Marcelo Fernández Font, who had replaced Raúl Cepero Bonilla as President of the National Bank, wrote "Development and Functions of the Socialist Banking System in Cuba", published in *Cuba Socialista,* in March 1964. In this article, he first outlined a brief history of the banks in general[9] and more specifically in the Soviet Union, then proposed that the banking system in Cuba wasn't moved by a desire for profit. He explicitly outlined the main functions of the country's National Bank, namely: regulating monetary circulation, granting credit, funding investments,[10] managing foreign currency, international operations, organization of savings [11] and economic banking control, which was the reason for harsh criticism from the Cuban Minister of Industry. Some time later, he disagreed with Guevara once again when he claimed that:

> ...to us, the financial system with the best characteristics in Cuba's current developmental stage is the self-management system. We estimate that this system provides better conditions for reaching two goals for our economy that can't be postponed: financial discipline and economic control. [...] As far as financial discipline is concerned, the relation of charges and payments that have their origin in the budgetary system's enterprises must be noted. Some of these enterprises don't seem to be motivated to charge their goods and services because their expenses are covered, and for them that only means that they don't contribute to the budget anymore; if, in order to pay their wages, they had to encourage the charging of their accounts, the situation would be different. The same thing can be said as far as their payments are concerned. (FERNÁNDEZ FONT, 1982, p.210-211)

He also said that:

> ...during the years 1961, 1962 and 1963, the state budget showed a deficit. In those same three years, the budgetary system's enterprises stopped contributing substantial amounts to the budget, that is, they didn't fulfill their programmed net incomes, and that was one of the crucial reasons for the budgetary deficits that occurred. What really happened was that the bank funded the budgetary deficits by granting automatic credit in the same amount as the deficits. (FERNÁNDEZ FONT, 1982, p.211)

But he concluded, apparently resigned: "The revolutionary government has decided to maintain, for the time being, both financial systems. Therefore, it is the bank's obligation to render the best service and to carry out the most efficient level of control possible for both kinds of enterprise." (FERNÁNDEZ FONT, 1982, p.212)

Another critic of Guevara's ideas at the time was Alberto Mora, the Cuban Minister of Foreign Trade. Mora believed that the law of value would regulate production and would work according to the plan. According to him, it would be demonstrated in the state sector by the fact that the products would be exchanged according to the value of each one. Influenced by the Soviet "reformist" economists, mainly Novozhilov (whom he quoted in his text "Around the Issue of the Functioning of the Law of Value in the Cuban Economy Nowadays", in *Comércio Exterior* magazine, in June, 1963), Mora said that the law of value was valid not only in the transition from capitalism to socialism, but also from socialism to communism. The Minister of Foreign Trade insisted that although the nationalized enterprises were owned by society it wasn't at all implicit that they constituted, in Cuba, "a single large enterprise". To support his ideas, he referred to the famous "manual" written by Stalin, as well as to texts by Rosa Luxemburg and Bukharin. Completing his criticism, Mora reaffirmed that the law of value would only stop working when the development of production forces could create "sufficiently broad" resources to meet the needs of man, and that in Cuba it would remain valid, as economic value and within the state sector.

The Belgian Trotskyist economist Ernest Mandel also participated in the debate. He supported Guevara and spoke directly with Bettelheim, in an attempt to explain some of the problems with his economic ideas. According to Mandel, Bettelheim made several methodological mistakes, made erroneous deductions from the works of Marx and Lenin, mixed up notions and applied the dialectic method in an insufficient manner. In the article "The Mercantile Categories in the Transition Period" (MANDEL, 1982a, p.241-260), he said that "while mercantile production exists, there will be a certain game to the law of value", in other words, that "therefore, the law of value plays *to a certain extent* a role before capitalism, during capitalism and after capitalism", but that, in a transition period, one should tenaciously fight against it, based on a long-term project, with the use of socialist planning. In another text (MANDEL, 1982b, p.168), he claimed that he continued to support "a democratically centralized self-management system in which the double risk of bureaucratization — that originates from excessive centralization and the excessive use of the market mechanisms — can be broadly neutralized by putting management into the hands of the workers in the labor centers, subject to strict discipline imposed by a central authority that is directly elected by the workers' councils". Specifically concerning the law of value in the transition to socialism, the Marxist theoretician claimed:

> Here there's also a clear relationship between the theoretical debate and the disagreements about the economic planning in Cuba. Those who confuse the survival of the mercantile categories with the regulatory role of the law of value must necessarily ascribe a greater role to the market mechanisms in the context of the planned economy, not only where the means of consumption are concerned — and we believe that this is broadly justified — but also, and above all, where the industrial means of production are concerned. On the other hand, that's why they insisted in introducing the game of the law of value in the relationship between the state-owned enterprises (where the "trades" are associated to a great extent with the means of production). And this "game" implies the need for autonomy in terms of investments, thus confirming, in its own way, that there's a historical antagonism between the imperatives of a real plan and those of a market economy (even though it's designated as socialist).
>
> Those who oppose the fact that the "law of value" continues to regulate production directly or indirectly in the transition period from capitalism to socialism don't deny in any way that the mercantile categories inevitably survive in this time. They also don't deny that in many realms the planners can easily leave certain adjustments between supply and demand to the market

> mechanisms. But they understand the fundamentally contradictory nature between the market and the plan, and thus agree more broadly on administration over the establishment of prices in several spheres, even if it's to uphold certain imperatives of the national economic development. That's why they reaffirm that the influence of the law of value is more limited than in the capitalist production manner, and that certain sectors — mainly the circulation of the means of production within the state sector — may escape from them. (MANDEL, 1982b, p.170-171)

Therefore, according to Mandel, in the transition to socialism it is necessary for, in objective terms: a serious calculation, which could be efficient for the cost control in *all* the socialized enterprises, starting with the means of production sector. A global pricing policy must be developed (using the operations of subsidy and indirect tax); attempting to avoid price distortions; *constantly* comparing production costs with average prices in the international market; incentives for small production, mainly in agriculture (offering industrialized goods in exchange for agricultural products of the small producers); and the establishment of a pricing policy approximately reflectomg the real values in the consumer goods sector. (MANDEL, 1982a, p.254-255) According to him, the improvement of the producers' living standard would be, consequently, an incentive for the yields and productivity of the labor to increase too. But those economicist measures would be in opposition to, or balanced by state policies of strict control and moral stimuli. All the analysis of economic categories should be tied to the concrete historical situation. In the transition to socialism, this should be taken into consideration in order to avoid mistakes that could jeopardize the economic advance, as well as that of awareness. According to that author:

> As a consequence, in order to avoid excesses that will certainly undermine the entire socialist plan ("excesses" which would

> imply extending credit, for the payment of wages, to the enterprises that operate at a loss, which would lead to the emergence of "socialist bankruptcy", of "socialist dismissals" and of "socialist unemployment"), one can only talk about financial autonomy within *certain limits.* Instead of openly discussing this issue, it is preferable to rationally assess these limits and the possibilities of autonomy that they allow to subsist.
>
> Even so, one immediately runs into a methodological difficulty when assessing a problem like that. The advantage of a "profitability" criterion (popularly speaking: of "profit") is precisely that profitability is the logic of *all* economic and commercial activities that take place within the examined organ (national economy; industry as a whole; industrial sectors; groups of enterprises; separate enterprises). But there is a corresponding *demand* to this benefit: the decision-makers of the organ in question can actually move *all* the levers of economic activity. From the moment when a series of levers is blocked because it's *managed from a distance,* profitability loses much of its effectiveness as optimum criterion of the *partial* economic activity examined. For this reason, profitability is not always used to rule the interconnected relations among the different workshops or plants that make up the trust within a gigantic capitalist enterprise that moves tens of thousands of workers. (MANDEL, 1982a, p.257)

According to Mandel, the central problem in the debate sparked by Bettelheim was the struggle to increase the yield and the productivity of labor. But that didn't mean building a system based only on technical terms, but being able to develop structures that are efficient in both administrative and economic terms and that *actually* build socialism. Che read Mandel's article, and agreed with his ideas. The intellectual of the Fourth International and Guevara took positions that were similar to each other and basically followed the same logic. Che's position concerning the organization and administration of the Cuban industrial apparatus during the transition to socialism was clear, a position that indirectly echoed Mandel's elaborations and those of other "heterodox" Marxist intellectuals, which often weren't directly tied to any practical experience of constructing socialism.

---

[1]The incentive system, socialist emulation and voluntary labor will be discussed in Chapter 6, "Socialism and the 'New Man'".

---

[2]According to Guevara: "As far as the pricing theory is concerned, we also have profound disagreements. In the self-management system prices are established 'according to the law of value', but it doesn't explain (as far as we know) which expression of the law of value is adopted. One starts from the socially necessary labor to produce a certain article, but the fact that 'socially necessary labor' is an economic-historic concept was neglected and, therefore, changing, not only [...] in a local (or national) [sphere], but also in global terms: the ongoing advances in the realm of technology, which result from the competition in the capitalist world, reduce the expense of the necessary labor and, therefore, the value of the product. A closed society might ignore the changes for a certain period of time, but it must always return to these international relations to compare its value. If a given society ignores them for a long period, without developing new and exact formulas to replace them, it will create internal interrelations that represent its own value scheme, coherent with itself, but opposed to the tendencies of the more developed technique (the example of steel and plastic); this can cause relative delays of some importance and, at any rate, distortions of the law of value on an international scale that makes the economies incomparable." (GUEVARA, 1982, p.195)

---

[3]The Ministry of Industry divided the costs into: costs of raw materials, of direct materials, of indirect materials, of the labor force, of depreciation and of social security.

---

[4]Michael Löwy (2001) is one of the advocates of that theory. Later, in 1970, Bettelheim, having already changed his position and gradually beginning to admire the Maoist concepts, in his *Economic Accounting and Forms of Ownership* quoted Stalin's text in a more moderate manner. That author explains several times that the answers of the ruler of the Soviet Union

concerning the mercantile categories within socialism weren't false, but insufficient. See Bettelheim (1972).

---

[5] It's about the survival of the mercantile categories in the Soviet Union based on the existence of two kinds of socialist ownership, that of the people and that of the kolkhozy, which attempts to explain the economic categories by means of the legal superstructure, something that Bettelheim didn't accept.

---

[6] Years later Bettelheim claimed, "the competition among capitals in the Soviet economy expresses itself concretely in the existence of *separate* production and trade units. Those units are placed under the authority of the directors who are actually autonomous to a large extent. […] The economic planning is itself one of the areas in which a specific form of competition takes place. [...] This form of competition is obviously a special kind of competition [...] different from the 'free competition' that the classic economists discuss and from the 'monopolist competition' analyzed by the contemporary political economy. Those differences are tied to the peculiar characteristics of Soviet capitalism, especially of what is subject to a *specific regulation manner*. […] The adjustments made are subject to corrections imposed by the relatively severe lack of existent products in a system where supply is often lower than demand (which engenders an inflationary process, partly open and partly hidden). Thus, the 'objectives' of the plan result from a *conflicting process that is not controlled.* They are rarely realistic and must constantly be changed as non-predicted shortages of products emerge or when the balance of forces among the enterprises, other economic agents and different social groups change. […] The plan is not the instrument through which the government imposes its decisions on an economy that doesn't work in an autonomous manner anymore. It's made up of a series of numbers modified so commonly, under multiple pressures, that nobody really knows to what extent its different 'objectives' were fulfilled." See Bettelheim (1986, p.31-32, emphasis by the author). It should be noted that this criticism of Bettelheim, made in the 1980's, expresses certain displeasure with the "financial self-management" in a system that can't impose truly socialist control mechanisms. In other words, the "financial self-management" of the enterprises, within the environment that he calls "Soviet capitalism" would lead to a distancing from socialism and to a return to capitalism. In a certain way, these observations are similar to those that Guevara made when

he was the Minister of Industry of Cuba. For further information about the origins of the degeneration of the Soviet system, see Bettelheim (1976a).

---

[7]Solius, who wrote *Political Economy of Socialism,* another one of the "official" manuals by the Academy of Sciences of the Soviet Union, claimed that "The objective nature of the economic laws of socialism is that their period of validity is determined by the socialist relations of production that exist objectively. The latter depend, in turn, on the level and the nature of the production forces. [...] The idealist distortions of the nature of the economic laws took place in several socialist countries in the transition period from capitalism to socialism. Those who had similar conceptions in the Soviet Union were the Trotskyists, who, overcoming the objective requirements of the economic laws, imposed on the party and on the government a socialist industrialization pace without support. [...] The lack of understanding of the objective nature of the economic laws of socialism or its denial, as well as the underestimation of the objective factors and the exaggeration of the subjective ones lead to voluntarism in the economic policy and offer possibilities for adventurous acts by all of the rulers of the national economy." See Solius (1976, p.58-59).

[8]For further information on Bettelheim's intellectual development, see Porcaro (2001).

---

[9]Guevara argued that Fernández Font showed the origin of the banks as advertisement, with scant theoretical depth. That was supposedly the reason for the emergence of his mistakes about how this organ and its rulers should perform. See Guevara (1982, p.223-224).

[10]Che believed that the banks could only finance investments if they did so with their own resources, which he considered absurd in a socialist economy. The bank should distribute the resources of the national budget determined by the investment plan and make them available to the corresponding investor apparatus. See Guevara (1982, p.219).

[11]Guevara believed that Fernández Font was overly influenced by the idea of divulging and advertisement, without clearly explaining his ideas. Font said: "The money being saved stops circulating, which contributes to re-establishing the balance between the product fund and the purchasing power of the population, which is especially useful in Cuba's current condition. Besides, the savings of the population are important to the Bank's ability to grant credit destined to finance the development of the national economy". Guevara claimed that "the money in savings stops circulating temporarily and this resource can only be applied in the

economic sense when private activity is financed through bank loans, since it would be absurd to believe that, in a socialist economy, the cost of the interest paid to those with savings is offset by the interest charged to the state-owned enterprises." He believed it would be much more interesting and useful to know the composition of saving and its cost, because then saving would take place according to the scale of the people taking part and, thus, more advisable economic measures would be taken. See Guevara (1982, p 219).

5

Trade union Organization and workers

Guevara clearly showed his position on the ideal form of economic management for the country. However, after that new questions emerged. One of the reasons for the economic decentralization in several socialist countries and, in the case of Yugoslavia, the implementation of financial and "worker" self-management, would be to allow greater decision-making power and participation of the workers in the industries. But what actual role would the workers play in the system proposed by Che? The trade unions would certainly continue to exist in Cuba. But what would their function be? In that regard, Guevara was categorical, having expressed his opinions on several occasions. Before discussing the positions of the Argentinean revolutionary concerning the trade unions and the performance of the workers in the plants, it's important to mention briefly how they organized themselves in Cuba before the revolution and what the role of the trade union organizations were in that country. We intend to outline some important events in the history of the Cuban labor movement and of the trade unions of the island so that, later, we can discuss Guevara's ideas.

Since the 19th Century, the Cuban workers had been accustomed to organizing themselves into associations and trade unions, and those traditions could hardly be left out. The creation of the *Asociación de Tabaqueros*, in 1866, and the publication of the newspaper *La Aurora*, were important elements of the embryonic Cuban labor movement, since, with harsh denunciations of the rough conditions of the workers in the tobacco industry, discussions and readings in the work place were advocated, which increased the political awareness of an important sector of the Cuban proletariat. Even with the prohibition of readings in the plants during the First War of Independence, other groups were created, and merged in 1878, becoming the *Gremio de Obreros del Ramo de Tabaquerías;* meanwhile, the anarchists were becoming more active, restructuring, from 1885, on the *Junta Central de Artesanos,* the platform which served to unify the workers' associations and to encourage several strikes in the country. (ALONSO JÚNIOR, 1998, p.30) Next, the anarchists founded the *Círculo de Trabajadores de La Habana,* as well as the periodical *El Productor.*

The Regional Worker Congress took place in Cuba at the beginning of the 1890s, with the attendance of representatives of several organizations from five Cuban provinces, except for Oriente. They decided to advocate the implementation of an eight-hour workday and an organizational model for the working class. There was also discussion about women and children working, racial discrimination and the incentive of gathering the workers into autonomous sections organized by categories, which would later be part of the Federation of the Cuban Workers. Alongside these events, one can see the great increase of government repression against the workers (DEL TORO, 1969, p.58-60), while the workers' press grew and became increasingly active, through several publications, such as *El Artesano* (1886), *El Obrero* (1888), *El Clarín* (1889), *La Claridad* (1890), *La Antorcha* (1890), *El Obrero Cubano* (1890), *El Acicate* (1891) *and La Batalla* (1891), among others, in spreading the concepts of the labor movement throughout the island.

In 1900, the Popular Party emerged, led by Diego Vicente Tejera. It only lasted for a few months and was replaced, in 1901, by the Popular Workers Party, made up of militants from the Cuban Federation of Labor.

(FCT) (DEL TORO, 1969, p.64-65) Although the anarchist groups had a strong presence in strikes and in workers' organizations from 1907-1920, in general they weren't able to maintain this level of participation in the proletariat struggles occurring in later periods. While they tried to engender some real activity in the country's political life, they gradually lost ground to the communists, beginning in the second half of the 1920's.

The socialists were also very active in the Cuban labor movement during the years before the revolution. After the formation of the *Club de Propaganda Socialista,* which was founded by Carlos Baliño in 1903 (considered the first Cuban Marxist group and which later changed its name to *Agrupación Socialista Internacional*) and the creation, one year later, of the Socialist Labor Party and its newspaper *La Voz Obrera,* run by Ramón Rivera, the Marxists started to politicize the workers and influence the struggle for socialism in the country. (DEL TORO, 1969, p.67) The party gradually became more radical, including in its new theses the conversion of individual or corporative ownership into collective or common ownership and the complete emancipation of the proletariat, starting with the abolition of the social classes. (DEL TORO, 1969, p.68)

In 1918, the year following the October Revolution, there was an increase in the number of strikes and protests in the Cuban labor movement. During the May 1st celebrations, there were several disturbances and stoppages in both industrial and commercial activities in Havana and other Cuban cities. There were also strikes by the miners in Matahambre and the shoemakers and tobacco workers in the capital. (BALIÑO et al., 1967, p.5-6) In that year, the *Agrupación Socialista de La Habana* was created.

On May 1st, 1919, workers gathered at the Payret Theater, in Havana, protesting against sending interventionist troops to Vladivostok, while in the Alhambra Theater cries of exaltation to bolchevism could be heard during that night's performance. (LEÓN EXPÓSITO, 1975, p.327-336) In April of the following year, there was a celebration in Havana for the first National Worker's Congress, and in November several entities gathered to organize the Worker's Federation of Havana, formally created eleven months later. (BALIÑO et al., 1967, p.7) In 1923, Baliño founded the *Agrupación Comunista* with several trade union leaders in its ranks and which, in 1925, helped form the Cuban Communist Party. The first Central Committee of the party was made up of leaders from the *Unión de Cigarreros,* the *Sindicato de Tabaqueros de San Antonio de los Baños,* the *Gremio de Pintores, Decoradores e Tapiceiros,* the *Federación Obrera de la Habana* and the *Universidad de La Habana.* In other words, a relatively representative group. (ALONSO JÚNIOR, 1998, p.34)

In 1925, the Cuban National Workers Confederation (CNOC), the first central national trade union was created. In this case, the communists had great influence because, in the year of its foundation, the second secretary of the CNOC was César Villar, giving the party greater field of action within the central. From then on, the Cuban CP and its ranks within the CNOC called several strikes, even though later they were forbidden, by the dictatorship of President Gerardo Machado, to act within the legal boundaries.

In retaliation to the CNOC, the Cuban Federation of Labor (FCT) was created, largely influenced by the American Federation of Labor (AFL) and by the Pan-American Confederation of Labor (COPA), conservative organizations that supported class collaborationism. According to Blas Roca, the CNOC represented the revolutionary, anti-imperialist and classist tendency of the Cuban proletariat, while the FCT was a reformist organization, which supported Machado and the interests of the United States in Cuba. (ROCA, 1961, p.162) It's worth mentioning another important feat that resulted from the strikes promoted by the communists, the creation of the Worker's National Trade Union of the Sugar Industry (SNOIA).

With the ongoing increase in the number of the strikes and of popular dissatisfaction, President Machado was overthrown and fled the country. He was replaced by Carlos Manuel de Céspedes, who stayed in power for a short period of time. After the revolt of the sergeants, led by Fulgencio Batista, the Presidency was taken by Ramón Grau San Martín who was overthrown in 1934 and replaced by Carlos Mendietta. In that year, the Cuban Revolutionary Party (PRC), also known as *Auténtico,* was established.[1] From then on, the succession of rulers demonstrates how complicated the country's political situation was: Batista and José A. Barnet took over the government and, in 1936, Miguel Mariano Gómez was "elected" and overthrown in the same year; he was replaced by Federico Laredo Brú. All of this took place with Batista, behind the scenes, as a leading player exercising the actual power. In 1939, Grau San Martín was the President of the Constituent Assembly and, in 1944, he returned to the Presidency of the country.

In 1938, however, still during Laredo Brú's term, the CNOC was dissolved and, in its place, the *Confederación de Trabajadores Cubanos* (CTC) was created, gathered its first National Council and elected the Communist Lázaro Peña as its secretary-general. From then on, the CTC was able to unite almost all the trade union organizations in the country. After discussion with its bases, the Central decided to join the Latin American Workers' Confederation (CTAL), organized in that same year in Mexico. To counter the new CTC, the National Workers' Commission (CON) was established, tied to the PRC. However it wasn't able to divide the most advanced sectors of the Cuban workers.

Batista won the 1940 election and a close collaboration with the communists began to emerge. The Cuban CP even occupied some ministry posts in that government. In 1942, the party itself stated that the workers, through the CTC, would cooperate with all who were willing to maintain national unity and fight against the foreign enemy of the "homeland", that is, Germany, even though the alliances were absurd compared to the party's earlier policies.(ALONSO JÚNIOR, 1998, p.44)

In 1943, the party changed its name to Popular Socialist Party (PSP), while important leaders, such as Juan Marinello and Carlos Rafael Rodríguez, became Ministers. Since the party backed Batista in the 1944 elections and lost, the CTC began to be persecuted by the government of President Grau San Martín, who decided that it could no longer be an instrument for the communists to manipulate the trade union realm. This started a policy of repressing the confederation and implementing a line of action that protected the members of CON. The result was an attack on the offices of oppositionist organizations, murders of socialist leaders, impositions of obligatory participation quotas on the workers, the creation of a system of exclusion and division within the CTC, the federations and the trade unions and the elimination of several democratic practices within the trade union movement. (ROCA, 1961, p.162-163) According to Blas Roca, with the increasing pressure on the communists, the CON, beginning in 1947, imposed the Mujalism on the CTC, which meant the institutionalization of corrupt practices, divisionism and conservatism in the workers' organizations. It also separated the CTC from the CTAL, tying the Central to the Inter-American Regional Organization of Workers (ORIT). In the same period, the Catholic Workers' Youth (JOC) began, more actively, to penetrate the trade unions, defending principles of class conciliation and attacks on the communists. Many trade union leaders, often tied to the government, accumulated great fortunes in that period.

In 1948, Carlos Prío Socarrás was elected the new President of Cuba and had to face opposition in several sectors of the country, from elements of the Army to the communists themselves. After Batista's coup, in 1952, and his "election", in 1954, the communists, who at first, had elements inside the new government in the Ministry of Labor, gradually became opponents of the regime. The CTC, linked to the *auténticos* and run by Eusébio Mujal, controlled most of the country's trade unions and started to collaborate closely with Batista. For some, like Rufo López-Fresquet, the leadership of the CTC had many reasons to remain neutral in the struggle against the revolutionary movement, since it could obtain benefits from the government. Meanwhile, Batista realized the importance of working with the CTC, considering that he would have an ally within the worker environment and that he would be able to avoid problems with other national sectors. (LÓPEZ-FRESQUET, 1969, p.37) In that period, the government began withholding 1% of all workers' wages and passed it along to the confederation. (ALONSO JÚNIOR, 1998, p.51)

For a long time, the relations between the PSP and the M 26-7 were not the best. Right after the attack on the Moncada barracks, in 1953, the party announced that it opposed those fighting methods, which they considered "putchists", peculiar to the middle class political factions. That was supposedly an "adventurous" attempt, based on a sterile and false heroism, guided by bourgeois concepts. (DRAPER, 1966, p.35) According to Carlos Rafael Rodríguez, the communists didn't think it was possible "that a group of petty-bourgeois revolutionaries was sufficiently strong to sustain an anti-imperialist revolution and later to transform it into a Socialist Revolution". (RODRÍGUEZ, 1983b, p.441) Fidel, in turn, "was not originally a petty-bourgeois. He was the son of an old, landed estate owner, and of course, that would be worse in formal terms. Fidel was an *ortodoxo* and he expressed — until the revolution — petty-bourgeois ideas. If we look at the problem only from the perspective of class origins and we examine Fidel, Raúl, Che and Dorticós, they were all petty-bourgeois, none of them had a proletarian background". (RODRÍGUEZ, 1983b, p.441) In the *Letter of the National Committee of the Popular Socialist Party to the July 26 Movement,* published in June, 1957, the PSP said that it had a "radical disagreement" with the tactics and the plans of Fidel's group, and that the M 26-7 had still not positioned itself in a sufficiently vehement manner against imperialism. (DRAPER, 1966, p.38)

The communists sabotaged the general strike brought about by Castro and they apparently attempted a rapprochement with Batista between June and July, 1958, by sending a committee, made up of Blas Roca and Joaquín Ordoqui, to talk to the dictator. They supposedly proposed to fight Fidel Castro if the Cuban President granted some favors to them, such as the legalization of the PSP, the control of the CTC, the return of the right of ownership of the periodical *Hoy* to the communists, the radio station 1010-4 and a lot of money to prepare a great campaign against the guerrilla leader. (ROMUALDI, 1967, p.194) None of the proposals were accepted. Shortly after the conversation with President Batista, the communists formed an alliance with Castro. When they were in the opposition, they helped create the Committees for the Defense of the Workers' Demands and integrated the United National Workers Front (FONU), which led the general strike on January 1959, against the attempt to install a puppet government right after the revolution.

With the triumph of the revolution, however, the trade unions began to play a different role and gradually adapted themselves to the historical changes that the country was undergoing.[2] Some years after the triumph of the revolution, Guevara claimed:

> The trade union is the workers uniting against the boss. It's class warfare. When the domination of one class over another disappears and the means of production become collective ownership, the contradictions will disappear. But the contradictions… as Lenin used to say. Let's see what's going on

> here. If we forget Lenin's observation, it is clear that the trade union would no longer have a reason to exist. While Lenin explains the need for the survival of the trade unions, which are necessary — I also acknowledge that — to avoid possible abuses. These contradictions exist and we must find an original to resolve them. I don't believe that permanently going back to the original division (of classes), treating every worker who leaves manual labor to take over a leadership position as an enemy of the working class, is the solution. (GUEVARA, 1982, p.72)

In the same conversation, Guevara recalled the debates over the trade unions that took place at the beginning of the Russian Revolution. In that sense, he specifically mentioned the debates between Lenin and Trotsky. According to the Minister of Industry of Cuba:

> ...it's worth reading carefully and writing down what Lenin says about these problems. But it's necessary to read his words very carefully, because they must be placed in the frontier of the controversy with Trotsky who, at the time, was beginning a work which would later become divisionist. Trotsky anticipated a series of claims concerning the activity of the trade unions and the economic direction of the trade unions; Lenin was supposed to make some concessions, since he, among other things — and I'm sorry if I'm repetitive, because I have already said that many times and maybe even here, is more than a revolutionary, more than a philosopher, he is a politician, and the politicians must make concessions. Anyway, whatever it is, at some point he must say things that do not reflect his way of thinking. And facing the proposal to grant greater power to the trade unions, to entrust several economic responsibilities to them, to create strategies for the economy, facing the real power that the trade union had... in Russia, Lenin was forced to use a kind of language that, personally, I'm sure was not in line with his way of thinking. (GUEVARA, 1982, p.73)

It must be recalled that Lenin believed that, if the trade unions remained concealed within limited horizons, in a "self-sufficient" struggle, they wouldn't be socialist at all, as happened in several cases. According to the Russian revolutionary, the proletariat was made up of a heterogeneous mass, which consisted of extremely diverse elements and levels of awareness. Many workers were conservative and were only interested in immediate material gain and in improving their standard of living. Therefore, it wasn't a function of the trade union, *but of the revolutionary party,* to organize the workers in a cohesive manner in the struggle for socialism.

In the first few years after the October Revolution, an intensive debate took place in Russia concerning the role of the trade unions. Mikhail Tomski, the most important bolshevik trade union leader, advocated that, in that moment, when the proletariat had already seized the political and economic power of the country and removed the bourgeoisie from managing the industries, the struggle of the workers to improve their social conditions should take new forms, in an organized action, using the trade unions and other regulating organs to deal with politics in general, subordinating the specific interests of the different categories of the Russian workers to the interests of the class as a whole. (DEUTSCHER, 1950, p.18-19) The mensheviks, in turn, argued that the October Revolution continued to be a bourgeois revolution and that the trade unions should go on with their usual activities. They believed that it was likely that capitalism would soon return to the country with all its might; for that reason, it would be important that the trade unions became stronger and prepare themselves to act in the traditional manner in that case. (DEUTSCHER, 1950, p.19)

Some bolshevik leaders even had doubts about the future of the revolution and of the new role of the trade unions. Riazanov believed that, while the socialist revolution had not triumphed in other Western European countries, the Russian workers should maintain their only means of fighting, the trade unions (DEUTSCHER, 1950, p.20), which, therefore, would be instruments to protect themselves from a counter-revolution, which could happen at any time. To refute those statements, Grigori Zinoviev asked why and from whom should the trade unions be independent, since they were part of their own government. Some, like Solomon Lozovski, didn't accept Zinoviev's theses that the trade unions should be organs of the State power, since there could be coercion and lack of spontaneous class solidarity. He believed that if the trade unions were only "organs of the State power", that would mean that the trade union decisions would be taken in a compulsory manner, without connection with the real activity of the workers. (DEUTSCHER, 1950, p.22)

In the First Trade Union Congress, the approved resolution stated that, during the deepening of the revolution, the trade unions should become state organs, but that even so, they would be hybrid organizations, carrying out several vital functions for the State, though staying outside the organizational sphere of the government. With the civil war, the trade unions took over a new role in the country, providing greater support to the Red Army by supplying soldiers and equipment. They would also help the government to press for an acceleration of the socialization process of all the Russian industries. In that period, worker control of the plants ceased and in 1918, the Commissariat of Labor was created: the trade unions quickly became appendages of the Soviet State.

The Second Trade Union Congress, in January 1919, established a greater emphasis on the functions of the central government, with an almost complete fusion of the trade unions with the state power, an idea advocated by many Bolshevik leaders, among them Tomski and Lenin. In that same congress, however, there was the elaboration of the famous "point 5", which stated that, in the future, the trade unions should concentrate the management of the entire national economy into their hands, that is, theoretically a form of struggle against the bureaucratization of the economic "apparatus". Other points reduced and hindered the statements of point 5, but that would be a subject of intense discussions.[3]

There were many debates concerning the functions and attributions of the trade unions, mainly against the Workers' Opposition, which some people considered anarcho-syndicalist. In that period, Lenin and Trotsky basically advocated the same ideas and attacked that group, thought to be "dangerous" to the stability of the regime. Beginning with the Fourth Trade Union Congress on this subject, the controversies and disagreements between Lenin and Trotsky emerged in a more outlined form. While the Workers' Opposition advocated that the entire organization of the economy be transferred to the trade unions, both Bolshevik leaders supported the thesis of economic "militarization". But according to Trotsky, the Party should, at that moment, stop backing the so-called "workers' democracy" and replace it with a "producers' democracy". In other words, a regime built on top of a public industrial apparatus, producing to meet the social needs, which would represent the real interests of the proletariat, as opposed to some temporary corporative benefits. Thus, the State would have the right to impose its policies on the working class, while at the same time the trade unions should serve the state power, without the possibility of being confronted by its traditional demands.

Lenin also advocated the thesis that the trade unions should defend the Soviet State, which he claimed was still not a workers' State, but that of both peasant and worker, bureaucratically distorted. This implied that the workers have the duty to defend the state, avoiding a systematic attack of the government: the ideal would be a constructive attitude towards it. But the workers, on the other hand, also have the right to defend themselves from the state apparatus, since its policies could represent conflicting pressures from different sectors of the population. It is also important that it be able to protect itself from occasional arbitrary acts by the bureaucratic apparatus. The trade unions, therefore, could have a certain degree of autonomy in relation to the government. The workers' adherence to the trade unions shouldn't be compulsory, as Trotsky advocated, but it should be obtained through persuasion. Even so, Lenin also insisted on the historical rights of the party in the leadership of the country's revolution. (DEUTSCHER, 1950, p.54-56) The difference between the two of them was mainly in the emphasis they gave to that matter: while Trotsky insisted on the supremacy of the party, Lenin emphasized the democratic, voluntary and educational character of the trade unions. According to historian Adam Ulam, at that time Lenin was extremely clever in the discussions:

> At first he [Lenin] played the role of a moderator between two factions of the Party. Trotsky, whose impatience with the worker was as great as his own but whose political ability and tact were considerably inferior, proposed a much more open attack to the "syndicalism nonsense". His wartime experience inspired Trotsky with respect for professional expertise, military discipline and a distrust of the "initiative of the masses". Now he believed that the trade unions should be made strictly subordinated to the State agencies, that not only should their claims to run the economic life be vigorously repulsed but that they should be put in their place, which ought to be that of military-like sub-agencies of the State and Party bureaucracy. With his sure political instincts, Lenin spent as much time attacking Trotsky's "theses", which were close to his own thinking, as he did those of Kollontay and Shlyapnikov, which he abhorred. Within the Party, Trotsky now became a sort of lightning rod attracting to himself the charges of authoritarianism and military thinking, and allowing Lenin to play the role of a broad-minded conciliator. (ULAM, 1969, p.615-616)

This is probably how Guevara interpreted that episode. Knowing about the need for pragmatism and political skill in an extremely delicate moment of the revolution, Che believed that Lenin had acted correctly according to the circumstances, which didn't necessarily correspond to his ideas.[4] The Minister of Industry of Cuba believed that the opinions of the Bolshevik leader were similar to his own as far as the role of the trade unions in the transition to socialism were concerned.[5] It was in that sense that he mentioned the debate between his peers within the government. Che Guevara believed that a way to resolve the contradictions inherent to the transition period to socialism should be sought. He said:

> The fact is that it's not so much about owning the trade union, or an association of the workers, but about resolving those contradictions. And this can be carried out, for example, with the system — which we have been testing — of "labor arbitration commissions", in which there are representatives of both the managers and of the workers. It's a first step, a test; let's see how it will develop and how they will react. We could already verify — and it was obvious — the importance that people place on the choice of their representatives. Indeed, we can't forget that the unionist democracy is a myth. The party meets and proposes to the masses such and such single candidate, and he's the one elected, with more or less, a consensus of the base, without the candidate actually participating in the election process. On the other hand, in the current system of the "arbitration commissions", the workers actually choose their representatives, and, as far as I know, with great enthusiasm. (GUEVARA, 1982, p.73)

It can be said that Guevara didn't agree entirely with the preservation of the traditional role of the trade unions, since that could lead to greater problems with the direction of the government. But he thought that the arbitration commissions could possibly be an interesting way to try to implement "democracy" in the plants and greater efficiency in the relations among workers, managers and State organs. According to the Argentinean revolutionary's conception, only the rulers and trade union bureaucrats would be dissatisfied with that new model. (GUEVARA, 1982) Most of the Cuban labor force, however, would completely agree with that system. The Minister of Industry believed that:

> "...the labor leader and the worker in general should have a share of responsibility in the production process. We can't advance further because there are many plants where discussion is impossible, because of a hostile trade union or because the workers still don't understand the marrow of the matter. And if the trade union talks to management, they believe that the trade union, the leadership of the trade union, is a going in a shaky direction. All those things must disappear, because our task, the task of the industrialization of the country, Cuba's greatest task nowadays, can't be carried out, absolutely, by the desire of a few, nor by the genius of others and of nobody. Our task is to see the best path and explain it, but the people's task is to see that right path, fully contribute to accelerating the journey on that path and always correct mistakes constructively. (GUEVARA, 1988b, p.72-73)

In Guevara's plan, both the administrative management and the responsibility should be unified, always based on collective discussions. For that reason, the business directors were in charge of: personally — or through trusted employees — supervising and managing the work in the sections, offices and production units; taking responsibility for the final elaboration and fulfillment of the state plan related to his or her enterprise; supervising the realization of the established policies concerning labor, wages, contracts, technology, finances, laws, regulations, security, hygiene and the correct use of resources; imposing the internal resolutions; informing, guiding, encouraging, training and qualifying the enterprise staff; signing the enterprises' documents without going over the limits established by the plan; presiding over the Boards of Directors; collaborating with the trade unions; and fostering the active participation of the workers in the direction and fulfillment of the plan. (GUEVARA, 1988b, p.132) The trade unions, in turn, would have two distinct functions: understanding the goals of the state plan and discussing them in the enterprises; and defending the interests of the workers in the plants. The transition to the socialist system wouldn't resolve the conflicts once and for all, but it would change the ways to handle them. Thus, the trade union would substantiate the opinions of sectors of the proletariat, who attempt to have their own needs met to the detriment of the national interest, that is, the development of socialism and fast industrialization. (GUEVARA, 1988b, p.133) As for the compatibility of the interests of the government and of the trade unions, Guevara believed that there would be no intrinsic conflict between them, since, while the government tried to develop the country as quickly as possible, using all available resources for the benefit of the majority of the population, this would also be, theoretically, the interest of the trade unions, which should be in charge of adapting the local real conditions to the state projects. According to Che:

> ...the trade union must carry out the dual functions of keeping an eye on the labor conditions of the workers and employees and providing them with revolutionary guidance about the necessary sacrifices or efforts with all the honesty that the members of the proletariat are capable of, since the general guidelines of the socialist revolution's economic policy are ruled by the desire to create greater wealth, for the greater well-being of the working class, of the peasants and of the entire people.(GUEVARA, 1988b, p.133)

Therefore, the trade unions would also be responsible for the increase of productivity, discipline on the job and the qualification of efficient managers, elevating, in that way, their technical and political level. They would also have a stake in the material and "spiritual" interests of the workers, using discussion and persuasion as basic methods to steer them into behaving in a manner that leads to the fulfillment of all their goals. Relations between the directors and the trade unions would have to be polite and harmonious, demonstrating mutual cooperation.[6] All conflict should be resolved by means of debates, taking pains to avoid greater tensions and worker strikes, which would be a terrible impediment to the development of socialism, not only because it would represent a failure of the management but also because it would indicate a low degree of political awareness in the workers. (GUEVARA, 1988b, p.134) In other words, the conception of the trade unions for Guevara was very close to Lenin's. They would be "schools of communism", organizations that should encompass an entire class, elevate the political awareness of the workers and be strictly tied to the revolutionary party. (LOSOVSKY, [198-?], p.198)

To make better relations within the plant possible, the Technical Advisory Council (CTA) was created, made up of the most qualified workers of each production department, who advised the administrators in the management of the plants. The CTA was in charge of solving technical problems, such as the lack of spare parts. It was an "experimental laboratory" where the workers engaged in activities that were crucial for promoting the industrial development of the country on the local level. Therefore, the CTA encouraged the technical instruction of the employees, working closely with the trade unions. The administrator of the production unit would also be the President of the CTA, and his decisions were irrevocable. But, if there were abuses by the administrator, the CTA could denounce him to the director of the public enterprise, accusing him of acting against the determinations of the ministry, and consequently harming production. If the denunciation wasn't heard, it could even be taken to the sub secretary of the ministry tied to that plant. In other words, that system, in theory, would make real control over occasional cases of abuses and corruption possible. The CTA, in general, was also concerned with rationalizing the processes of production and increasing labor productivity, as well as with helping to structure the labor regulations, together with the Ministry of Labor and other government organs. (GUEVARA, 1988b, p.135)

Therefore, Guevara believed that the Technical Advisory Councils, the trade unions and the management would have several common tasks and relations and should work together, with broad integration. But some people, mainly the Trotskyites, criticized the councils, which annoyed the Argentinean revolutionary. In a televised conference, for the opening of the Seventh Economy and Planning Cycle, halfway through 1961, Guevara said that:

> A few days ago we were reading a satirical newspaper we have here; it's not particularly worth mentioning, but it's a Trotskyite newspaper, I'm not exactly sure about its name ... *Voz Proletaria!* It criticized the Technical Advisory Councils from the Trotskyite point of view. So it said that the Technical Advisory Councils had been created by that fearful petty-bourgeoisie, that exists within the government, in an attempt to provide something to the masses who are claiming the management of the plants, without actually giving anything. (GUEVARA, 1988b, p.51)

He went on:

> And, from a theoretical point of view, this is absurd, but from a practical point of view it's an infamy or a great mistake. The sin of the Technical Advisory Councils is precisely that they weren't created by pressure from the masses, but from a bureaucracy, top to bottom, in order to provide to the masses a vehicle they didn't ask for. That's where the sin of the masses is located. We, the "fearful petty-bourgeoisie", created a channel so we could hear the voice of the masses; we created, with the imperfections that such things are very likely to have because it's our idea, our creation, the creation of people who lack experience with those problems, the Technical Advisory Councils. The masses must be interested in knowing what's an economic plan, what's industrialization, what's due to each plant, what's their duty, how can that duty increase or decrease the interests of the working class in each plant. These are all elements that must agitate the masses. (GUEVARA, 1988b, p.51)

In practice, maybe the participation of the workers was not so considerable. In the elaboration of the plan, for example, JUCEPLAN indicated the main terms, according to the directives of the Board of Ministers. After that phase, the document was sent for evaluation by the ministries and other governmental organs, after which it would be delivered to the enterprises, and they would pass it along to the industries. Then, in the labor centers, the workers would meet to discuss the plan elaborated in the superior levels, make suggestions and send the outline back to each link in the chain, until it got back to the Board of Ministers. They would make the necessary changes and approve the document. (MESA-LAGO, [197-], p.41)

Even so, for some scholars, perhaps it was possible that a combination of centralized organization in the upper tiers and relative flexibility in the lower levels was an efficient form of industrial management and worker participation. According to Maurice Dobb:

> ...it's true that such attitudes and responses will not blossom overnight: they will not be created automatically by a government proclamation that industry was socialized... For this very reason the institutional set-up of a socialist economy may make a world of difference to the outcome. Too much centralization — a period of economically necessary centralization dragged out for too long — may cramp and smother any such new attitudes and responsibilities as new socialist situations ("industry now belongs to *us*") may spontaneously create. On the other hand, situations in which the initiative from *below* is encouraged and appropriately mixed or blended with a planned co-ordination coming from above; in which the democratic participation is combined with the "collective discipline" that modern productive techniques demand — this may serve to develop these new attitudes, leading to new levels of "collective conciousness" such as in an individualist, exploiting society (with its pay-packet bias) was unknown. (DOBB, 1970, p.58-59)

As has been said before, after the triumph of the revolution, the trade unions should adapt themselves to a new historical moment. In April and

May 1959, union elections were called. From then on, the M 26-7 held majority control of the CTC. Over the following months, congresses of several federations of national industrial trade unions tried to ensure the main posts were held by anti-communist elements. Just before the elections for the Federation of the Workers in the Sugar Industry — which represented around 40% of all the members of the CTC — the newspaper *Hoy* made direct attacks on several leaders that it considered anticommunist. Emotions were so stirred up that a group of unionists who were against the PSP invaded the periodical's offices, forcing the writers and journalists to ask for police protection.

With the disputes between communists and anticommunists growing increasingly tense, the Cuban Humanist Workers Front (FOHC) was formed in May 1959. It was made up of twenty-eight industrial federations, governed mainly by anticommunist leaders of the M 26-7, who had won the union elections. This was an attempt to control and even to impede the members of the PSP from directing the trade unions. (RIVERO, 1963, p.41-42) At that time, in a meeting at the CTC, attended by several commanders, ministers, trade union leaders, members of the M 26-7 and of other revolutionary organizations (but without the presence of Raúl Castro, Ramiro Valdés and Che Guevara, some of the most notoriously pro-Soviet elements of the new regime at that moment) there was a debate over the communist infiltration and how to stop it. That meeting was crucial in defining the two "communists" groups, as well as in determining, once and for all, the stance of the anticommunist elements of the government. (FRANQUI, 1981, p.63) According to Carlos Franqui, since the communists were the minority within the CTC, they decided to use other methods to take control of the central machine. Raúl Castro himself would have advocated that Augusto Martínez Sánchez take the place of Manuel

Fernández in the Ministry of Labor, and thus be able to control the trade union movement.

On November 18, 1959, the CTC carried out its congress, with a free, direct and secret vote, to choose 3,200 delegates among all the trade unions of the country, 3,000 of which were from the M 26-7. The other 200 were from the PSP and the other organizations participating in the event. (FRANQUI, 1981, p.72) In the congress the so-called "unit ballot" was imposed among the members of the M 26-7 and the communists, apparently at the request of Fidel, Raúl and Che. The trade union delegates of the movement would have agreed, although there was a wide majority. Even so, they didn't want to risk the possibility of the communists gaining more influence. (FRANQUI, 1981, p.73) Regardless of this fact, from then on almost all of the anti-communist labor leaders were expelled from the CTC, including catholic workers and anti-communist leaders of the M 26-7 itself, since the powerful machine of the Ministry of Labor was controlled by pro-Soviet elements of the government. At the same time, a purge committee was created with the goal of tracking down and expelling all of the trade union rulers who had opposed the rise of the communists in the CTC.

Until that convention, the communists had less than 15% of the delegates in the confederation. Another group, led by *auténticos,* commanded a considerably large alliance with several experienced trade unionists. David Salvador, himself, laid off Conrado Bécquer, Reinol González and J. A. Plana, three influential anti-communist leaders who had been on the board of the CTC since January of that year. He was replaced by Octavio Loit, a well-known anti-communist, who was the "number two" of the former directorate. Nevertheless, he was placed in a secondary position, without any real power. That ensured the appearance of a broad division of power, but the leaders who were tied to the communists retained a greater share. On that occasion, there was also the approval of a resolution demanding the withdrawal of the CTC from the International Confederation of the Free Trade Union Organizations (CIOSL) and from the Inter-American Regional Organization of Workers (ORIT). It's worth recalling that, right after the revolutionary triumph, the CIOSL had published a note expressing satisfaction with Batista's withdrawal from power, but at the same time showing concern that the CTC could become a target of "power measures", insisting that the labor movement maintain the right to vote on its leaders.

The secretary-general of the ORIT, Alfonso Sánchez Madariaga, had already stated, on January 3rd, 1959, that he wished that the new government was "authentically democratic" and that it facilitated the trade union's ability to exercise their rights in the country. (ROMUALDI, 1967, p.202) Next, Luis Alberto Monge, a representative of the ORIT, was sent to Cuba. He confirmed that the greatest concern of the Cuban trade unionists was with the issue of Mujalism. All the former collaborators of Eusébio Mujal were being fired. Monge also noticed that few revolutionary trade union leaders were willing to continue their relations with the ORIT. Shortly after that, George Meany, the main leader of the AFL-CIO, made his first proclamation about the revolution, in a letter sent to David Salvador, leader of the CTC. In it, Meany claimed that "our organization, having consistently fought dictatorial regimes, rejoices over the prospect of consolidating democracy in Cuba by strengthening the independent democratic labor movement, free of any totalitarian control or influence". (ROMUALDI, 1967, p.203)[7]

As the revolution unfolded, the Executive Committee of the ORIT, began to demonstrate concern and, in an emergency session that took place in Mexico City on February 3rd and 4th, 1959, it concluded that members of the trade union should have the exclusive right to elect their leaders, suggesting that elections take place within the trade unions as soon as possible. (ROMUALDI, 1967, p.203) In other words, the international trade union organizations tied to the US gradually started to pressure and try to influence the Cuban labor movement, which was unacceptable to the new government.

Every trade union, on all levels, joined the FONU, represented at the time by all of the revolutionary groups. Later, the FONU was reorganized, keeping only individuals linked to the M 26-7, most of whom weren't communists. The trade union leaders who had fought against Batista in the exile were also fired from management posts. Ángel Cofiño, for example, a former leader of the electricians, was prohibited, when he returned to Cuba, from continuing his activities and his leadership functions were suspended for ten years. In turn, Vicente Rubiera, leader of the trade union of the telephone and telegraph enterprise workers, who had been against the old regime, was replaced by members of the movement.

Still in the beginning of 1959, Serafino Romualdi, envoy of the AFL-CIO invited by the CTC, went to Havana to talk to the Cuban trade union leaders. Paradoxically, everyone ignored him when, upon his arrival to the island, he was vehemently attacked by the newspaper *Revolución,* run at the time by Carlos Franqui, which accused him of being tied to Eusébio Mujal, and of being a millionaire and a gangster. Romualdi immediately left Cuba. (ROMUALDI, 1967, p.204) Even though some anti-communist trade union leaders still wanted to keep the CTC in the ORIT, pressure for the confederation to withdraw from that organization began to increase. As the months went by, the discomfort grew, culminating with the withdrawal of the CTC from both international organizations inspired and influenced by the United States.

On January 7th, 1960, the new Executive Committee of the CTC adopted a resolution proposed by Jesús Soto, the new director of the organization, who advocated purging all of the anti-communists. After that, several rulers were arrested or lost their posts in the country's trade unions.

Many changes were taking place in the labor legislation. In March 1960, a law eliminated the collective contract. This meant that the right of negotiation with the patronage, which had been held by the trade union, now belonged to the Ministry of Labor, giving it maximum authority over labor disputes. Next, several laws were promulgated, extending the ministry's jurisdiction to every aspect of the relations between workers and business owners, and to labor conditions, organization and wages. The collective contract was all but abolished in April 1962, when the ministry was authorized by the government to suspend all collective agreements that, according to its interpretation, violated any legal socioeconomic regulations. In September, the Minister of Labor, Martínez Sánchez, publicly announced that the system of collective contracts would be transformed into a system that ensured the fulfillment of the production plans. (ROMUALDI, 1967, p.214)

In June 1960, the Ministry of Labor had already been granted the authority to freely intervene in the labor organizations. This made it easier for the new communist leaders to remove the elected leaders who displeased them and to replace them with men they trusted. In January 1961, striking was deemed a counter-revolutionary act and was prohibited, while the trade union organization Law, of August 3rd, 1961, completely dismantled the country's former labor structure, judging that the workers in the same type of business should belong to the same organizational unit, regardless of their occupation.

At the CTC convention, in November of the same year, its former leader, Lázaro Peña, returned as secretary-general of the organization. On that occasion, the number of federations was reduced from thirty-three to twenty-five; the members of the eight federations that had been dissolved were redistributed among those that remained. The convention also decided on some benefits for the Cuban workers. Resolutions were approved which ensured thirty days of paid vacation; nine paid sick days; twenty-six days of extra pay, in the range of four hours per week, even if the work week was reduced from forty-eight to forty-four hours and payment continued on the same fort-eight hour schedule; an annual Christmas bonus; longer weekends in summer, that is, in the four month season, between one day and one and a half days were added to the weekend, which amounted to twenty-six additional paid vacation days because of the shortened work week; four national holidays; and four days for optional holidays. With the Third Organic Law, of May 1962, all the workers were forced to carry their work cards, a fourteen-page document with detailed information about each individual, such as his or her attitude about work, the regime and the indoctrination methods. In order to get a job, everyone must have his or her card. Citizens who opposed the regime had their cards revoked by the government. Until then, the workers were unable to freely change jobs whenever they wished.

Already in 1960 — that is, even before returning to the board of the CTC — Lazaro Peña demonstrated his concept of what the role of the trade unions should be in the revolution. According to him:

> ...the role, the position, the responsibilities and the tasks of the trade union movement can't be the same now, under a revolutionary government, as before, when there was tyranny, a product of the coup d'État, now that the popular classes are in power instead of being the servants of the Yankee imperialists and of the classes that are the worst and most voraciously exploitive of the workers and of the people.... The defeat of Batista's tyranny and of the semi-colonial regime, combined with the subsequent establishment of the revolutionary regime, created the conditions for restoring the internally democratic operation, the true role, of the entire trade union movement of the CTC, of the federations and of the trade unions. (MIRANDA FERNÁNDEZ, 1984, p.284-285)

Thus, he believed that the Mujalist elements should be eradicated from leadership positions, that the methods and procedures of those individuals should cease and that what he called “false concepts” of subordination to imperialism, to economicism, to egotism, to anti-communism and to divisionism, which were supposedly encouraged by the “agents” of imperialism should be eliminated. (MIRANDA FERNÁNDEZ, 1984, p.285-286) The trade union movement would also have the task of defending the interests of the workers, protecting their rights and their working conditions, always supporting the revolutionary government. According to him, the “protection of the workers” shouldn’t be mistaken for the interests of specific groups. The most urgent demands would be short-lived and untenable if they didn’t contribute to advancing the revolution, agricultural and industrial development and increasing productivity. For that reason, Peña believed that the workers should have a revolutionary attitude and should not ask for higher wages. In other words, the main obligation of the trade unions would be to elevate the awareness of the workers and to support the new regime. For that to happen, they should encourage more meetings, “discuss Fidel’s speeches”, explain the problems of the revolution and attack its enemies in a consistent manner. (MIRANDA FERNÁNDEZ, 1984, p.291) It would be crucial for the trade union members to learn how to use weapons and join the workers’ militias. Also crucial, was internationalist solidarity, which should improve relations with other trade union organizations on the continent by providing solidarity andwhatever additional help was deemed necessary.

In theory, these ideas are very similar to those advocated by Guevara in the beginning of the revolution. On the other hand, one cannot find practical examples of positive wage differences in a considerable share of the Cuban working class. In 1968 — many years after Peña’s statements — the wage differences were quite large. While a judge of the Supreme Court earned 900 pesos per month, university professors earned 750 pesos, Cabinet Ministers 700 pesos and government employees, 250 pesos, construction workers earned 166 pesos, metalworkers, 161 pesos, sugarcane cutters, 96 pesos and youngsters in the compulsory military service earned only 7 pesos per month. (BONACHEA; VALDÉS, 1972, p.363) Since it was hard to balance the payments among the citizens in general and the productivity levels didn't always present the desired rates at certain moments, greater emphasis was sometimes placed, on moral stimuli and the development of communist awareness. Even many years after the revolution, Havana's workers continued to earn and consume more than those in other parts of the country. In that same year, 1968, Havana, which contained 27% of the island's population, earned 38% of the national income, consumed 35% of the goods and had 49% of all the commercial services. (BONACHEA; VALDÉS, 1972, p.364)

However, according to James O'Connor, based on information disclosed at the time,[8] "the great majority of the workers believed they had more influence on the government after the revolution than before; a great majority rejected general elections; and almost three-fourths of the workers had "favorable" attitudes towards the revolution, while the rest were undecided or hostile". (O'CONNOR, 1969, p.53) The workers who had suffered from unemployment or underemployment before the revolution were more likely to support the revolutionary government and had been, in the previous period, the group most approving of the communists. The revolution also received equal support from both the workers who earned low wages and from those with high wages. (O'CONNOR, 1969, p.53) In general, black people demonstrated more support for the revolution than white people, but both the unskilled workers and the specialized ones supported the new regime to a similar degree. (O'CONNOR, 1969, p.53-54) In turn, men had a more favorable attitude towards the revolutionary government than women, while there were no significant differences in support for the revolution among groups of workers from different social backgrounds. The workers of the small and large enterprises also equally supported the revolution at that time. (O'CONNOR, 1969, p.54)

It is clear, anyway, that in the first few years of the revolution, there was a great effort by the CTC, by the trade unions and by the Ministry of Labor, as well as by such rulers as Guevara to actually help the workers attain a better standard of living and, at the same time, develop their awareness and support of government decisions.

---

[1] The Cuban Revolutionary Party, or *Auténtico,* was established by Grau San Martín and by student leaders from the *Directorio Estudantil.* Created with the purpose of continuing the struggle for the revolution in Cuba, frustrated by Fulgencio Batista's intervention, it drew its inspiration from the first Cuban Revolutionary Party, founded by José Martí on January 5th, 1892. The program of the *auténticos* advocated political and economic nationalism, social justice and civil liberties. The party opposed Batista during the 1930's and half of the 1940's. When Grau San Martín was elected President in 1944, the party started to use violence against those who opposed it and became known for several corruption cases.

---

[2] From the beginning of the Cuban revolution, the AFL-CIO tried to destroy the new government by means of old contacts with trade union leaders on the island who could be useful in internal subversion. But all the old leaders were removed and Eusébio Mujal was fired; most leaders went to Miami and they soon joined organizations supported by the AFL-CIO. Eusébio Mujal became leader of the CTC in exile in Mexico; José Artigas Carbonel, former treasurer of the CTC, representative of the American Institute for the Development of Free Labor (IADTL), in Central America; and Esteban Rustan, former secretary-general of the Confederation of the Bank Workers, became a representative of the ORIT in Costa Rica. The CIA and the AFL-CIO influenced the trade union policy on the island for many years. See Morris (1967, p.77-79).

[3] Point 6 stated that the next task of the Soviet government would be the maximum use of all the available labor force, its correct distribution and redistribution geographically and in the several spheres of the economy. Point 7, in turn, advocated a re-education of the masses, by means of their disciplined work, to be coordinated by the trade unions, which should adopt and put into practice the job accounting, production rules and responsibilities of the workers. In point 8, the program asked the trade unions to learn with the bourgeois technicians and experts, in order to end ultra-radicalism and the lack of trust. Thus, the government would pay greater wages to the bourgeois experts for their technical knowledge and egalitarianism would only be a project for the future.

[4] About Lenin and the trade unions, see Lenin (1979a, p.433-462; 1979b, p.408).

[5] From the economic point of view, it should be recalled that, to a certain extent, the ideas of the Minister of Industry were similar to those of Preobrazhensky, that is, it is important for an increase of productivity to occur in the short term, an economic acceleration. In that sense, the trade unions would have to be interpreted according to their economic function and, as well as other instruments of the proletariat, they would be directly conditioned by the fact that the industry was state-owned and that it merged with the proletarian State. See Miranda (1980, p.172-173).

[6] According to Che, "each human grouping is more important than the individual, and each one of the groups of a workers' sector is more important than the trade union of a labor center, and all the workers are more important than one. This is something that must be understood; it's necessary to reorganize in order to change the previous mentality". In other words: "To change the mentality of the head of the trade union, who's responsible for speaking out against the boss, of sometimes imposing absurd measures within the production order, but who tends to falsely have a worker there earning wages, even though he's not making anything. The worker who currently demands a wage without earning anything, without doing anything, is actually conspiring against the Nation and against himself." See Guevara (1988b, p.71-72).

[7] To give an idea of how the American trade unionists interpreted the Cuban labor movement, it's useful to read the statement by Ernst Schwarz, executive-secretary of the Latin American

Business Committee of the CIO, in 1956, a part of which is reproduced here: "the Confederation of the Workers of Cuba brilliantly resisted the last political storm caused by Batista's coup, in March, 1952. Thus, it was able to preserve its union and its strength as a powerful Cuban institution, which not even the new dictatorial regime dared to touch. The CTC made possible for the Cuban workers to set an example, for others, of what can be accomplished by the union and by the strength of the workers. The wages are much higher than what is paid in many other parts of the Caribbean and even of Latin America, [...] the eight-hour workday is the basis for everything in the collective contracts made by the organizations tied to the CTC. Modern rules of social protection and security are arranged in laws, regulations or contracts of the trade unions; at the same time, funds maintained and managed in common by the workers, employers and authorities ensure adequate means to put them into practice. [...] Besides, the CTC took over a role of complete responsibility within the Cuban community as a whole, and it is currently developing its own economic program to make up for the periodic nature of employment and of production in the sugar industry" (RIVERO, 1963, p.59). Those opinions are very different from what the PSP and the M 26-7 thought about the same issue at that time.

[8] James O'Connor based himself on the information prepared by Maurice Zeitlin (1970).

6

Socialism and the "New Man"

The concept of "new man" has often been analyzed in an extremely vulgar and simplistic manner by most critics who deal with the issue, they often emphasize only the ethical, "philosophical" and "humanistic" aspects of the term, which, in practice, doesn't contribute much to the understanding of its real historical meaning and only reiterates romantic views which lack a greater political or economic content. According to Fidel Castro, for example, Cuban "humanism" would be a third way, an option between capitalism and communism. He claimed that there shouldn't be "either dictatorships of men nor dictatorships of classes; dictatorships of the groups nor dictatorships of caste, or class oligarchies: a people's government without dictatorship and without oligarchy; freedom with bread and without terror — in other words, humanism". (CASTRO apud DRAPER, 1966a, p.302) Besides, he claimed that "capitalism may starve a man to death" and that "communism kills the man by denying him freedom". (CASTRO apud DRAPER, 1966a, p.302) After claiming that he believed there shouldn't be bread without freedom or freedom without bread, he concluded: "We call this humanism. We hope Cuba becomes an example of representative democracy with authentic social justice". (CASTRO apud DRAPER, 1966a, p.302) That couldn't have been further from the political ideas that Che Guevara tried to implement later! Of course, Fidel Castro made these statements at a specific historical moment — in 1959, the beginning of the revolution — and, of course, these statements were made in light of the influences and concrete needs of that time and place. It's also known that Guevara didn't necessarily need to agree with the opinions of the *jefe máximo* of Cuba. Even so, it's clear that, according to the future Minister of Industry, humanism couldn't be separated from the political and economic aspects of socialism. The term "humanistic" in itself is vague, generic and can be applied to many situations, offering only a minimal and confused reference to the complexities and specificities that the term may encompass.[1]

Michael Löwy proposes a distinction between the philanthropic, "beyond class", "bourgeois humanism", and the "revolutionary humanism" advocated by Guevara. Löwy's strives to show the importance of the humanistic aspects of Marx and Engels in opposition to other "dry", more scientific interpretations spread mainly in the Second International, and less tied to "sentimentalist" elaborations. According to Löwy, Guevara better understood this humanistic character of Marx's undertakings, which was not in opposition to his scientism, but which was related to it in a dialectical and reciprocal manner (LÖWY, 1976). Löwy defines as such, the aspects of Guevara's "revolutionary humanism":

> What are the characteristic features of that new man, the communist man or "the man of the 21st Century"? Rejecting the utopia, Che limits himself to some general hypotheses, necessarily abstract, hypotheses, by the way, based on the Cuban reality itself, in which the first prefigurations of that future already unveil: the revolutionaries, the guerillas who fight among themselves to undertake the most dangerous tasks with the single satisfaction of fulfilling their duty ("our combatants' attitude already showed the man of the future"); the popular masses themselves, for their courage and sacrifice in the critical moments of the revolution: the invasion of Playa Girón, the missile crisis in 1962, the Communist Youth, a living example of revolutionary fervor and of internationalist spirit. The communist man must necessarily be a richer man inside and more responsible, tied to other men by a bond of real solidarity, of concrete universal fraternity, a man who recognizes himself in his undertaking and who, once the chains

> of alienation are broken, "will reach the full awareness of his social being, his full realization as a human creature". A man whose potential condition is what Marx called, on the *Theses on Feuerbach,* "the socialized humanity": in other words, overcoming the split orchestrated by bourgeois society between the "private" and the "public", the "private" interest and the "general" interest, the "man" and the "citizen", the individual and the community. (LÖWY, 1976, p.37-38)

Of course, Löwy based his remarks on articles and speeches by Guevara, himself. However, he omitted an analysis of the historical conditions and the motivations that led the Argentinean revolutionary to express such opinions. According to the those assessments, Guevara is seen as a man moved more by factors of ethical and almost "religious" inspiration — by that we don't intend to establish any direct correlation with the Church, but only to suggest a an attitude of "faith" and "mysticism" similar to religious fervor — leaving the practical aspects of the concept of "new man" as a minoritarian factor, related to the development of the Cuban production forces, to the mobilization of the masses, to technical improvement and to political awareness. Löwy (1976) deals with these topics in subsequent chapters of his book about Guevara, but he doesn't make the association of the Argentinean revolutionary's economic theories with the concept of "new man".

Even Leopoldo Zea is carried along by the emotion and by the current stream of a more generic left, when he talks about Guevara's "new man" as being "the man who can recognize himself in other men". (ZEA, 1997, p.84) According to the Mexican intellectual, "moving away from the conventional would be important in order to create the new man. New, not because he denies his background, but because he accepts it in order to overcome it". (ZEA, 1997, p.84)

Raúl Fornet-Betancourt, in his *Marxism in Latin America,* best shows Guevara's relation with "revolutionary humanism". Outlining that trend in a more detailed way, Fornet-Betancourt states that "the task of the ongoing critical examination of the social process in socialism represents, according to Guevara, a task that points to the view of the new man, to the extent that the conscious perception of this task, basically, reflects only the concrete subjectification of men [...] But this understanding is precisely the quality that Guevara places in the center of the new man's humanism". (FORNET-BETANCOURT, 1995, p.272) And he comments:

> Since, according to Guevara, Marx's communism represents a humanistic program, the specificity of which consists precisely in the fact that this "goal of humanity can only be reached in a conscious manner", he interprets Marx's theory in the sense of the new man's humanism, so it can, thus, emphasize precisely the decisive importance of the subjectification of man in historical development, as the result of a consciously executed process of self-liberation. Because Guevara believes that the humanism of the new man means progress, along this dialectic of emancipation that is, precisely, liberating because the concrete man in his historical situation executes it. The man grows with this dialectic, which is the historical embodiment of his own humanization. Well then, this dialectic of emancipation — expressed in another way — is a successful convergence between the modifications in the socio-structural realm of the society and transformation of the awareness of men. (FORNET-BETANCOURT, 1995, p.273)

The author demonstrates his knowledge of the subject and he explains it in a profound manner, but he's not willing to venture into a more specific study of other factors that also relate to this issue. Assuming there is a connection between "humanism" and the concept of "new man" in Guevara's theories, it is important to analyze other relevant issues that the term denotes — which are not often discussed as belonging to our theme — mainly those concerning the Cuban necessities when Che belonged to the ruling strata of the country. Thus, it's essential to observe some details related to the formulation and to the concretization of this idea, details that are present in both the political and in the economic realms.

In order to understand Guevara's "new man", it's necessary therefore, to explain three crucial elements that make up this idea, these are, basically, the *incentive system*, *voluntary work* and *socialist emulation.* These concepts are interconnected and intrinsic parts of Che's political and economic vision. Put into action during his term as Minister of Industry, they are closely related to the creation of the new man, and for that reason they will be discussed here in detail.

In a Cuba that needed quick development of the production forces and an increase and diversification of agricultural and industrial production in a short period of time, the discussions about building socialism by means of moral or material incentives, the use of voluntary work and "fraternal competition" proved to be useful and necessary in the first few years of the revolution. To talk about the new man only in terms of the technical and economic aspects, to the detriment of the "spiritual" and "ethical" realms, would be a complete misrepresentation of its most universal meaning, But to discuss this idea as something abstract and excessively "romantic", leaving aside the concrete factors of the historical moment in which it was elaborated without pointing out the political and economic elements with which the new man was imbued, shows a lack of profound knowledge on the subject and little care when dealing with something so broad and important. Since the "humanistic" aspects have been strongly emphasized in most texts about the new man, my concern will be primarily to emphasize the historical and economic aspects that led to the elaboration of the concept, as well as its consequences in the Cuban scenario.

As previously mentioned, in 1959 Cuba was lessening its dependence on the United States, and their control of the "export sector", electricity, banking credit and the fuel supply. The Americans owned approximately 1.2 million hectares of land, among which were 25% of the best agricultural estates in the country. Cuba was mainly an agricultural nation, and sugar was its staple product. There was chronic unemployment and underemployment, in levels that were proportionally much greater than those of other countries on the continent. At times, it was estimated that about 300,000 workers were consistently unemployed. (RODRÍGUEZ, 1978, p.66)

For some critics, the Cuban revolution was not made in a single block, as something unique and watertight. Beginning as a democratic-bourgeois revolution or, for some, "national-democratic" or only "democratic", it moved in quick stages towards socialism. Therefore, authors such as Abelardo Villegas (1986, p.272-273) and Carlos Rafael Rodrigues don't consider it indicative of Trotsky's "permanent revolution", as stated by Kevin Devlin (1968), among others. For them, it was an example of the V. I. Lenin's "uninterrupted revolution"[2], which according to its basic assumptions didn't conceive the "democratic" phase as necessarily extended or stable, but as an important yet transitory stage; the Cuban revolution saw the need to move towards socialism because of external contingencies and internal political and economic demands.[3]

There were many interpretations of that period. According to Sergio de Santis, the redistributive phase, having facets identifiable with democratic and socializing tendencies, indicated the beginning of the revolutionary process, and became known, in 1959, for the promulgation of the Law of Agrarian Reform. With the transition phase — and here we emphasize that the term denotes a specific moment of the Cuban revolution and not the "transition from capitalism to socialism" or from "socialism to communism" in broader terms discussed in the realm of Marxism — there was a difficult attempt at a relationship with the United States, a slow approximation of the Soviet Union, nationalizations and "State capitalism", with increasingly anti-imperialist tendencies. And, finally, the socialist phase, from 1961 on, when the Marxist-Leninist ideology and alignment with the Soviet Union prevailed. (DE SANTIS, [197-?]) It could be argued that, to a certain extent, the Cuban revolution in its general sphere was possibly closer to the concept of "permanent revolution" as elaborated by Mao Tse-tung and also, related to the process of "uninterrupted revolution" as discussed by other authors.[4] As it is known, in this specific case the two terms wouldn't exclude each other and could theoretically coexist as parts belonging to a same whole. Other models or theoretical outlines were also developed in an attempt to understand that period. According to the Italian Trotskyite Roberto Massari, the Cuban revolution underwent phases different from those proposed by De Santis: according to him, there was a first phase, from 1959 until the first few months of 1960, with the initial aggression of the United States against Cuba, the creation of JUCEPLAN, and the agrarian reform; a second phase, from that date until the beginning of 1962, with a realization of the public sector's potential, the beginning of the economic embargo, greater relations with the Soviet Union and the declaration of the revolution's socialist nature; and a third phase, with the Missile Crisis, the ministerial restructuring and the Second Law of Agrarian Reform. (MASSARI, 1993, p.157) It's hard to tell which of these models is correct, since all of them are imbued with substantial political content, at the same time that they are often self-justified according to authoritative arguments. Anyway, a study of the revolution based on a "phases" model — with all the problems that these models may present — would at least be useful for understanding the more subtle characteristics of the process.

In 1961, Guevara had outlined the plans for Cuba's industrial development, which were elaborated before Fidel Castro proclaimed the socialist nature of the revolution. The intentions were: to reach an annual production of 500,000 tons of steel; to build several plants for generating electricity with an approximate capacity of 600,000 kw, in order to double production until the middle of the 1960's; to double cement production in five years; self-sufficiency in fabric production; to produce 2,000 tractors, 5,000 trucks, 3,000 motorcycle engines, 100 fixed engines, the capacity to manufacture automobiles until 1965; and to create a shipyard for building fishing boats and later 10,000 ton ships for the foreign trade. (RIVERO, 1963, p.89-90) As can be seen, the Cuban projects were ambitious and demanded great effort by the population in accomplishing them. As Florestan Fernandes would say:

> Nevertheless, if it was hard to bring down the satellite republic and build the economic base of the revolution, it was even harder to erect, one by one, the girders of the new social order. In fact, the revolution had overcome itself many times. When it reached the socialist level, which was its highest possible historical level, it provided the revolutionary movement, mainly its frontline, with the tough task of crossing, from 1959 to 1964, the cultural and political distance that other proletarian revolutions of this century went through *before they took over the power.* It was necessary to do two vital things at the same time. First, the revolution should generate its *political philosophy:* the nucleus of ideas that mark its historical meaning and, at the same time, its utopian potential. Second, to transfer these ideas, such as what K. Mannheim designated as *principia media,* to the realm of effectiveness, of the formation of a planned society in Cuba. Due to the quick superposition of "phases" and "transitions" (which still today confuses the analysts of that revolution), the two things combined. And it was often the case that what should come before emerged later, in a climate of historical urgency and of political tension that precipitated the crystallization of the main ideas by means of the pressure of the facts, or, to the contrary, built revolutionary awareness directly as a clarification of practical activity. (FERNANDES, 1979, p.145-146)

And he insisted that:

> ...as the revolution unfolds, constantly changing shape and content after the socialist awareness becomes universal and hegemonic, the *new man* and the *new society* emerges. Their interaction engenders a civilization (a technology, a pedagogy and a culture), which leads socialism to its peak and exhausts it. Abstracted from the immediate historical crisis which nurtures the emergence of socialism, the economic element is crucial — because it's the substratum of the existence or the survival and the axis of social reproduction — but it appears within the reality that it must have fully established and developed under the plan (and not under the market, as in capitalism). Therefore, the economic element can't be used as an excuse to blame socialism for a static essence or for a stabilizing impulse. The plan reduces and, finally, extinguishes the economic determinism. Within it and through it labor emerges as the sociodynamic factor of the liberation of the individual and of society. (FERNANDES, 1979, p.147)

And he concludes by saying that "the *new man* and the *new society* should be considered according to your perception and to the explanation of your own behavior in the concrete situations of daily life". (FERNANDES, 1979, p.154)

The Cubans did not invent the idea of the "new man" and the tendency toward the *sobornost* (the collective awareness, which represents the opposite of Western individualism), nor did they have their origin in Guevara's thought. From Marx and Engels, through Mao Tse-tung and other socialist thinkers, there are constant elaborations on these themes. In the beginning of the Russian Revolution, for example, there was the idea of freedom as an active change, an act performed by man not only as an individual, but also as a social being. Regardless of how outdated that attitude might seem in light of the Soviet Union's collapse, it was spread in the beginning of that nation's revolutionary process, it was even a part of the slavophiles' and *narodniki's traditions,* as well as the French utopian socialist ideas, spread in the 19th Century, and of Marxism itself. (NORMANO, 1945) The Russian *furor technicus* encouraged the creation of a new society. As J. F. Normano used to say, "the Soviet Union abandoned the idealization and idolatry of the industrial worker and the peasant, leaving both of them subordinate to intensive industrialization. And as for the petty-nobility and bourgeoisie the Soviet Union united them with the nation, identifying them with the working class who encompasses everyone". (NORMANO, 1945, p.170)

The creation of the new man and the building of socialism and, later of communism, necessarily went through morality; but the communist morality, according to V. I. Lenin, should be seen in a different manner and it had both specific functions and clear objectives, which were explicitly related to the building of the Soviet State. Because of its political and economic implications in a particular historical period, Lenin's observations are very close to Guevara's conceptions. In other words, the "communist morality" was not something transcendent, separated from humanity, but totally subordinated to the class struggle. At the same time, this "morality of the future" had an edifying character, and the young people, the main builders of socialism, should develop awareness of the objective conditions, fight ferociously against the bourgeoisie and against alienation of labor. (CHAMBRE, 1960, p.226-229) Another Russian revolutionary who showed concern about the issue of the new man was Trotsky, who discussed the matter. In 1924, he wrote:

> The human being that is capable of moving rivers and mountains, of building palaces on the peak of Mont Blanc and deep in the Atlantic Ocean, naturally will also know how to grant not only wealth, color and intensity to his or her daily life, but also the greatest dynamics possible [...] The human being will call upon him or herself to dominate his or her own feelings, to raise his or her instincts to the maximum level of awareness, leaving them transparent, to instill direct

> communication between desire and awareness, in such a way that he or she elevates him or herself to a superior degree, that is, he or she will transform into a higher being from the social and biological points of view, or still, if we want, will change into a superman [...] The human being will become incomparably stronger, more intelligent, more refined. His or her body will become more harmonious; his or her movements will have more rhythm; his or her voice will become more musical; the shapes of the being will gain a dynamic theatrical nature. The average human will rise to the level of someone like Aristotle, Goethe, or Marx. And new peaks will rise over that level. (apud LEONHARD, 1997, p.23)

But Trotsky went further. He also explained other details of how social relations would evolve from the creation of that new man. He said:

> The concerns related to feeding and education, which currently weigh as much as a tombstone over the institution of the family, will be taken from him, becoming the goals of the social initiative and of the inexhaustible collective actions. The woman will finally free herself from her state of semi-slavery. Along with the technique, pedagogy — in its broadest sense of psychophysical formation of new generations — will become the queen of the social idea. Pedagogical systems will gather powerful "parties" around them. The experiences of social education and the competition among several methods will go through an unfolding that we can't even imagine today. The communist lifestyle won't develop completely [...] it will be consciously formed: verified, calibrated and corrected according to the idea. (apud LEONHARD, 1997, p.23-24)

Early mentions of the conception of the CPSU can be traced to the *New Program of the Communist Party of the Soviet Union* itself, published on June 30th, 1961, which was theoretically elaborated in a period of "bureaucratic socialism" and not particularly related to an idealist goal. It's worth recalling that, in the Soviet Union, this was considered the "Communist Manifesto of the 20th Century", since it would be the "scientific program" for building communism. Guevara read it and praised some aspects of the program; according to him, "Marx, in his fantastic view of all that was going to happen, talked about labor under communism as a moral need of man, and that's present, for example, in the program followed by the Communist Party of the Soviet Union." (GUEVARA, 1982, p.145) The document says that the new order will be made up "of a new man who will combine, in a harmonious manner, spiritual health, moral purity and a perfect body". (EASTMAN, 1969, p.23) Besides:

> ...the organs in charge of planning, accounting, economic management and cultural advance — currently government organs — will lose their political nature and will become public organs of a self-government. The communist society will be a highly organized community of workers. Universally acknowledged rules of communist behavior will be established and its inspection will become both an organic need and a habit of everyone. (EASTMAN, 1969, p.23)

The theses of the program also stated that the Soviet Union would become "communist" in 1980, since the material bases would undergo enormous development in the following decades. The Soviet Union, according to the document, would overcome the per capita production of the American population between 1961 and 1970, and all workers would enjoy a good quality of life and a quality dwelling. The collective and the state-owned farms would become highly productive enterprises with high incomes, and physical labor would disappear until 1970, transforming the Soviet Union into the nation with the shortest workday in the world. Through 1980, the differences between the city and the countryside would disappear, as the collective villages would become cities. There would also be the establishment of an average wage for the entire population. And, the national boundaries between the several Soviet republics would be eliminated. As for the Party, there would be elections every four years in order to renew at least one-fourth of the CC and of the *Politburo* members, and the leaders would be chosen by the people on a rota basis. (LEONHARD, 1977, p.78-80) But there would no longer be so-called political elections. These would be "apolitical" elections, only for technical and economic positions.

Even after the disappearance of the State, however, the party would continue to exist under communism, in order to coordinate the many activities of several organizations, which would operate within the self-management system. The party would only cease to exist upon the victory of the global revolution. (LEONHARD, 1977, p.84-85)

In the communism imagined by the Soviets, production would be highly organized and the character of labor would change. Thus, each person could work at whatever he or she pleased and would have only twenty to twenty-five hours of work per week, which should gradually be reduced. For that to take place, mechanical tasks should be eliminated through greater automation and computerized planning. Only then would the moral incentives replace the material ones. People would have more time for leisure and idleness, and they could use that time to dedicate themselves to science, inventing, literature and art. This would lead to the emergence of thousands of new scientists and artists. Biological needs, such as eating and sleeping, would occupy ten hours per day, while compulsory work wouldn't occupy more than four hours per day, leaving plenty of free time available to the workers. Products would be distributed for free, and there would no longer be an obsession with profit. But the official manual called *Principles of Marxism-Leninism* stated that the communist order didn't intend to fulfill every desire and exaggerated whim. According to the document, the people would already be cultured and conscious enough not to demand nonsense, such as receiving new cars or TV sets every week. If that took place, it would be an exception, rejected by the majority of the population, and wouldn't be enough to destabilize the new order. Private ownership would be abolished for the most part, restricted only to objects for personal use, such as clothes and shoes, although it would still be possible to own some articles, such as musical instruments and books, for example. (LEONHARD, 1977, p.82-86)

According to Khrushchev, the main features of the new man would be the loyalty to communism, the lack of reconciliation with his enemies, awareness of social duty, active participation in work to benefit the society, comradeship, care, honesty, sincerity and intolerance of disrespect for the order. The communist men would also no longer have any attachment to capitalist habits and they wouldn't be egotistical. (LEONHARD, 1977, p.86) According to him:

> The communist society, which will have an abundance of material and spiritual wealth, is able to fulfill the needs of each individual, as well as those of each nation [...] Under these conditions, the old concepts of boundaries will disappear. With the triumph of communism on a global scale, the boundaries of the States will disappear, as Marxism-Leninism teaches us. It's likely that only the ethnic boundaries will survive for some time, and even these will exist only as a convention. Naturally, those boundaries, if they can be called that, won't have any guards, customs employees or incidents. They will merely mark the historical location of a certain people or the nationality of a certain territory [...] The foundations of the communist relationships among the people were established in the Soviet Union and in the entire socialist field [...] Comprehensive cooperation in all spheres of economic, social, political and cultural life is being developed in the sovereign countries of the socialist field. Speaking of the future, it seems to me that greater development of the socialist countries will probably follow in the path of the consolidation of a single socialist global economic system. (BRZEZINSKI, 1965, p.401-402)

Similar ideas concerning the new man can also be found in several official manuals, such as *The Principles of Scientific Communism,* by V. Afanassiev, who describes its characteristics similarly to the ideas of the

Soviet ruler, even though it was written later, after he stepped down and lost prestige within the party. (AFANÁSSIEV, 1985, p.176-177) In turn, according to the manual *Principles of Marxism-Leninism* there would no longer be crime under communism and half the population would have a college level education, while the other half would have specialized, technical, college level education. People would no longer live in houses, but in "communal palaces", buildings erected in areas of up to 40,000 square meters and would hold between 2,000 and 2,500 people. In those "communal palaces" there would be maintenance areas, as well as a ward, post office, hairdressers and laundries. The adults would live on some floors, the children on others and, on still different floors, the elderly needing special care. There would also be specific floors reserved for married people, single people, young workers and students. Each floor would have an area between 800 and 1,000 square meters for dining, reading, leisure and music rooms. Nobody would be forced to live in these "palaces", but according to the "intellectuals" of the party, few people would want to miss the opportunity!

The "scientists" of the Academy of Sciences of the Soviet Union even described the life of the communist "new man" in the 21st Century, as well as the main technological characteristics of the time. They believed that the men of the 21st Century would enter their synthetic phase, wearing and eating synthetic products that would be of a higher quality than the natural ones; meanwhile, the metals could last for centuries, and would be lighter and easier to handle. Coal, iron, copper and salt mines would no longer exist: man would produce metals according to the desired composition and nuclear metallurgy would originate a new sphere of industry. It would be possible to transform an electric current directly into nuclear power. In turn, the electrical networks would have normal tensions of approximately 2 million volts, while the long distance networks would have higher voltages. The technological development would make it possible to create conventional explosions, which could destroy mountain chains such as the Himalayas and, therefore, create new possibilities for transportation and communication. All of the diseases known in the 20th Century would be eliminated by 2007, which would allow physicians and scientists to focus on improving the human organism, mainly the higher nervous system, rather than curing disease.

In the agricultural sector, chemical fertilizers would be developed to foster plant growth, while, at the same time, protecting against diseases and other harmful elements. Many minerals would be obtained from the bottom of the sea and the sea plants would become a common food source.

The men of the new millennium would also create an artificial sun, placed at a height of twenty or thirty kilometers, which would be able to light an area equivalent to the entire city of Moscow. There would be a system of electromagnetic rays emitted by four high frequency stations, which would cross over the Red Square, and a reaction would cause the incandescence of nitrogen and oxygen molecules, which would make it possible to light the entire region of the Soviet capital.

As for the means of transportation, some people believed that there would be mobile sidewalks, made up of parallel lanes that would move horizontally at a speed of twenty km/h, through all the streets in both directions. There would probably be benches or chairs in the sidewalks, as well as places to sell juice and cigarettes. Those large sidewalks would cover the entire urban area of the cities; the buses and trams would only circulate in the peripheries. There would also be an increased use of helicopters in the city limits. Man would conquer and create cities on the Moon and on other planets.

All those discussions don't seem to have been noticed by the population, which wasn't interested or at least wasn't duly informed about them. In fact, it can be concluded that in the Khrushchev era there was a lot of exaggeration and not much pragmatism. His government showed how far the irresponsible enthusiasm for the development of socialism could go. With the rise to power of Kosygin and Brezhnev, the exaggerated expectation of reaching the United States in per capita production by 1970 and to reach total abundance and communism by 1980 were set aside and replaced by more realist prognoses. Nevertheless, no other political program was presented in the XXIII Congress so, officially Khrushchev's "program", despite all its extravagances, continued to be the Party's official document.

The Maoist concept was also interesting. Unlike the ideas by such thinkers as Marx, Engels and Lenin, Mao advocated concepts of "new man" and of "new society" in a line centered largely on the age-old Chinese traditions themselves. The Chinese leader didn't believe in the occasional disappearance of a political authority and advocated the inevitability of a "dominant leadership" in any historical situation. (EASTMAN, 1969, p.21) He believed that communism would be characterized by the abolition of the classes; even so, there would still be other kinds of contradictions as well as anti-social attitudes within the society, since man is an imperfect being, who maintains these characteristics in any circumstances. For some Maoists, the work of the "young Marx" should even be ignored and considered "counter-revolutionary", since it was supposedly written by someone with an "immature mind", influenced by "mechanic materialism" and "utopic socialism". (EASTMAN, 1969, p.25) According to Chou Yang, some Marxists believe that, in order to "eliminate the 'alienation of man', it's necessary to destroy the dictatorship of the proletariat and the socialist system. When they advocate the return to the self, they are actually advocating absolute individual freedom and asking the people who live under socialism to return to the human nature of bourgeois individualism and to restore the capitalism that creates it." (EASTMAN, 1969, p.25)

It's important to note Guevara's relation with the ideas of the "young Marx", as well as his interpretation of them. In the article "The Budgetary Finance System", published in *Nuestra Industria* in February 1964, the Argentinean revolutionary quoted the economic manuscripts of the "young Marx", even though, according to him, the German philosopher's ideas about economics were still vague. Che believed that Marx was in the blossom of his youth then, and had already decided to care for the humble, even though he hadn't reached the level of scientific rigor of his later writings. He believed that although Marx's quotation came from his younger years it was no less worthy, since it accurately expressed the philosopher's thoughts. (GUEVARA, 1982, p.183-184)

In this sense, Guevara seemed to agree with some trends that were counter to a "structuralist" interpretation of that thinker's work, which was gradually beginning to be outlined in the academic world. Some intellectuals, such as Louis Althusser[5], for example, began to make epistemological "cuts" that identified how the author of *Capital* developed his ideas, with a much more "academic" and "philosophical" viewpoint than one of practical political intervention.[6] Speech analyses, the use of psychoanalytic techniques and the "decoding" of texts were beginning to be seen as important tools for understanding the German author's work. The importance of searching for the "conscious" and the "unconscious" between the lines in Marx's background and readings, the search for the hidden discourse in each chapter of his books created a tangle of ideas which would, in theory, illustrate the philosopher's great complexity and would permit a broader understanding of his work.

Therefore, his writings could be understood as a superposition of explicit and implicit texts, which would articulate themselves and become richer, making a simultaneous reading of these two dimensions crucial to a full appreciation of the text. Some authors believe that Marx's works can be divided according to the periods in his life. Beginning between 1840 and 1844, in his youth — when the philosopher wrote his doctoral dissertation and the *Holy Family;* later, in 1845, the "cutting" works, with *The German Ideology;* next, the first mature period, between 1845 and 1857, made explicit in *Capital;* and finally, the second mature phase, between 1857 and 1883. According to Althusser, the works Marx wrote when he was young could also be separated into two distinct periods, the liberal-rationalist one, with the articles of the *Rheinische Zeitung,* and the communitary-rationalist one, between 1842 and 1845, with the works quoted above. The Marxologists asked themselves if there was continuity and unity in Marx's thought, and what changes or variations could have taken place in his ideas, etc. The "young Marx", therefore, would be Marx, but not necessarily a Marxist, that is, not the same Marx of *Capital* and of his other mature works.

As a young man, Marx supposedly elaborated his ideas by relating History to the human essence, according to such criteria, as "freedom" and "reason". From 1845 on, there was a break until Marx started to discuss History according to concepts like "social background", "production forces", "production relations", "superstructure", "ideologies" and "economy". That is, what represented the denial of a supposed "scientific nature" of philosophical humanism, since this concept wasn't related in anyway to reality of the political economy. Of course, these "structuralist" trends were criticized by several intellectuals and Marxist militants of the time. (GLUCKSMANN, 1971) The difference between "real object" and "object of knowledge" didn't satisfy many of those critics. To go from the concrete to the abstract, and not to go back to the concrete, but only to produce "thought" based on other knowledge, was unacceptable to some engaged scholars.

In practice, regardless of how intense the desire was to show the differences between the "young Marx" and the "scientific Marx", man was always his greatest concern. In this sense, even though the emphasis was different in various elaborations and depths of political economy issues, the creation of an unalienated and complete man, who cut the moorings of capitalism to build a world where he could fully develop his skills, was always present. (OELGART, [ca. 1970], p.131-167) It becomes clear that when Guevara read Marx he gave special importance to the element of consciousness and was not very interested in distinguishing Marx's phases because he was more concerned about the practical issues of the construction of socialism in Cuba than about merely academic discussions, which did not directly affect him at that time.

As a student, Marx was already expressing his social concern and interest in the transformation of man.[7] He took it further, in college, when he explicitly advocated the importance of "consciousness" in his doctoral dissertation. From then on, "self-consciousness" became a central concept in his political thought. The philosophy of the future would have to be oriented towards the society, becoming something "practical", which would help in the development of the consciousness. According to him:

> Philosophy has, therefore, to resign itself to becoming mainly *applied* philosophy; and just as the poetry of art transformed into the prose of thought, so philosophy must descend from the heights of theory into *praxis*. Practical philosophy, or, more accurately, the philosophy of *praxis* (whose concrete impact on life and social conditions amounts to the employment of both within the concrete activity) — this is the future fate of philosophy in general [...] Just as thought and reflection overcame the *beaux-arts*, so the deed and social activity will now overcome philosophy. (apud MCLELLAN, 1970, p.65)

Marx's way of thinking may have varied during his life, but he always maintained the possibility of creating a complete man. Each individual, free, fully realized, relating him or herself "in a human manner" with others exemplified a new man, which would not necessarily be equivalent to a naive desire or to an ethical postulate. The ultimate goal was not the "ideal", something created to oppose the "inhumanized" and "individualized" man, or a utopian dream.

Neither Marx nor Guevara, when speaking of the new man, meant to project the distant image of an idyllic and fanciful society, a world made up of abstractions. When he outlined the features of the "man of the future", Marx approached it with the same seriousness as when he described the individuals within capitalism, relating the emergence of the new man to the evolution of the capitalist society, out of which emerged the necessary conditions for the transformation of the individuals. The worker would become conscious of his own degradation and, from then on, he would start a process which would actually turn him into a man, when he recognized the products of labor as belonging to him. In order to build the new society, the workers would have to recognize what alienation means in relation to the products of labor, to his activity and to the means of production. Therefore, they would have to create the right conditions for converting their activity into full human accomplishment, as well as condemning the very bases of capitalism, trying to avoid the reproduction of their relations. Such consciousness would impel the revolutionary struggle.

But the new man is not only the product of the revolution: he builds himself in its process, since it's the creation of the human *praxis,* that is, the transformation of nature and of social relations. Therefore, that revolutionary process is a long one. In his *The German Ideology,* Marx said:

> The large-scale transformation of man becomes necessary for the mass creation of this communist awareness, as well as for the success of the cause itself. Well, such transformation can only take place by means of a practical movement, by means of a *revolution;* this revolution is necessary, however, not only because it's the only way to overthrow the *dominant* class, but also because only a revolution will allow the class that *overthrows the other* to sweep away all the rotten stuff of the old system and be able to establish society on new bases. (MARX; ENGELS, 1986, p.108-109)

The need for the revolution is justified not only by the taking of the bourgeois superstructure apparatus, which will be used to keep it in power, but also because it's the only possibility for the actual transformation of man; in other words, the actual process of the creation of the new man. By changing the means and relations of production, man would change himself. The new man, therefore, can be found after the revolution, but also during its process and among other men who were responsible for its triumph. The German philosopher stated:

> When the communist workers get together, their goal is initially the doctrine, the propaganda, etc. But at the same time, they acquire with that a new need, the need of the society, and what seemed to be the means becomes an end. The most brilliant results of this practical movement can be seen when the French socialist workers get together. They don't need unions anymore or reasons to meet, such as smoking, drinking, eating, etc. The society, association, conversation, which in turn has society as an end, are enough for them. Among them, the fraternity of men is not a phrase, but a truth, and the nobility of man shines in the faces hardened by labor. (MARX apud GUIJARRO DÍAZ, 1975, p.317)

The revolutionary workers would be the initial model for the man of the future. In Marx's conception, they supposedly felt the need of association and to construct a society according to new terms. With their "fraternal" integration, they built the bases for a real community of men. This wouldn't be the new society, but the embryo of socialism would already be seen within it. The new man would be forged in the school of "labor". It would form the moral character of the proletariat, showing, in his environment, the reality to be transformed. The workers' strength of character and the possibility of committing to advanced ideas would be provided by their own environment, and their own attitude towards it.

The man within bourgeois society, had become an "individual", but his "individuality", instead of being related to the community, was expressed in intensive competitiveness with it. As Marx insisted, liberty as a right of man wouldn't be based on the relations between men, but on the separation of men. In other words, "none of the supposed rights of man go beyond the selfish man, of the man as a member of civil society; that is, as an individual apart from the community, confined within himself, to his private interest and to his personal fancy" (MARX, 1964a,p.58). According to him:

> In that way, man didn't free himself from religion; he got religious freedom. He didn't free himself from ownership; he got ownership freedom. He didn't free himself from the selfishness of commerce; he got the freedom to dedicate himself to commerce. [...] The *selfish* man is the *passive* result, only *given,* in the dissolution of society, an object of immediate certainty and, as a consequence, a *natural* object. The *political revolution* breaks civil society into its components without *revolutionizing* these components and submitting them to the criticism. This revolution considers the civil society, the world of needs, labor, private interests and civil law as the *basis of its own existence,* as a totally subsistent assumption, therefore, as his *natural basis.* Finally, man as a member of the civil society is identified as the *authentic man,* the *homme* opposed to the *citoyen,* because it's man in his sensitive, individual and *immediate* existence, while the *political* man is only the abstract, artificial man, the man as an allegorical, moral person. Thus, man as he really is, recognized himself as the *selfish man,* and the *real* man, only as the *abstract citoyen.*

> *All* emancipation is a *restitution* of the human world and of the human relations to the *man himself.* Political emancipation is the reduction of man, on the one hand, to member of the civil society, an *independent* and *selfish* individual and, on the other hand, to a *citizen,* to a moral person.
> Human emancipation will only be complete when the real and individual man has within himself the abstract citizen; when, as individual man, in his empirical life, on the job and in his individual relations, has become a *generic being;* and when he has recognized and organized his own forces (*forces propres*) as *social* forces, in such a way as to never again separate this social force as *political* force. (MARX, 1964a, p.61-63)

Therefore, it is important to transform that individualized man into the socialist man, who depends on the community to develop his individuality. According to the “young Marx”, socialism begins with a theoretical and practical perception of man and of nature as crucial elements, not starting only from denial of religion and of capitalism, but from a positive self-consciousness, which would later develop into communism. The latter, however, despite being a necessary form for the near future, isn’t the goal of human development, the ideal form of community, but the search for “positive humanism”, that is, the life of man as a complete and full expression of all his potential. (FISCHER, 1978, p.21) Communism, therefore, would mean the beginning of the development of humanity; but, in order to reach that historic level, the role of thought and of ideas would precede that of actions.

Thus, consciousness plays a predominant role in forming the new man and overcomes the limits of historical progress. When he develops consciousness, man is able to go beyond his moment and facilitate the arrival of more advanced stages of social organization. Even after achieving communism, the self-consciousness process should continue, since consciousness will take man further than the initial goal of overcoming the contradictions and the conflicts of capitalism. In his mature phase, Marx continued to believe in the abolition of private ownership of the means of production, in the scientific nature of labor and in maximizing the use of machinery rather than the workers as elements for liberating man and enabling him to fully develop and use all of his potential.

Therefore, Guevara's interpretation of Marx seems to be generally correct. As has been said before, the Minister of Industry of Cuba was concerned about the practical aspects of the island's economic development. But his "philosophical" interpretation of Marxist ideas is also important. In debates with comrades from the government, he claimed that some "false" Marxists could say that men are equal and that neither their intelligence nor their character could be changed. That would be a strict dogmatism. According to him, the Cubans had developed the first "socialist" "Marxist" system, with "man" as its protagonist; a system in which one talks about the individual and of man's importance to the revolution. But he insisted that, despite this, they were still incapable of making man give his best, and that he was likely to become a machine. (GUEVARA, 1982, p.66) Consciousness, finally, would be the main aspect. According to him, "Marx thought about freedom of man and he saw communism [not only] as the solution to the contradictions which produce his alienation, but [also as] a conscious act. In other words, communism can't be seen merely as the result of class differences in a highly developed society, which would be resolved in a transition stage to reaching the peak; man is the conscious agent of History. Without this *consciousness,* which includes that of his social being, there can be no communism". (GUEVARA, 1982, p.184)

6.1 Incentive system and socialist emulation

The incentive system was one of the most debated issues in the first few years of the revolution. While one group, led by Charles Bettelheim and Carlos Rafael Rodríguez, advocated the use of material stimuli, Guevara and his closest collaborators were great promoters of the moral incentives. Bettelheim believed that the behavior of men wasn't determined by consciousness, but by their insertion into a specific production process, influenced by whatever stage of development the production forces had reached at the time.[8] Thus, the behavior of the people would only change in direct relation to the production process. According to him, "the stimulation techniques can be reduced to the level of the different technical units which make up a production unit, strictly speaking (for example, in the level of the workshops, by means of the establishment of awards granted to that level); thus they can go down, of course, to the teams and even to the jobs. In the latter case, it's about a motivational technique related to a certain wage policy". (BETTELHEIM, 1976b, p.255) In other words: pricing, wage and credit policy. Later, Bettelheim would agree that it was important to add further "non-economic" stimuli, such as "spirit of solidarity", "sense of honor" and "socialist competition". Such principles should develop throughout the process, even though priority was given to the material stimuli. The Czech economist Ota Sik also believed that, "in the current developmental stage of the production forces, and due to the current nature of the labor process, material incentives are, no doubt, the primordial stimulation". (apud SOLGANICK, 1967, p.46)

Che Guevara's opinion was opposite to that of Bettelheim's basic assumptions. The high official of the Cuban government believed that it was necessary to create the new man and develop technology and technical skills simultaneously. He thought it was absurd to believe that the material stimuli would disperse over time, even if consumer goods were produced with a surplus and they were abundant in the marketplace.[9] This is a contradiction in terms within a socialist society, where that kind of stimulus leads to individualization and selfishness, hindering the improvement of a communist consciousness. In other words, the material stimulus would be a "leftover" from the capitalist world, which should be set aside on behalf of a more efficient economic line of reasoning in practical and "cultural" terms. Thus, Guevara believed that the material stimuli could create a bureaucratic layer within the governmental organs and the enterprises and industries in general, as well as the elitist and technocratic groups and this layer would become a parasitic caste within the socialist society that was being built. He didn't deny the objective need for material stimulus; he only insisted that the latter couldn't be the basic driving lever of the economy and of the development of the socialist State. (GUEVARA, 1982, p.189-190) Ernest Mandel explained the situation clearly. According to him:

> ...all those who place the absolute assumption of the *previous* development of production forces, before the socialist consciousness can be expanded from mechanist thought similar to those who believe that they can arouse, by purely subjective means (education, advertisement, agitation etc.), an identical consciousness immediately. There's a constant interaction between the creation of a material infrastructure necessary for the expansion of the socialist consciousness, and the development of this same consciousness. (MANDEL, 1982b, p.169)

The more concrete economic aspects must also be observed. Cuba, at that moment, was a country with material and financial shortages and was poorly industrialized, to a certain extent. The advocates of moral stimuli saw the possibility of encouraging production by inexpensive means, which would demand more from the worker without additional reward. Thus, the moral stimuli would play the role of creating a "group spirit" and a "consciousness" of each individual worker's importance in the construction of socialism. That revolutionary surge, rewarded with bonuses, medals and certificates, would be valued in the entire country and would lead other people to follow the example of the most devoted proletarians. Of course, the material stimulus would still be necessary, since the nation would be undergoing a transition phase and would still be dealing with men from the old capitalist society. But Guevara believed that these incentives should be applied with restrictions, used together with the moral stimuli, always as a secondary support; they should gradually be eliminated, mainly by means of education. Priority should be given to the material stimuli of a social nature, such as aid to labor centers that demonstrated greater dedication to socialism, in terms of building houses, schools and health centers, regulating wages according to skills of the proletarians and providing the workers with better study conditions for improving their educational and technical levels. Che's intention was to gradually eliminate the material incentives, mainly according to concrete conditions, such as increasing the quantity of consumer goods in the country. Anyway, he was aware of the implications of his project. In comparative terms, he believed that — even though there was no way to measure or make calculations on the subject — in a relatively short period of time the development of "consciousness" would provide more favorable results in economic terms than material stimulus would. (GUEVARA, 1982, p.190)

At the time, Guevara studied several variants of the incentives system. Among them were material incentives based on the wage scale plus the payment of a bonus for completing or overcoming the labor standards and the production plans; material disincentives for failing to reach production goals or quality; material incentives as collective prizes; and improvement of the workers' quality of life. (TABLADA, 1989, p.194)

According to Che's conception, the system of standards that he advocated had the merit of establishing compulsory professional training, which would allow for the rise from one category to another, making an increase in the technical level of the business professionals possible. Therefore, the person who didn't fulfill the standard wasn't fulfilling his or her social duty and would be reprimanded by "society" with a decrease in wages. In that case, business control and ideological control would be crucial, with the party acting as an ideological "engine", using production labor, training and participation in the plant's economic issues as examples to the workers, in order to actually become a part of their life. (GUEVARA, 1982, p.193)

Polish economist Oskar Lange considered the incentives an important aspect of building socialism. But they must be defined according to each specific case and to the development stage of the country in question. He believed that people who participated in the enterprises would have to be interested both economically and morally in the satisfactory fulfillment of the enterprise. In other words, the incentives "must be created in such a way that the personal and collective interest of the staff of the enterprise is identical to the social task that it must carry out". (LANGE, 1966a, p.91) But he reiterated that there are two properties of the means of production in socialist enterprises, the national and the group, such as the cooperatives. They are both trustees of the workers' interests, but they operate differently. Theoretically, the "group" enterprises would permit, in some sectors, greater harmony between the incentives of the employees themselves with the general social interest, while in the "national" enterprises the workers should be substantially "self-governed", otherwise the economic and moral incentives wouldn't work and the enterprise would become bureaucratized and inefficient. (LANGE, 1966a, p.91-92) According to him:

> ...as a result of the social ownership of the means of production, incentives can also be determined by the business

> superstructure of the economy, the planning methods and the fulfillment of the plan, the principles of the economic accounting adopted, the methods for wage payments, the kinds of participation in the profits of the enterprises, the role of the market, and so on. All of these things help to determine the incentives of the workers. Thus, the adequate organization of the business superstructure of the economy is crucial to promote the operation of the necessary incentives to ensure the adjustment of production to the needs of the society, the rational use of resources and the promotion of the technical progress. (LANGE, 1966a, p.93)

In other socialist countries, such as China, the system of incentives was also widely discussed. Mao Tse-tung believed that Chinese economic constraint and the development level of the production forces in the country at the end of the 1950's were an advantage for the people of the "Middle Kingdom", since they would make a greater enthusiasm for communism possible. In the first stage of the Chinese economy, which coincided with its first five-year plan (1953-1957), the Chinese Communist Party adopted the Soviet model and the use of material incentives. However, with the "great leap forward", which began in 1958, emphasis was put on moral incentives because the Maoists believed that by resorting to the virtues of personal detachment, of asceticism and of collective well-being, they would be able to speed the path to communism. The members of the Chinese Communist Party's staff became experts, with refined ideological and technical backgrounds, trying to reduce the distance between the countryside and the city by industrializing country's heartland, and building a number of schools and health centers. The "intellectuals" of the party were sent to the countryside to carry out handwork, and both children and peasants were sent to the cities, in a regimen of working half of the time and studying half of the time, in order to become "masters of technology" and, in that way, reduce the gap between the two kinds of labor in the population. The result would be greater economic efficiency and, perhaps, as a result of that, the creation of a new man.

As it is known, the "great leap forward" was a huge failure. Even so, Guevara admired some of their assumptions and the use of moral incentives. A great advocate of moral incentives, Guevara had to face the criticism of many adversaries within the Cuban government itself, who thought his opinions were unrealistic and impractical. One argument of the advocates of moral stimuli was that, without consumer goods to meet the needs or the "fancies" of the workers, there could be no material incentives. According to Adolfo Gilly, "the shortage of consumer goods, as it exists in Cuba nowadays, after a certain point affects the worker very much, since he can't buy what he wants. As a consequence, if material concerns are his priority, he would prefer to earn less and make less effort". (GILLY apud MESA-LAGO, [197-], p.122)

Gradually, however, Guevara's ideas started to lose strength, as his economic project seemed as if it wasn't producing the expected results. In 1965, based on suggestions by Carlos Rafael Rodríguez, material incentives became prevalent once again. The incentives proposed by Fidel at the time were trips to other socialist countries, refrigerators and motorcycles. In that year, 1,500 refrigerators, 1,000 motorcycles, 500 trips to socialist countries and 2,000 trips to Varadero beach were distributed to the workers. However, only eighty of the international trips were accepted: most workers preferred to exchange them for durable consumer goods. (MESA-LAGO, [197-], p.141)

The moral "rewards", on the other hand, consisted of medals, banners, buttons and certificates. The greatest titles that could be obtained were "National Hero Worker" and "Worker of the Nation's Vanguard". The moral "punishments" would be the display, in the Cuban industries, of the names of the workers and the labor centers that had produced less, denouncing to all the “laziest” workers in the country. At the beginning of the experiments with material and moral incentives, money was given in addition to consumer goods and “certificates”. As time went on the financial compensation gradually stopped being a part of the rewards to the most innovative and productive workers. Even so, some mechanisms continued to exist, with the explicit goal of “rewarding” the “vanguard” workers, who devoted themselves to the revolution without material interests. A social security law promulgated on March 27th, 1963 granted health benefits to all Cuban workers, cash payments for the entire time of treatment up to one year, or for retirement. The citizen could withdraw up to 40% of his wages from the pension funds if he was hospitalized and 50% if he was being treated at home. But the “vanguard” workers had access to 100% of their wages for necessary health benefits. (BONACHEA; VALDÉS, 1972, p.361)

In 1968, the government went even further in extending the benefits, but only to the workers who showed a “communist” attitude toward the job. That meant giving up payment for overtime, working forty hours or more per week, no unauthorized absences from the job, surpassing the labor quotas and being an active participant in voluntary work. However, one year later only 6% of the Cuban citizens satisfied that criteria. (BONACHEA; VALDÉS, 1972, p.362)

The system of incentives is closely related to the socialist emulation, which was a way to build socialism by means of maximizing the country’s labor, a way to increase productivity, as well as an instrument for raising the consciousness of the workers. The method consisted of rewarding the best workers and showing them to the others as an example using an intensive advertising campaign and political propaganda. The other workers would then be encouraged to produce more and better, inspired by their fellow employees. Both in the Soviet Union (where the emulation was implemented based on the formulations made by V. I. Lenin and gained momentum mainly from 1929 on, with the first Five-Year Plan) and in China, this idea was used to promote faster development of the nations. The main goal of the emulation would be to increase each worker's productivity and production in general, promoting quality control and, at the same time, putting "pressure" on the workers to produce more; it also worked ideologically, since it encouraged a "fraternal competition" among the workers and praised the virtues of socialism.

The emulation began in Cuba in 1960, first with cutting sugarcane, then agriculture in general and later in the industries, partly in an effort to resolve the problem of absenteeism, which was growing in the country. Halfway through 1962, absenteeism had reached unacceptable proportions for the Cuban leaders, which forced them to take "coercive" measures. Gradual punishments were introduced in Cuba starting on August 27th of that year, varying from wage reductions to job transference. Even so, the results remained unsatisfactory, while a part of the population expressed their displeasure. Until 1964, other measures were taken to discourage poor discipline and increase productivity, since a system of goals and standards was carried out with the objective of ensuring that each worker reach certain production levels in order to receive his or her full wage. If the worker couldn't reach the goal, his or her wage would be reduced proportionally. If the individual produced more, he or she would receive a wage increase.

Despite an apparent failure of the emulation in several sectors, the government decided to extend the system to the entire national economy. (MESA-LAGO, [197-], p.131) Even so, by the end of 1962 only 9% of the country's labor force participated in that activity. (BONACHEA; VALDÉS, 1972, p.369)

The emulation was divided into individual and collective forms. The former would encourage the worker to produce as much as possible with maximum effort and devotion and would reward him with material or moral incentives. The latter, in turn, would "organize" a competition among sectors, sections and departments of the plants, farms or labor centers in general. This process would occur in places where the different sectors depended on one another and through competition for greater productivity, would encourage others to follow their example and to maintain, and even increase, the production rate. (BONACHEA; VALDÉS, 1972, p.136-138) Since the system still was not working as the leaders of the island wished and absenteeism still hindered production, a new labor law was enacted in 1964, considering the non-fulfillment of labor quotas or schedules, unjustified absence, damage to tools, carelessness and disrespect towards superiors as serious infractions. This law was managed by the workers themselves through their boards, made up of members who fulfilled certain requirements, such as having a "socialist" attitude towards the job; having discipline; not being considered "absenteeist"; and never having been reprimanded by any organ of the labor judiciary. From 1965 on, however, when it noticed that those measures weren't very popular, the government decided to gradually change its emphasis by reducing or eliminating sanctions and praising the development of the socialist consciousness of the workers. (BONACHEA; VALDÉS, 1972, p.370-371)

6.2 Voluntary work

Voluntary work played an ideological role, at the same time that it carried out an extremely important economic function, since it was often critical for the sugarcane harvest, for example. Voluntary work was a concrete bond between intellectual and manual labor, it should be carried out with pleasure and required the conscious participation of the workers, preventing them from feeling alienated and expediting the transition to socialism. As Michael Löwy would say, "Che's theses about the voluntary work and its meaning for the development of the new man don't depend exclusively on 'voluntaristic', 'utopian' problematics, foreign to Marxism (as advocated by some of his 'materialist' critics), but are inserted in an authentically *Leninist* tradition". (LÖWY, 1976, p.101)

Volunteering could consist of many different things, such as by workers who were employed in a certain field of production using their spare time to work in another field for free; the assistance of unemployed women; students, as part of their "socialist education"; tasks imposed on political prisoners as a means of social rehabilitation; and the work considered to be part of compulsory military service. (MESA-LAGO, 1972, p.385) Work done by employed men and women outside their normal working periods could be carried out in different manners such as, extra hours after the work day; on the weekends, mainly on Sundays; during vacations; or for a period of many months in a row, during a leave of absence from their regular jobs. The latter was known as long term voluntary work and meant an absence of six months from their usual work place to volunteer mainly in the countryside. Those who remained in the industries were expected to make an effort to maintain the production levels even though that meant working more than they normally did. Between 1962 and 1967, the number of voluntary workers increased from 15,000 to 70,000 in the most varied sectors, from cutting sugarcane and harvesting coffee to repairing houses damaged by hurricanes and erecting buildings. The workers weren't paid for those services, but they were given lodging, and the tools for carrying out their tasks. From 1963 on, they could use the hours of voluntary work as service time for receiving a pension.

In the beginning of the revolution, that volunteerism was spontaneous, for the most part, but beginning in 1962, the citizens were recruited and organized into battalions and brigades. The government was in charge of regulating the work and several measures were introduced: self-criticism among the workers; annual contracts stipulating a certain number of unpaid working hours; management and inspections of the trade unions to ensure the quantity and quality of the work done; weekly reports made by the battalions themselves about their performance; inspection teams to maintain discipline; and punishments for violations of the regulations. (MESA-LAGO, 1972, p.388-389)

Both the Federation of the Cuban Women and the Union of Young Communists were extremely active in spreading and organizing the voluntary work. Thousands of housewives were recruited to work in the countryside, while a great number of students completed their volunteer activity during school vacations. In 1964, the Ministry of Education made this compulsory.[11] One year later, the same ministry asked the universities for their students to participate in voluntary work for a period between three and six months per year. They received food and lodging for this time.

Political and military prisoners were also expected to take part in unpaid work. Government employees who committed errors and transgressions while carrying out their functions, as well as those imprisoned for ideological reasons were punished by being compelled to carry out certain unpaid tasks as a form of rehabilitation and re-education. This served as one more element that contributed to the increase of labor and to a small increase in general productivity. The "crimes" were adjudicated by the Administrative Disciplinary Committee (CODIAD), which, after analyzing each case, sent the guilty parties to labor camps run by the Ministry of Interior. According to official figures, between 1964 and 1965 there were between 15,000 and 20,000 political prisoners on the island.[12] As in the other cases, the prisoners received food, clothes and lodging.

With the goal of putting an end to the idleness of a considerable number of people, in 1963 compulsory military service was established for men, between sixteen and forty-five years old, for a period of three years. The recruits were divided into two groups: the "not completely politically integrated" and the "unsuspected". The first group of soldiers was stationed with the Military Units of Support to Production, working in the agricultural sector for their term of service, while the "unsuspected", who were more trusted military, joined regular training together with the production work. In 1966, the number of recruits in the Cuban military service reached at least 84,000 soldiers. (MESA-LAGO, 1972, p.391)

In 1967, the unpaid workers made a substantial contribution. From a labor force of 2.5 million people, between 200,000 and 300,000 volunteered for the Cuban government. The greatest participation quota was that of regularly employed male workers: between 60,000 and 70,000 volunteered. Next were women, between 5,000 and 10,000, who also participated in this activity. With a number varying between 18,000 and 23,000, youngsters and high school students made up another significant sector of unpaid workers. Over 90,000 recruits from the military service helped increase production without getting wages. And, finally, between 20,000 and 75,000 political prisoners, who were forced to carry out these functions as punishment. (MESA-LAGO, 1972, p.391-392)

In the Ministry of Industry itself, Guevara decided to create what was called the Red Battalion, with 120 to 130 militants, who would have to serve at least 240 hours of voluntary work per individual in order to obtain the "communist work certificate" and to remain as a member of the battalion. Che called this group, the "supervanguard" of the revolution and he believed that its goal was, not only to increase production, but primarily to set an example. (GUEVARA, 1982, p.144) The Argentinean guerrilla emphasized, in conversations with other government members, that he thought about making it "compulsory" for all people to work 240 hours for a period of six months in order to obtain their "certificate", but he explained that it should be a "voluntary" obligation.

Guevara also insisted on the success of his project, even though some time later it was confirmed that the results were not as favorable as hoped. Even so, there were individual cases of impressive effort. On January 11th, 1964, in a speech at the CTC-R, Guevara mentioned some examples of exceptional devotion to voluntary work, such as several workers who, in four months, had worked 980 hours, that is, more than eight voluntary hours per day during that period. The woman who completed the longest unpaid work period accumulated 340 hours. Until the beginning of that year, the government organ that had accumulated the most voluntary hours was the Vice-Ministry for the Light Industry, with 774,344 hours. Within this ministry, first place went to the mechanical sphere, with 404,000 hours; next, the textile sector, with 141,000 hours; then came the chemical sector, which accounted for 117,000 hours; and finally the food sector, with 110,000 hours.

Che presented awards to forty-five workers who stood out the most in the Ministry of Industry, on April 30th, 1962. After praising the achievements of workers who had cut thousands of kilos of sugarcane in a relatively short time, he expressed his idea of what one goal of volunteering should be. According to him, the watchword should be: produce more everyday, with greater enthusiasm and work hard to increase production in every enterprise in the country. On August 15th, 1964, however, in another ceremony to present "certificates of communist labor", this time to the workers of the MININD at the CTC theater in Havana, Guevara approached the theme in another way:

> ...voluntary work must not be viewed in terms of the economic importance that it represents to the government; voluntary work, fundamentally speaking, is the most important factor in developing consciousness. And even more so when these workers carry out their labor in unusual places, cutting sugarcane, sometimes in very difficult situations, or when our management or technical workers get to know the Cuban fields and get to know the factories because they participated in voluntary work. A new cohesion and understanding are established between both factions that the capitalist production technique had always kept separate and hostile to one another, because this was part of its endeavor for constant division in order to keep a host of unemployed people, desperate people, ready to fight for a loaf of bread, against long-term conveniences and, sometimes, against their principles. (GUEVARA, 1982, p.76)

And he insisted: "Voluntary work becomes a conduit for understanding and connection between management and manual workers which sets the course towards a new stage of society, in which class doesn't exist and, therefore, differences between manual and intellectual workers, or between workers and peasants don't exist". (GUEVARA, 1982, p.76)

During the first semester of 1964, the only provincial delegation to earn the "certificate" was that of Matanzas, with one worker. Among the enterprises, the consolidated enterprise of the Basic Chemistry had the least prominence in that period, with only one worker from the management sector. In the Ministry of Industry, in turn, 1,002 workers were able to earn their certificates. (GUEVARA, 1982, p.82)

Gradually Che began to place greater importance on the "educational" aspects of this kind of activity. The crucial facet was developing consciousness, since this would allow a faster transition to socialism. Guevara himself made a great effort to stand out in volunteering. His activities demonstrate that he did more than simply set an example for use as propaganda. On July 31st, 1962, in the José Antonio Echeverría mills, in the village of Regla, Havana, he participated in an intensive undertaking and closed the one-thousandth bag of wheat flour produced in that month. Between February 4th and 12th, 1963, he operated a machine for cutting sugarcane in several places in the Province of Camagüey, for twelve hours per day. On that occasion, he cut 81,900 *arrobas* of sugarcane. (PÉREZ-GALDÓS, 1987, p.125) But he understood the difficulties of making voluntary work an intrinsic part of the Cuban citizens' life:

> Nowadays voluntary work must become a phenomenon of the masses; which also requires a qualitative leap in organization, so those who volunteer will not feel that they're wasting their time, which is the most unpleasant sensation there is. Last Sunday I got tired of volunteering and something that never happens to me, except when I work with sugarcane, occurred. I was looking at my watch every fifteen minutes to see when the workday would be over so I could leave, because what I was doing made no sense. I mean that the identification of the man with his job must be developed, must be organized. (GUEVARA, 1982, p.59)

Later he insisted that:

> ...we still have not been able to find the way in which man gives something that is his. We created an apparatus by means of which society extorts volunteer work [...] The drive to work through his own internal determination or by the environment around him are different things [...] The environment must help man to feel this need within himself, but if it's only the environment, if it is only moral pressure that drives him; in other words, he won't achieve something that is his, something new, made freely. He will continue to be a slave of the work. (GUEVARA, 1982, p.67)

For that reason, voluntary work should permeate the lives of the Cuban citizens from childhood and effectively expose them to values of comradeship and mutual help. With adolescents, military training and collective unpaid work are also an attempt to prevent the formation of a parasitic quality in the new generation, and to instruct them on how to work together as a team for the development of the country. Adults, in turn, would have that as a form of late education. Governmental bureaucrats, who supposedly had "bad habits" from previous times and commit errors that could "harm" the revolution, would rehabilitate themselves and also contribute to the new government being established through that kind of work.

It can be said that the direct antecedent of "voluntary works" in Cuba were the "Communist Saturdays" established by Lenin in the first few years of the Russian Revolution. That example certainly inspired Guevara in the development of socialism on the island. According to Lenin:

> The "Communist Saturdays" have a great historical importance precisely because they show us the conscious and voluntary initiative of the workers in developing labor productivity, in the transition to a new work discipline and in the creation of socialist conditions both in the economy and in life. [...] [They] are initiated, not by those working in extremely favorable conditions, but by workers who are experts in several areas, as well as non-expert workers, servants in the usual conditions, that is, *the toughest ones*. We all know very well the basic condition of the decrease in productivity that takes place not only in Russia, but in the whole world: the ruin and the misery, the exasperation and the exhaustion caused by the imperialist war, diseases and undernourishment. For its importance, the latter is first. [...] And to overcome hunger it's necessary to increase labor productivity in agriculture, as well as in transportations and in industry. Therefore, we're facing a kind of vicious circle: in order to increase productivity it's necessary to escape from hunger, and to escape from hunger it's necessary to increase productivity. [...] And these starving workers, surrounded by the wicked counter-revolutionary restlessness of

> the bourgeoisie, of the mensheviks and of the revolutionary socialists, organize the "Communist Saturdays", work extra hours *without any payment* and achieve a *great increase of productivity,* despite being tired, tormented and exhausted by undernourishment. Wouldn't that be magnificent heroism? Isn't that the beginning of a journey of universal historical importance? [...] The great initiative of the "Communist Saturdays" must also be used in another sense, namely: to *purify* the party. It was absolutely inevitable, shortly after the revolution, when the mass of people who were "honest" and had a petty-bourgeois spirit was particularly scared, when the bourgeois intellectuals, including, of course, the mensheviks and the revolutionary socialists, sabotaged without exceptions, as servants of the bourgeoisie, [...] who added ruler adventurers and other harmful elements to the party. [...] It is important for the party leader, resting on the developed class, healthy and strong, to know how to purify his ranks. (LENIN, 1979c, p.152-158)

The "Communist Saturdays" were established in 1919 and, one year later, their importance was surpassed by compulsory and more coercive kinds of labor. Lenin himself changed his previous position to a certain extent, and the voluntary and compulsory work co-existed in Russia for some time. Since the proletariat (the "conscious" and "reliable" group tied to the bolsheviks) was small compared to the rest of the population, thousands of workers were transferred to several functions, joining the Army ranks, participating in supply detachments, propaganda groups, political management and the business sector, as a consequence, its constant presence inside the plants was reduced. Thus, the "Communist Saturdays" also took charge of keeping the "old" proletariat — transferred to the Red Army or to bureaucratic functions within the apparatus of the Soviet State — in direct contact with the production sector. (LINHART, 1983, p.144-145) In that case, the ideology functioned as an incentive to the activities. In other words, the ideological stimuli would be the most important in that situation, without the use of any material incentive.

During the "Communist Saturdays" both the intellectual and manual workers would get together, but there wasn't an explicit attempt to eliminate both kinds of activity. The bureaucrats who participated in the voluntary work could come closer to understanding the reality of the manual workers, but the opposite didn't take place, since there was no policy to raise the technical or intellectual level of the proletariat specifically in that kind of task. Even though Lenin advocated, in theory, the end of the differences between the countryside and the city, between manual and intellectual workers, in practice the main function of the "Communist Saturdays" was to increase productivity and the economic development without much cost to the government. In theory, it would be crucial to join capitalist science and technique with the conscious individuals, working together to build socialism.

The voluntary work was one of the best means of solving the serious structural problem of the Cuban economy, mainly in terms of the lack of labor in agriculture and the surplus of the tertiary sector, concentrated in the cities. At the beginning of the revolution, there was an intensive domestic migration to such cities as Santiago and Havana. Many of those workers were absorbed by the Armed Forces, by several mass organizations and by the construction sector. But a considerable number of Cubans couldn't find a job, leading to unemployment or underemployment, which was mainly a result of the problems in the industrial sector. With nationalization, many of the foreign enterprises left Cuba, reducing the number of jobs in that sector; the elimination of the private contractors, in charge of real estate building, cost many people their old jobs. The combination of these factors had a decisive influence on the employment situation of the country. Based on the need to improve the agricultural sector, much of that labor surplus should be transferred to the countryside. The voluntary workers in agriculture, therefore, were mostly recruited from the large urban centers. In 1967, the voluntary workers represented as much as 8% to 12% of the country's labor. (BONACHEA; VALDÉS, 1972, p.359)

In a sense, the idea of creating the new man can be related to Guevara's own life and to his understanding of the world based on his personal experience. On the other hand, we must give due credit to the concrete and practical aspects of his theories, not only within the scope of Marxism, but also in the Cuban revolution. The ideas of the Argentinean guerrilla were certainly very influential, not only in the general conception of the island's government but also in the imagination of several leftist movements of Latin America. His ideas had a real effect on the Cuban economy while he was one of the main rulers of the country.

---

[1] It would be possible to argue that Castro was referring to the "humanism" as advocated by Marx when he was young, but it's not very likely that this was his intention at that moment.

---

[2] According to V. I. Lenin, "from the democratic revolution we will then move to the socialist revolution, and precisely to the extent of our strengths, of the strengths of the conscious and organized proletariat. We are supporters of the uninterrupted revolution. We won't stay in the middle of the way". According to E. Batálov, (1985, p.96, 100-101) "the revolutionary process, being an *uninterrupted* process which, only when reaching its end, concludes with the establishment of the socialist regime, can last longer or for less time and give birth to intermediate, *transitory structures,* of a democratic revolutionary kind, which, as Lenin had said, '*was still not* socialism, but *it wouldn't be* capitalism anymore' [...] In the countries with a low level of capitalist development, where the proletariat is in the initial stage of its formation; where they're strong (in the economy and in the culture) the survival of the pre-capitalist relations; where the formation of the material premises of socialism are still in process, conditions emerge for the existence of a democratic revolutionary State of socialist orientation. The emergence of that State and of the entire system of the democratic revolutionary dictatorship is, as a rule, a result of the national liberation movement, of the struggle of the national democratic revolutionary forces against imperialism, colonialism and

neo-colonialism. The democratic revolutionary dictatorship is able to carry out measures that open the way to socialism and prepare for the successive transfer of power to the hands of the working class". Advocates of the theory of the uninterrupted revolution were pro-Soviet Marxists or those who were politically tied to the Soviet Union, often using this and other theoretical schemes to oppose Trotskyism or other leftist currents and to legitimize their positions.

[3]The "stage nature" of the Russian and global Revolution appears in several articles by V. I. Lenin. He claims, for example, that, "judging from the scarce available data in Switzerland, the first stage of this revolution, in concrete terms, of the Russian Revolution of March 1st, 1917 was over. This [...] will certainly not be the last stage of our revolution." He insists: "Without the three years of enormous class struggles and the revolutionary power of the Russian proletariat, in 1905-1907, it would be impossible for a second revolution to occur so fast, in the sense that its *initial stage* was concluded in a few days." Or still: "In another article [...] we will show what the particularity of the current moment is made of, of the *transition* of the first stage of the revolution to the second one, and the reason why the watchword, the "task of the day", *in this* moment, must be: *workers, you achieved prodigious proletarian and popular heroism in the civil war against tsarism, now you must achieve prodigious proletarian organization and of the entire population in order to prepare your victory in the second stage of the revolution*". See Lenin (1978, p.1-9)

[4]Mao's "permanent revolution" would be "the idea that the attainment of communism could only take place through incessant waves of struggle, in which the radical ideological advance moved along with (or was even a requirement for) an increase in the economic production". See Bailey (1996, p.443)

[5]It must be recalled that Althusser had already written several essays about the "young Marx" since 1960, in French magazines, which were later gathered and published in 1965 in the book *Pour Marx*. Anyway, Althusser didn't participate at any moment in the "economic debate" and wasn't even quoted in the debate. See Althusser (1966).

[6]According to Professor George Kline, of Bryn Mawr College, the essays written by "young Marx" were a clever adaptation and variation of Hegelian themes but, in philosophical terms,

they were neither original nor profound. According to Irving Fetscher, of the University of Frankfurt, in turn, only through the understanding of the texts written during the younger years would it be possible to understand what led him to write the criticism of the political economy, which contains, in an implicit or explicit way, a criticism of alienation, which is a central part of the texts he wrote as a young man. Soviet scholar E. V. Ilienkov, from the Academy of Sciences of the Soviet Union, in turn, believed that there wasn't a fundamental difference between the thought of the "young Marx", of the "mature" Marx and of the "old" Marx. In practice, what happened was that the style of the essays he wrote as a young man grew into a more concrete and elaborate style. See Demaitre (1966, p.29-35). Another author who disagrees with a "separation" between the "young Marx" and the "mature Marx" is Stanley Rothman (1966, p.52), who claims that the essays written by the philosopher in his mature phase were based on the concepts of the previous period, despite changes in his vocabulary and in some of his concerns.

---

[7] In his youth, Marx claimed: "History calls those the greatest men who ennoble themselves by working for the universal. The experience praises as the most happy the one who has made the most people happy. [...] When we have chosen the vocation in which we can contribute most to humanity, burdens cannot bend us because they are only sacrifices for all. Then we experience no meager, limited, egotistic joy, but our happiness belongs to millions, our deeds live on quietly but eternally effective, and glowing tears of noble men will fall on our ashes." See McLellan (1970, p. 8).

---

[8] A similar opinion can be found in some texts written by Stalin, who claimed: "If the consciousness of men, their uses and habits are determined by the external conditions, if the inadequacy of the juridical and political forms is based on the economic content, it's obvious that we must contribute to the radical transformation of economic relations, so that together they change, starting from the bottom, the uses and habits of the people and its political order." See Stalin (1990, p.121-122).

---

[9] Western intellectuals and those from the socialist block criticized the predominance of material incentives in the transition to socialism. For example, the editors of the *Monthly*

Review, as well as the Albanians and the Chinese. According to the editors of the *Monthly Review,* "if the rewards of the workers and directors are closely related to material gains, the seeds of the disintegration of socialism and the restoration of capitalism will bloom there, even though that's not the intention of the interested parties". See Solganick (1967, p.42).

---

[10]Among the reasons for the failure of the "great leap forward" are natural catastrophes, inefficient transportation systems, and the use of workers from the countryside for a gigantic and exaggerated industrial irrigation project. There was a considerable decrease in agricultural production and an increase of hunger in much of the country. See Bailey (1996, p.443).

---

[11]According to Carmelo Mesa-Lago (1972, p.389), between 150,000 and 180,000 high school students worked on state-owned farms and plants, on the weekends and vacations, and approximately 1.28 million elementary school students undertook a work called "socially useful", with the goal of minimizing the differences between physical and intellectual labor, as well as inculcating in the children a sense of obligation to the country.

---

[12]Other sources indicate that the figures varied between 50,000 and 75,000 political prisoners. See Mesa-Lago (1972, p.390).

7

CHE GUEVARA AND THE MARXIST TRENDS

Although already exhaustively analyzed by several scholars, Che Guevara's political thought is still the subject of intensive debates in the academic and Party environments. Both its anti-dogmatic and anti-bureaucratic character and his heterodox and dynamic Marxism made Guevara the target of much criticism by his contemporaries, who often accused him, among other things, of having Trotskyist and Maoist tendencies, even though he absolutely disagreed with that kind of judgment. But what, after all, was the real relationship between Guevara and the Marxist trends? How did he interpret the ideas of such personalities as Stalin, Mao Tse-tung and Trotsky? Unlike the previous chapters, which emphasized the economic aspects of his thought, the intention here is to outline the similarity between Che and the debate of political trends, mainly in Latin America. Not only to better understand the ideological side which certainly influenced his economic ideas, but also to try to present a more complete portrait of the revolutionary.

As it is known, Che's political maturation occurred later in his life. It's obvious that, as a young man, Guevara was aware of the Argentinean socio-political environment and of the economic problems in his country. The son of anti-Peronist[1] parents, young Ernesto was exposed to all kinds of debates that took place at his home. Not only the issues related to Argentina but also those concerning the Spanish Civil War and World War II permeated his family environment. It is also known that he read books by Bertrand Russell, Aldous Huxley, Joseph Stalin, *The Communist Manifesto,* some texts by Lenin and parts of Marx's *Capital,* but he didn't deepen his study of Marxism, even though he wrote for some years his *Philosophical Notebooks,* a collection of essays about general themes. Politics in itself, however, wasn't his main concern, and he didn't participate in any party or social movement, nor did he actively participate in political events during his student years. Guevara's first actual revolutionary experience happened on his second important trip, beginning in 1953, when he saw for himself the process of agrarian reform of the Bolivian revolution, which had triumphed in the previous year and was in full development.

The Bolivian revolution of April 9th, 1952 was certainly a reference in Latin America, but it had, nevertheless, a clearly reformist nature. Despite appealing to the masses — mainly miners and peasants — and proposing, theoretically, changes that would improve the life of the marginalized population (at that time, approximately 78% of the Bolivian population was rural and indigenous), increasing the participation of the natives and of the illiterate people, besides strengthening, to a certain extent, the miners — through the nationalization of the mines and the creation of the *Central Obrera Boliviana* (COB) — it wasn't accompanied by profound economic or technical transformations and demonstrated, according to Halperin Donghi, (1989, p.256) "only a more radical version of the policy favoring the redistribution of the political power and, to a certain extent, of the well-being within a structure that is basically unvaried". Later, Guevara himself said that it was a "very timid bourgeois revolution, extremely weakened by the concessions it had to make, with its economy totally tied to the imperialist economy and being solely a mono-producer, made of tin exporters, and a bourgeoisie that was partially maintained by imperialism". (GUEVARA apud VILABOY; DE LA NUEZ, 1989, p.308)

Despite that, the debates about the unfolding of the revolution and its development to socialism were present at that period. In that sense, the contribution of the *Partido Obrero Revolucionario* (POR), founded in Córdoba, Argentina, in 1934, by Guillermo Lora (who was linked to Trotskyism), José Aguirre Gainsborg (who was inclined to the Leninist ideas of revolution) and Tristán Maróf (considered a "leftist nationalist") was important. Both the POR and Maróf were tied to the heterodox Marxism of Mariátegui, with a more "indigenist" than necessarily proletarian character, seeking their inspiration in the Inca collectivist traditions. In 1938, Maróf founded the Bolivian Labor Socialist Party (PSOB). The POR gradually freed itself from Maróf's influence in the 1940's, when other groups became more influential within the party.

Better known, was Lora's increasing importance and growth within the political and intellectual environment. In 1946, for example, he was able to obtain the approval of his *Pulacayo Theses* by the Federation of Miners of Bolivia, which proved, for the first time in Latin America, the official acceptance, by a meaningful group of workers, of Leon Trotsky's ideas of "permanent revolution". But the POR lost its great opportunity in the 1952 revolution. According to Maria José Lourenço:

> ... nobody knows very well what the policy of the POR, the party that claimed to be Trotskyist and was the strongest in the entire left, was. The POR did the opposite of everything the bolsheviks did in Russia and of the Trotskyism preached in all the revolutions. This party, impressed by the "revolutionary" speeches of the [Revolutionary Nationalist Movement] MNR, impressed because there were cases such as those of Lechín (the greatest trade union bureaucrat) who claimed to be a "clandestine Trotskyist", that is, he didn't assume that position in public and provided a "critical support" to MNR's bourgeois government, didn't fight for the COB to be kept independent from the government and to prepare itself to seize the power. Instead of fighting against the MNR, he made it stronger. With these positions, the POR gave up, in practice, the most basic

> principle of a revolutionary leadership, which is never support a bourgeois government, regardless of how socialized its style is. In that sense, the POR is greatly responsible for the defeat of the Bolivian proletariat. (LOURENÇO, 1980, p.5)

According to Omar de Barros Filho, after the revolution of 1952, the *Partido Obrero* wouldn't be the leader of the Bolivian masses. It would serve as a bridge between them and the MNR, and it didn't prepare itself for (nor did it understand in all its depth) the revolutionary situation that came with a visible feeling in the dominant classes, incapable of controlling the country, of overcoming its own power crisis and of keeping the workers under permanent punishment. The masses burnt stages, and both the POR and the direction of the Fourth International itself, led by the Greek Michel Pablo, expired before the crude reality of the Bolivian revolution. (BARROS FILHO, 1980, p.33)

The revolutionary environment and the debates that took place between the Stalinists from the Bolivian Communist Party, the Trotskyists from the POR and the members of the MNR couldn't go unnoticed by Guevara. The young adventurer, when in the country, had the opportunity to see, up close, the different ways to interpret that historical moment, to talk to politicians and to have direct contact with the miners. Guevara criticized the "double power", where the national government and the COB, labor and peasant militias and the Army co-existed in the same reality, in constant contradiction and opposition. According to him, that "unstable balance" favored the absorption of the power by the bourgeoisie, which eventually happened. The proletariat and the peasants should be able to seize the power and keep it. Otherwise, the bourgeoisie, re-establishing the Army, would massacre the workers and peasant masses, would absorb the popular movements and would take care of the revolution. (ALMEYRA; SANTARELLI, 1994, p.37)

Young Ernesto's other crucial experience was the time he spent in Guatemala. The military coup against the government of Jacobo Arbenz, in 1954, ended a process of social changes inspired, in part, by the communists of the *Partido Guatemalteco del Trabajo* (PGT) themselves. Arbenz had claimed that the three basic goals of the revolution were: to convert the country, from a dependent nation and one with a semi-colonial economy, into an economically independent country; from a backward and mostly "feudal" economy into a modern capitalist country; and to raise the living standard of the masses. (ARIET, 1988, p.45) Although the project was extremely naive and conceptually mistaken, it influenced Guevara, who claimed to defend the positions of Arbenz's government and, within it, of the PGT. (ARIET, 1988, p.47) After the government's defeat, there was a great debate about the nature of the Guatemalan revolution, mainly between the Stalinists and the Trotskyists. As Raúl Fornet-Betancourt stated:

> The Bolivian and the Guatemalan revolutions [...] besides, contributed to a better understanding of the sociopolitical context of this stage, because of the debate that took place between Stalinism and Trotskyism. The framework of their experiences explains the circumstances of why Latin America's forms of social analysis, as well as political programatics, fit consciously to the left of the official communism and required a more radical interpretation of the Marxist inheritance. Together with Trotskyism, of course Maoism must be mentioned here, the influence of which, however, became systematic only after 1956, after the conflict between China and the Soviet Union. (FORNET-BETANCOURT, 1995, p.221-222)

Guevara, as an observer and participant of some important political events of his time, must have been aware of the debates, engaged in among different political trends, nor could he refrain from taking a stance, though still without much instrumental base in relation to the stances discussed.

But his direct contact with Trotskyist and Maoist sources was still very limited, although not non-existent. With only a basic Marxist background, originating from his observations, debates with Hilda Gadea, his first wife, and with some leftist militants, and readings of some classics "in the moments of rest, which were rare", as he himself stated, young Che was far from having a profound knowledge of Marxism. His main point of reference, in the 1950's, was Stalin. It is known that Guevara even signed letters as "Stalin II". (GÁLVEZ, 1997, p.336) In 1953, for example, he said, in a letter, that he swore before daddy's picture and cried over comrade Stalin, claiming that he wouldn't rest until he saw these capitalist leeches destroyed". (MASSARI, 1993, p.108) Even so, he never joined the Argentinean CP, or the PGT, when he was in Guatemala, since he felt that they had an excessively rigid discipline. (MASSARI, 1993, p.109)

It's also true that between 1963 and 1964, during the economic debate in Cuba, he occasionally quoted *Uncle Joe*[2] in his texts. But his attitude would ultimately change radically in relation to the Stalinists and to the Soviet Union, and the claims that Guevara was "a great friend and admirer of the Soviet Union" (GRIGULÉVICH, 1988), as some people insisted, are a distortion. In fact, it was exactly in the period of the economic debate that Guevara began to have greater contact with the Trotskyist literature, in addition he became the interlocutor of some intellectuals tied to the Fourth International, such as Ernest Mandel himself, who broadly advocated the ideas of the Argentinean guerrilla. But in the early 1950's, Guevara would hardly have access to materials that were critical of the Soviet Union, to Stalin and to Trotsky himself. It must be recalled that most of the books published by the Academy of Sciences of the Soviet Union, were of dubious quality, and excessively biased. The Academy of Sciences of the Soviet Union published, for example, a long biography of Lenin in which Trotsky was hardly mentioned. The name of the founder of the Red Army appeared in few passages, as if he hadn't participated in the Russian Revolution at all. (ACADEMIA DE CIÊNCIAS DA UNIÃO SOVIÉTICA, 1984)

Stalin, on the other hand, was almost always praised in the Soviet publications as a fantastic leader of the people and a great scholar of the works of Marx, Engels and Lenin. He was described as one of the greatest men of his time. *Stalin and the Armed Forces of the Soviet Union,* a text written by K. Vorochilov published in 1953, described the Soviet leader as a tireless man, who was, very nearly, in several places at the same time, staying up for entire nights studying, for days in a row, organizing the militants of the party, preparing the Red Army, and leading the country. At the same time, he was unforgiving of his enemies, against the "panic spreaders" and saboteurs. Of course, Trotsky is almost absent from the book and, when his name is mentioned, he's often attacked. In discussions with Trotsky, "comrade" Stalin was "always" right, even in relation to the Red Army, since he was, according to Vorochilov, his closest and dearest friend. According to that author, Stalin was the true founder of the Red Army and, together with Lenin, one of the greatest military strategists of all time. According to Vorochilov, "Stalin is not only the personification of bolshevism and of Soviet power, but he also embodies the triumphant socialism that encourages and inspires our people to heroic action and to creative work, instilling them with boldness; he embodies the hopes, enthusiasms and horizons of the workers worldwide. Stalin is a name that has overcome all borders, becoming the banner of combat for the great ideals of humanity". (VOROCHILOV, 1953, p.46-47) The book ends with a great deal of praise for Stalin, described as "wise", "fantastic chief" and "master" of the workers and of progressive humanity, as well as a "magnificent man" and "great friend of all progressive people of the universe", that is, a man with almost all the qualities that someone could have. (VOROCHILOV, 1953, p.134) Considering that many of those materials were disseminated in Latin America and that at the beginning of the decade, the Soviet Union and Stalin were seen as symbols of the struggle against the American imperialism and as an alternative to capitalism, it's understandable that Guevara, until that time, was an enthusiastic supporter of the Soviet regime.[3]

On May 16th, 1934, Stalin and Molotov signed a decree related to the teaching of History in the Soviet Union, completely reversing the previous canon, which was led by historian Mikhail Pokrovski, author of the famous *History of Russia,* considered to be the "Bible" of Soviet historiography, admired by Lenin himself, and which had editions sold in several countries. After the decree, many of Pokrovski's old disciples were accused of being "enemies of the people", "agents of Trotskyism" and even "fascists". Shortly thereafter, texts by the professor were banned and a five-hundred page book by the Academy of Sciences of the Soviet Union, *Against the Conception of History of M. N. Pokrovsky,* was used to destroy his reputation for good. This new historiography spread by the Soviet Union represented the aspirations of all humanity and made "predictions" or "anticipations" of what would take place in the future based on the logic of mankind's journey toward communism. Such words as "proletariat" and "workers" were gradually replaced by the word "people", while praise of the Soviet State, and of some leaders, increased. Even the terms "homeland" and "patriotism", which had been out of use for a long time, started to resurface again, with greater emphasis. That's how the "History of Soviet Union" was produced, beginning with the first civilizations on the planet, since, according to the new school, all that had happened in the world throughout several centuries led to the Russian Revolution and to the new Soviet State. The History of the Soviet Union became the History of the world. A "messianic" view of History was officially adopted in the country. On the fifth anniversary of the Soviet victory in World War II, the *Pravda* published an essay claiming that:

> ...the Russian people have created the most abundant culture: they have given the world an entire constellation of great scholars, writers, composers, artists, thinkers and inventors. Russia became the home of Leninism, the peak of the world's science and civilization. The Russian people gave mankind that thinker of great genius, Lenin [...] The Russian working class has played an eminent rôle in the history of mankind. It was the first in the world to carry out a soviet revolution, and thereby to institute a new era [...] The great Soviet Union is on the march today as the vanguard of the whole of progressive humanity. (MEHNERT, 1952, p.31-32)

It seems that Stalin, himself, read and revised several materials before they were published. Some people claim that he wrote the *History of the Communist Party of the Soviet Union.* (MEHNERT, 1952, p.108) The fact is that, from the new Soviet historiographic school, a somewhat distorted view of reality and the cult of personality became accepted facts in the country's publications.[4] Even the political economy manuals were extremely biased, with little theoretical depth or originality. Those same publications, which seemed more like instruments of propaganda, were spread throughout other parts of the world, including Latin America. For that reason, it's not surprising that Guevara read some of those works and was impressed.

Guevara's first informal relationship with the Soviets was in Mexico, right after he moved to that country. In 1956, in the Mexican capital, Raúl Castro introduced him to Nikolai Leonov, a young employee of the Ministry of Foreign Relations of the Soviet Union who had met Fidel's brother a few years earlier. Since young Ernesto didn't have a profound knowledge about what was actually going on in the Soviet Union, he spoke extensively with his interlocutor from the "Iron Curtain", who told him details of his homeland and recommended some books on socialist realism to him. At the end of 1955, Che patronized the Russian-Mexican Cultural Exchange Institute, where he attended courses to learn Russian and increased his knowledge about the Soviet Union. Those facts, which don't seem to be very significant, led some authors to imply, years later, that Guevara had been an agent trained and used by the Soviets to infiltrate the M 26-7 during the revolutionary process in Cuba, to influence the leaders of the movement. This, of course, was not true.

During the revolutionary war in Cuba, Che also became acquainted with individuals from several political trends. Most of the members of the M 26-7 weren't communists, and those who considered themselves close to Marxism weren't tied to any party, not even to the PSP, which advocated, at the time, "peaceful means" for seizing power. The only important leader of the M 26-7 who had been affiliated to the PSP was Raúl Castro, and he was removed after the assault on the Moncada headquarters. It's also known that some Trotskyists from the Oriente region had minor participation in the revolutionary process, but no important leader came from their ranks. (MARTÍNEZ HEREDIA, 1999) It's certain that Che Guevara, Fidel Castro, Camilo Cienfuegos and Raúl Castro advocated Marxism, even though some of them were, on the other hand, heterodox and open to other ideas and political trends. Some scholars even believe that Cienfuegos himself had been a Trotskyist when he was younger and a member of the POR, which doesn't seem likely.[5] It can be said that he certainly wasn't a great admirer of the PSP, even prohibiting the distribution of the periodical *Hoy* at Camp Columbia, after the revolution. (BANDEIRA, 1998, p.175)

Guevara's disenchantment with the Soviets began in 1962 with the "missile crisis", mainly because he felt "betrayed" by the Soviet Union, which removed its weapons from Cuba without informing the island's government and capitulated to the United States. Next, he was disappointed with the industrial equipment that Cuba bought from the socialist block, which he considered to be outdated and of horrible quality. Increasing industrial production was always a concern for Che, but he considered the quality of the products crucial.[6]

Guevara certainly began losing faith in the bureaucracy of the Soviet Union. According to Alberto Granado, Che was riveted by Stalin because of the books he had read, but later, already a member of the Cuban government, "he started to discover a world that was made up of more than just slogans and manifestos — an important world — and I believe that this intoxicated him and made him think that the solution to life was in the Soviet Union, that everything he had read would be carried out there. However, in 1963 and 1964, when he saw that he had been deceived — you know that Che couldn't stand being lied to — he had a violent reaction". (GRANADO apud ANDERSON, 1997, p.645)

Between November 4th and 18th, 1964, Guevara visited Moscow, leading a Cuban delegation. After discussions with Vladimir Trapeznikov, one of the main advocates of the economic reforms in the Soviet Union, with members of the CPSU and with students, he was accused of being a Trotskyist. Disappointed, he later wrote the outline of a book counter to the Soviet political economy manuals, openly criticizing the principles of so-called "scientific socialism" and advocating his theory of the budgetary finance system. According to him, since Lenin was rarely added to updated interpretations of Marxism, the Soviet Union would become a capitalist country in the future, if it continued with its reforms. However, the book was never officially released during his lifetime. (BORREGO, 2001a) As to the accusations of Trotskyism, Guevara stated that, "on the other hand, there were several accusations of Trotskyism. In this sense, I believe that either we have the ability to destroy the opposite opinions or we must allow them to express themselves [...] We can't destroy opinions using force, because this blocks all free development of intelligence." He goes on: "Also many things can be taken from Trotsky's thought, even if, to my way of thinking, his basic concepts were mistaken, his later performance was mistaken, and, in the end, even his work." And he concludes: "Anyway, there's always someone who accuses me of Trotskyism." (MASSARI, 1993, p.113) Anyway, Che had read very little of Trotsky at the time, not only because there were no official editions of that revolutionary's work in Cuba, but also because the information about him came, in general, from Soviet books. (MASSARI, 1993, p.114) The first serious work that Guevara read about Trotsky was the trilogy written by Isaac Deutscher. From then on, he began to understand him more deeply.

But Guevara was often misinterpreted, both by orthodox Marxists, who accused him of being Trotskyist, and by some Trotskyist groups, which considered him to be pro-Soviet. In Punta del Este, in August 1961, Guevara gave an interview to the magazine *Quatrième Internationale,* despite the opposition of the Uruguayan CP. The communists disapproved of that gesture, and it seemed to be an extreme concession to the Trotskyists. The "ambassador" of the Cuban revolution, however, had supposedly attacked, on television, a newspaper published by the Cuban Trotskyists. The news spread quickly, making it seem as though Che was an enemy of the members of the Fourth International. Some time later, he apologized to the "Trotskyist comrades" for having been misinterpreted. Thus, while groups such as the Socialist Labor League (SLL), led by Gerry Healy, were against the support given by other Trotskyist associations to the Cuban revolution *as it developed* and to their interpretations of the process, other organizations, such as the Socialist Workers Party (SWP), led by Joseph Hansen, openly advocated the revolution as it was being carried out by the leaders on the island — even though at some moments they had to defend themselves against accusations from some Cuban Stalinists — and they supported Che unconditionally.

After the triumph of the Cuban revolution, different Trotskyist trends often presented divergent positions about its nature. The supporters of Michel Pablo, of Greece, considered that Castro's positions were, *to a certain extent,* aligned with the Fourth International, praising the events in Cuba as an "unheard of phenomenon". The Unified Secretariat considered Cuba a "proletarian State", maintaining its support of Castro's government; unlike other Trotskyist trends, the Unified Secretariat thought that Fidel and his group contributed greatly to the success of the revolution on the continent. Meanwhile, the International Committee — the Lambertists and SLL, for example — didn't see the island as an example of a proletarian State, and had difficulty fitting the revolution into its traditional schemes. According to the IC, there was no revolution in Cuba; the expropriation of the American interests was only the result of the pressure exercised by that country on the new government; and the masses only participated in the process after being "called upon" by the leaders of the island. Gerry Healy even supported Aníbal Escalante and his "microfraction" — tied to the most conservative groups of the Soviet Union and identified with Stalinism — against Fidel, considered by the group as "semi-fascist". In Argentina, some trends influenced by Nahuel Moreno (who had ties with the leftist Peronism) even describe Castro's regime as "gorila", a strong allusion to the military dictatorships, relating Fidel and his group with petty-bourgeois trends and suggesting he was favorable to American imperialism, certainly a biased position. (COGGIOLA, 1990, p.90-97) According to another source, however, the Trotskyist leader said that his admiration for the leaders of the Cuban government was unlimited, and that, together with Lenin and Trotsky, both guerrillas were among the greatest revolutionary geniuses of the century. (MASSARI, 2001b, p.348)

Inside Cuba at the time, the Trotskyists were a small group, mainly located in Guantánamo and without much political power. But that didn't deter the newspaper *Hoy* from attacking them. It not only reproduced the same versions of Trotsky that were spread in the Soviet Union but it also tried to accuse Eusébio Mujal, a former member of the Cuban CP and close aide to Batista, of being "the Trotskyist leader in Cuba". (HANSEN, 1994, p.296) The periodical even claimed that George Meany, the main trade union leader of the AFL, had Trotskyist characteristics! According to the newspaper *Hoy,* the Trotskyists worked to "combat the Revolution by presenting themselves as more revolutionary than the Revolution itself", (HANSEN, 1994, p.299) and their labor would be "to try to sow confusion, to divert people from serious revolutionary work by enmeshing them in senseless discussions, to instill doubt about the Revolution's future and to create whatever obstacles they can to its development". (HANSEN, 1994, p.299) And the criticisms went on. According to that periodical:

> The Trotskyists complain that in the socialist States they have no freedom of action.
>
> In the Soviet Union, they had it until 1927.
>
> What did they use it for?
>
> To attack the Party, to foment division, to distract militants from the constructive revolutionary work with interminable discussions, to weaken confidence in the possibility of the Soviet Revolution triumphing in face of its enemies and constructing socialism among the peoples of old Russia, to conspire and sabotage.
>
> The Soviet people, because of this, had to end their freedom of action. (HANSEN, 1994, p.300)

On June 23rd, 1962, *Hoy* continued its attacks, this time reacting to a speech by J. Posadas in Brazil, published later in the edition of May 7th of the *Voz Proletaria,* of Buenos Aires. In relation to the Trotskyists, *Hoy* said:

> For them, "the policy of the Cuban leadership continues to be that of limiting the extension of the Latin American revolution".
>
> Why?
>
> Because in "all the speeches, in all the Cuban press, not a word appears indicating that the definitive victory of the Cuban revolution depends on the triumph of the world socialist revolution or of the triumph of the colonial revolution. Everything is placed exclusively upon the construction of socialism in Cuba.
>
> This is the conception of socialism in one country". (HANSEN, 1994, p.302)

As for the freedom of opposition and propaganda, once again the newspaper attacked the Trotskyists. It claimed:

> With this propaganda they contribute directly to the campaign of imperialism on the lack of liberty in Cuba. Consequently, they demand:
> "The masses of the continent must perceive that a revolutionary opposition exists in Cuba."
> Neither the masses of the Continent nor the masses of Cuba need, in the least, the existence of an opposition in Cuba which, either with slogans from the left or with arguments from the right, would serve imperialism in its aims of promoting disturbances in our country and promoting favorable economic-social conditions for their criminal plans of new armed interventions against the Revolution. (HANSEN, 1994, p.304)

Later, when Che was no longer acting as a member of the Cuban government, Fidel Castro made vehement attacks on the Trotskyists, which he considered to be "the main speakers in the imperialist campaign of intrigue and defamation against Cuba in relation to comrade Guevara", and that "Trotskyism had become, in recent years, a vulgar instrument of imperialism and of reaction". This fact led the Unified Secretariat of the

Fourth International to publish an "open letter" to Castro, maintaining its support of the revolution, but defending itself against all of the accusations.

It is known that Guevara talked to supporters of Posadas in Cuba on April 15th, 1965, when he apparently informed them that "shortly all the works by the revolutionary, Leon Trotsky, will be published in Cuba"; in the same interview, he supposedly said that "the communists call me a Trotskyist and you Trotskyists call me an adventurer". (HANSEN, 1994, p.318) And he supposedly completed with: "We will shortly sweep away all these conservative bureaucrats." (HANSEN, 1994, p.319) All of these statements, however, must be viewed with all the necessary precautions. Castro's criticisms were directed to the Trotskyists in an extremely delicate moment, and the accusations that he had gotten rid of Guevara came both from the capitalist countries and from his leftist critics, among whom were Adolfo Gilly and J. Posadas. That might have been the reason for such a violent reaction by the Cuban leader. At that specific time, Fidel couldn't reveal where Guevara was, or what his mission entailed. In fact, despite all criticisms, Fidel and Che were always closely bonded by friendship, which is almost undeniable. Castro, therefore, didn't betray Guevara in any way, as some people still insist. When Che went to fight in Bolivia, with full support from Fidel, he tried, among other things, to create a rearguard of the Cuban revolution, since he didn't trust the Soviets very much and he believed that Cuba couldn't be isolated in any way. He wouldn't export the revolution, but would encourage and help prepare the conditions for other revolutions to take place with their own characteristics in other countries on the continent.

Even with a greater openness by Guevara in relation to Trotskyists and Maoists, the position of some pro-Soviet rulers of the Cuban government, years later, would enable the publication or distribution of books that were extremely contrary to those trends.[7] The book *La lucha del*

Partido Bolchhevique contra el trotskismo después de la Revolución de Octubre, by the Academy of Sciences of the Soviet Union, is a clear example of that kind of behavior. The text tries to destroy Trotsky's reputation and to accuse him of being revisionist and counter-revolutionary.

After attacking the Latin American Trotskyists in general, it insists that China followed a line that was very close to Trotskyism, also stating that Mao advocated the cult of violence and war and that, therefore, was irresponsible. The book goes on, saying that Mao agreed with the Fourth International, fighting the peaceful coexistence, the general disarmament and believing that China would be the center of the global revolutionary movement, subordinating the communist movements and those of national liberation to its selfish interests, using the rhetorical and intellectual background developed by the Trotskyists. That is, the objective of the Maoists was to disorganize and to cause a rift between the several revolutionary movements fighting together against imperialism. (IGNÁTIEV, [197-?])

According to a "dictionary" of "scientific communism" published by the Soviets, Maoism was a pseudo Marxist doctrine closely related to the cult of Mao's personality, a state ideology of an anti-popular and bureaucratic-military regime, which also had nationalist, anti-Soviet, voluntarist, "adventurerist" and egalitarian characteristics, moving away from what they considered to be true socialism. (RUMIÁNTSEV, 1981, p.253-255)

As for the Maoists, Guevara apparently also had a more flexible position than that of many other members of the Cuban government. Che had three meetings with Mao and reportedly left the meetings "persuaded" of the purity of Maoism as a more dynamic variant of the Marxism of his time. (CASTAÑEDA, 1997, p.217) He said that "some Soviet comrades tend to understand my points of view — about such themes as guerrilla warfare being the main means for the liberation of the Latin American people, or the problem of self-management against the budgetary finance system — as Chinese positions, and from there they reach the conclusion that Guevara is pro-China". (CASTAÑEDA, 1997, p.295) And so, he asked if he couldn't have his own opinion, regardless of what the Chinese thought. Those statements show well Che's discomfort about possible pressures within the Cuban government and from some Soviet staff members. Supposedly, in 1963 he reprimanded Ambassador Alexeiev for not having visited him, because he believed Che favored the Chinese. As far as it's known, the diplomat avoided meeting Guevara, so as not to create problems in his chancellery. (CASTAÑEDA, 1997, p.295) Anyway, the Argentinean revolutionary claimed, "The Chinese government has a position regarding Cuba which is hard to criticize. It provides us with considerable help, which we can't ignore. We asked, the Czechs for arms, and they refused. The Chinese agreed in a matter of days and they didn't even charge us, saying that arms are not to be sold to friends." (CASTAÑEDA, 1997, p.296) For this and other reasons, the CIA considered him an admirer of Mao Tse-tung and his ideas.[8]

It must be recalled that between 1950 and 1960 China engaged in a great propaganda effort in Latin America, and that the "cultural diplomacy" policy might have influenced young Ernesto, even though the literature coming from the Soviet Union was still prevalent among the leftist groups of the continent. Although the Chinese still didn't have either the material resources or a more profound interest in the region in the first few years of the 1950's, they intensified their interest to the extent that they noticed the importance of a more active stance among the leftist movements that were gradually starting to annoy the United States. This policy also created a favorable position for China among the Latin Americans, being an opposition to the Soviet influence. Already in 1958, Prime Minister Chou

En-lai stated that the Latin American people represented the vanguard of the struggle against imperialism. (RATLIFF, 1969, p.55) In that same year, a long justification was published, in that country, for the armed struggle in Latin America, even though the Chinese leaders thought that it was not very likely that the conditions for it to take place would exist for some time. Even with the triumph of the Cuban revolution, they still believed they had greater participation in the field of ideological propaganda than in direct support for the guerrilla. Halfway through 1960, however, an article in the periodical *Hung Ch'I* (Red Flag), the official organ of the Chinese Communist Party's CC, praised the guerrilla warfare in Cuba and pointed to that country as an example for the entire continent. In November of that year, at a dinner in honor of Che, Prime Minister Chou En-lai stated that the Cuban people were the hope and the example for all people of the region. In a joint statement signed by both rulers, they said that:

> ...the Chinese side expresses admiration and happiness for the great victory of the Cuban people who, maintaining unity and persisting in their armed struggle, increased their forces from small to large, from weak to strong, and were finally able to overthrow Batista's reactionary dictatorship. We believe that the struggle and the triumph of the Cuban people provided an abundant experience and is an example to all the oppressed people in the world, mainly the Latin American people, in their struggle to gain and to maintain their national independence. (RATLIFF, 1969, p.56)

The main objectives of the Chinese propaganda on the continent were to spread an anti-American feeling in the region, and to propagate the Maoist model of revolutionary struggle. They were also looking to improve their country's image in order to obtain some support in the international Courts. Among the different kinds of "cultural" exchange, there was a great increase in the number of Chinese people visiting Latin American countries, as well as several Latin American delegations going to China.[9]

There, these delegations, made up of artists, intellectuals, journalists and political leaders, visited cities, villages, farms and industries. They were introduced to important Chinese leaders and encouraged to write about the progress of the "New China" in their respective countries. (RATLIFF, 1969, p.56)

In the same way, the Chinese began sending envoys such as students, dancers, musicians and even an opera to Latin America. In 1960, some young people were sent to participate in the First Congress of the Latin American Youth and to participate in volunteer work. The Chinese Ambassador and his employees arrived in Havana in December of the same year. In the Cuban capital, in April 1959, the New China News Agency was already operating. It spread the Chinese ideas throughout the entire Latin American continent. The NCNA cooperated with the *Prensa Latina* agency, even organizing, and extensively advertising, a Chinese movie festival. In March 1961, the Museum of Fine Arts of Havana opened an exhibition entitled "The Economic Edification of the Republic of China", with displays of machinery from both the light and heavy industries, art and culture. That exhibition was successful and very well received by the Cuban people.

A great number of Chinese publications were translated into Spanish and distributed in the region, while such authors as Euclides da Cunha, Jorge Amado, Pablo Neruda, Ricardo Güiraldes, Nicolás Guillén and José Martí, among others, had their works translated into Chinese. Many exhibitions of art and movies from that Asian nation circulated, and cultural associations were installed in those countries. With the restrictions imposed by several Latin American governments on the Chinese propaganda materials and the attack by the Soviets on the policies of the "Middle Kingdom", the Chinese influence on the continent decreased somewhat, even though there were supporters in some Maoist parties of the region, which didn't have much influence in the political struggles of the time. Even so, it's understandable that Che had suffered the influence of the Maoist ideas *in a certain way*, which went beyond the simple discussion between China and the Soviet Union and the concrete pressures of the pragmatic policy of the Cuban government.

The Anshan Charter must also be recalled. It was re-edited by Mao Tsé-tung in 1960 and it established several basic principles to "revolutionize" production relations. The document advocated that politics should be placed, as the main element, above the economic decisions, the party's management should be reinforced, mass movements should be encouraged, the participation of employees in the productive work should be encouraged as well as that of workers in the management of the enterprises, the regulations that didn't improve efficiency should be reformed, the cooperation among employees, workers and technicians should be increased and technical innovations should be encouraged. (JOBIC, 1973, p.200) The Chinese rulers even emphasized that making the revolution and promoting production was a "totally" fair principle, which properly maintained the relationship between the "spirit" and "matter", between "super production" and the "economic infrastructure", between the "production relations" and the "productive forces", that is, assigning an equal dimension to the political and the economic aspects of the production sector. (JOBIC, 1973, p.201)

During the Khrushchev era, the Chinese government claimed, in a document, that the Soviet ruler, "advocating the material stimulus, reduced the relationships between men to a relationship with money and led to individualism and selfishness. It was he, who put down manual labor once again and praised the pleasures obtained through the seizure of the fruits of other people's labor. The moral climate and the habits encouraged by Khrushchev are 10,000 leagues away from communism". (BABY, [ca.

1970], p.281) When Kosygin and Brezhnev took power, the Chinese continued their criticism. According to them:

> The report about the industrial problems presented by the President of Board of Ministers, A. Kosygin, during the last plenary session of the Central Committee of the CPSU, and the resolution that was adopted, show the great step the Soviet economy has taken towards the restoration of capitalism [...]
> The "new system" of industrial management introduced by the new Board of the CPSU mainly reapplies the principle of capitalist profit, when it "reinforces the economic stimuli" and when it makes profit the main motivating force of production within the enterprises [...]
> It granted the right to hire and fire workers, to establish the wage structure and the rewards, and to freely make decisions about important funds to the directors of the enterprises. Thus, they are, in fact, the owners of the enterprises, and they can, as they wish, mistreat and oppress the workers and seize the fruits of their labor. That means, ultimately, the restoration of capitalism, the exchange of socialist property of the entire people and the gradual transformation of the Soviet Union's socialist enterprises into capitalist enterprises of a specific kind. This is not at all a "new creation". It's a copy developed from the old "experience" of the restoration of capitalism in Yugoslavia by Tito's followers. (BABY, [ca. 1970], p.282)

Guevara, as one of the main officials responsible for Cuban economic development and for the industrial management of the island, was probably aware of those documents. The influence of the Chinese, according to statements by Che himself, was not only related to the revolutionary struggle, but it, certainly, also extended to several aspects of industrialization and of the Cuban economy in general.

As has been seen, Che Guevara's positions concerning the Stalinists, Trotskyists and Maoists gradually changed during the first few years of the revolution. Members of the Cuban POR — a small party with limited penetration into the great mass of workers on the island — accused of being Mujalists and "provocative agents" — were repeatedly arrested and removed from their work places. In addition, they were periodically surveiled, and their publications were censored and often seized. The attempts by some militants to invade the American Base of Guantánamo caused discomfort to Cuban authorities, for whom that kind of action could make, the already delicate, situation in the country even more complicated.

For some time, Che Guevara supported the measures taken by the government. The sequence of the facts is significant: on August 18th, 1962, Juan León Ferrera Ramírez was arrested for making Trotskyist "propaganda"; next, celebrations of the 22nd anniversary of Trotsky's murder were prohibited in Guantánamo; shortly after that, Idalberto Ferrera, Secretary-General of POR, and José Lungarzo, representative of the Argentinean section of the Fourth International (Posadist) were arrested. However, in 1965, when a lawsuit against Trotskyist militants for being "imperialist agents" began, Guevara's attitude had already changed enough for him to intervene in the matter himself. (TENNANT, 1998, p.172-173) Thus, several militants were released, such as Roberto Tejera and Ángel Fanjul. Guevara also began to periodically receive a copy of the *Voz Proletaria* at his office. And Roberto Acosta, a member of the POR, was appointed director of Standards and Metrology. When Acosta was arrested, he told Che that he couldn't abandon his Trotskyist activities. Guevara supposedly agreed and stated that, if he and the Trotskyists believed in their ideas, they should continue fighting until they reached their goal. (TENNANT, 1998, p.174) Many Trotskyists worked in the Ministry of Industry with Guevara's permission. On one occasion, he received complaints from members of the *Unión de la Juventude Comunista* (UJC), who complained that the former made political propaganda while volunteering, as well as inside that government institution. Che responded to the young communists, stating that ideas can't be attacked by means of force or censorship, but with different ideas and by example. If they wanted to combat the Trotskyists, they would have to work harder than ever to demonstrate that their concepts were better. Next, he called the Trotskyists to his office and asked them which books by Trotsky they had read. When they said none, Che suggested that they get to know the work of the founder of the Red Army so that they could discuss his ideas in a more profound manner. (BORREGO, 2001b) When Guevara left Cuba, some jailed Trotskyists were released, with the commitment that they cease their independent political activities and stop publishing their newspapers.

In Bolivia, Guevara contacted several leftist organizations, with the intent of recruiting different groups to participate in the revolutionary struggle. According to him, although they had occasional conceptual differences there was a common reality and a common enemy, which made the unification of the different socialist organizations easier. For that reason, he didn't have a problem with speaking to different parties and asking for their support, including the Trotskyist POR and the Maoist PC-ml. It must be noted, however, the theoretical differences of the Bolivian Trotskyists and Maoists and of Guevara, to better understand each of these political players' actions.

According to Guillermo Lora, main leader of the POR, a guerrilla could only be successful in a country with a democratically elected government if the military were clearly subordinate to an imperialist power, such as the United States, or if there was a party sufficiently organized to lead the revolution. (LISS, 1984, p.187) Thus, the guerrilla *should always be subordinate to a party.* According to Lora, it was up to the "social-democrats and members of the orthodox Communist parties" to wait for the ideal conditions for the guerrilla. He demonstrated that he not only believed in the feasibility of guerrilla warfare, but he also thought that it could and should be carried out, even without all the necessary conditions in pace at the time, since the conditions *could be created* if there was a party as vanguard. Despite that, Lora thought that the level of political and historical development was different in the Latin American countries, and, for that reason, the Cuban model couldn't be applied in all cases, as a "formula" for revolution. Juan Lechín (1995) stated that Lora and his group joined the "peaceful struggle" and didn't want to support Guevara. The latter only began to advocate armed combat later. According to Lechín, Lora and the POR wouldn't submit themselves to a single front against a common enemy, imperialism, for example.[10] The POR wouldn't have agreed to participate in this kind of block in certain circumstances, such as when it insisted on facing Lechín and the National Leftist Revolutionary Party (PRIN) within the movement of the miners.

Another view points to a different path. Loyola Guzmán, treasurer of the guerrilla, claims that in the beginning of 1966 some members of the ELN, including herself, made contact with a sector of the POR that was willing to fight with the guerrillas. Thus, small groups were organized to provide training for the POR members, with the goal of starting actions in the cities. That POR group, however, was tied to González Moscoso, who sent addresses of likely collaborators in La Paz to Rodolfo Saldaña, the urban contact of the ELN. Even with a very small, extremely limited and extra-official participation in Guevara's continental project, it is known that the POR tried to participate in the Tricontinental congress, showing a clear interest in the communications that were taking place about the guerrilla warfare in Latin America, but it was barred by recommendation of the Bolivian CP.

Guillermo Lora states, "The Bolivian POR was the party paying the most attention to the problem of the guerrillas. This fighting method was not only discussed and written about, but the preliminary groundwork of its constitution was laid". (LORA, 1978, p.159) He believed that guerrillas in

Bolivia could only have been successful if they were led by the *Partido Obrero Revolucionario.* According to the Porista leader, Fidel Castro's anti-Trotskyism represented a "suicidal sectarianism", which became a rule when it had to do with support agreements for guerrilla movements and proved to be disastrous. According to Lora, what used to be an imposition by the Soviets eventually became a rule of action. Besides, "the Bolivian situation requires another kind of guerrilla, one that's the result of a single front in the workers' trends". (LORA, 1978, p.159) Even so, in the official document in relation to the guerrillas published in the periodical *Masas,* the POR demonstrated its solidarity and support of the ELN, even claiming that it, alone, wouldn't resolve the main problem of the revolutionary process, which they claimed was the issue of management, and it also didn't believe that the guerrillas could place themselves at the margin of the country's problems. According to the POR, the guerrillas, "despite all of the limitations" they could have, were part of the armed vanguard of the people.

According to the Trotskyist leader, the idea of the continental revolution as an "excuse" for guerrilla aims in the region of Ñancahuazú was attractive, but the simultaneous subversion of several countries based on that concept would be simply utopian. As he himself states:

> ...it can't be a justification to argue that Ñancahuazú was a simple link in a continental plan: to install guerrilla groups in most Latin American countries, moving under Cuban leadership, to facilitate the struggle against imperialism and the *criolla* dictatorships. From that point of view, the emergence of new guerrillas is a very important achievement because it plays a supporting role to the continental movement; nevertheless, their isolation, their lack of relation to the masses will become, as time goes by, one of the causes of their progressive weakening. The Latin American revolution will begin uniting within the boundaries of a country and then it will expand to the continental realm. (LORA, 1994, p.182)

Lora never had a personal interview with Fidel at the time of the guerrilla — despite having represented POR at the CODEP, in the Tricontinental — nor did he mobilize himself *clearly* on behalf of Guevara's armed struggle. On the other hand, the Cuban leaders didn't officially invite him and his party, nor did these leaders seek them out to join the ranks of the ELN, or to provide any kind of support for the guerrillas, even though some members of the urban group had made this sort of contact.

The *Partido Comunista-marxista-leninista,* a dissident of the pro-Soviet Bolivian CP, founded on April, 1965 and run by Oscar Zamora, didn't have any actual participation in the guerrillas led by Che nor did it officially supported them. Zamora believed it would be necessary to promote a popular war, which would have to be led by his party. Some dissidents from the PC-ml fought in the ELN next to Guevara, but none of them was formally tied to the party anymore.

And the Bolivian CP, which for years had been working in close collaboration with the Cubans for other guerrilla purposes, providing logistical support to combatants fighting in Peru and in Northern Argentina, in the specific case of the ELN campaign in Bolivia, put aside its work with Castro's government and chose not to support Guevara. Even though Mário Monje, First-Secretary of the Party, decided not to help Che, some dissidents of the CP, already without any ties to their organization, participated and stood with the guerrillas.

Due to his internationalist, anti-bureaucratic and libertarian style, Guevara was often accused of being a Trotskyist, a term he didn't accept, he was even, implicitly, thought of by some as the "Trotsky" of the Cuban revolution. (RADOSH, 1974, p.60) It's true that some Trotskyists, such as Ernest Mandel and Roberto Santucho, were sympathetic to Guevara's ideas and supported them. Santucho, who liked a syncretism among several

Marxist trends in the struggle against a common enemy, exemplified the unification of Guevarism with the spectrum of political-military lines relevant to the revolutionary war, as he was the main guerrilla in his native country, Argentina. But Che never considered himself a Trotskyist, even though some critics have pointed out similarities between his ideas and those of Trotsky. Guevara once mentioned:

> In Trotsky's thought one can also gather several things, even when, in my opinion, his basic concepts were mistaken, his successive action was wrong, and, in the last period, not very clear. The Trotskyists didn't contribute in any way to the revolutionary movement, anywhere; where something was done, such as in Peru, it failed, because their systems are flawed. That's why comrade Hugo Blanco, personally an unassailable man and full of sacrificial spirit, is bound to fail. Anyway, [this kind of discussion provokes a reaction] there's always someone who makes the accusation of Trotskyism. I believe that this doesn't depend so much on the position adopted concerning this or that problem, but on the fact that about this issue [the management method] there's a fervent, violent and bitter discussion and, as in all such discussions, each side is inflexible and loath to acknowledge other people's opinions. I have expressed opinions that are similar to those of the Chinese comrades about several things: about the guerrilla warfare, about the people's war, about the voluntary work, about the material incentives, in short, several things that the Chinese also advocate. But when my interlocutors identified me with the budgetary system, they mistook this for a Trotskyist position. As for the rest, people also say that the Chinese are divisionists and Trotskyists and they hint at that about me, personally too. On the other hand, when I'm abroad, I represent the government, and since I'm a disciplined person, I don't strictly express opinions that imply that the Cuban government is Trotskyist, which is something that's impossible. (GUEVARA, 1982, p.68)

Both Guevara and Trotsky favored an international block against capitalism. Thus, they both considered peaceful co-existence a deceptive proposal. But the Argentinian, unlike the Soviet leader, placed more emphasis on the role of the guerrilla, and of the peasantry than, on the proletarian struggles in the cities, without ever, of course, rejecting them. His ideas concerning the trade unions were also relatively different from Trotsky's: he believed that they should be subordinate to the government, but insisted that the workers should also carry out truly voluntary work, without coercion. Supportive of the freedom of thought and expression, in 1961 Guevara condemned, the destruction of the printing plates for the book *Permanent Revolution* by a subordinate employee, stating, "this shouldn't have happened".

It's true that Guevara took a copy of Trotsky's *History of the Russian Revolution,* with him while he was fighting in Bolivia, and that he read it in the last few months of his life. It was found in his backpack at a guerrilla camp, by the Bolivian army. This shows Guevara's interest in better knowing the work of the founder of the Red Army, although it doesn't indicate that he had necessarily opted for Trotskyism.

Guevara's thinking changed quickly from the beginning of the Cuban revolution to his guerrilla fight in Bolivia, from a rather superficial Marxism, still influenced by Stalin's image, to a heterodox, agile and dynamic Marxism, open to many different readings and interpretations. As the Cuban historian José Tabares de Real would say, "Che wasn't a Trotskyist, or a Titoist, or Maoist. Che was Che, just that." (TABARES DEL REAL, 1999) In this sense, one can understand his interest in the works by authors as varied as Stalin, Mao and Trotsky and his great willingness to debate with militants from different political trends. Guevara was never a Trotskyist or a Maoist, but there's no doubt that he demonstrated respect for differences of opinion and for open debates concerning his ideas.

---

[1] Even so, Guevara seemed to consider it important to support Perón. In a letter to his father, in February, 1955, he stated that "Argentina is the oasis of America, one must give all possible

support to Perón to avoid going to war, which is likely to be horrible; whether you like it or not, that's how it is". See Gálvez (1997, p.335). It must be recalled that Guevara nicknamed his guerrilla group, in the revolutionary struggle in Cuba, Los Descamisados (*The Shirtless*), and that later, when he was a member of the Cuban government, he talked to leftist Peronist groups to try to obtain occasional support for his revolutionary project.

---

[2]Stalin had that nickname in some Western countries, such as the United States, for example.

---

[3]According to Jorge Castañeda, in 1956, while in Mexico, Guevara was supposedly reading the *Principles of Leninism According to Stalin,* and stated that Khrushchev's briefing in the 20th Congress against the former Soviet ruler was only imperialist propaganda. See Castañeda (1997, p.108).

---

[4]For further information on the "new" Soviet historiography, see Ulam (1964). Another cutting criticism of the "falsification" of History can be found in Mandel (1979).

---

[5]See Bandeira (1998, p.175). None of the Cuban people interviewed, including William Gálvez, Camilo's right-hand man, nor the consulted bibliography, indicated that the guerrilla leader was or had been Trotskyist at any time.

[6]During a speech at the opening of the cookie plant Albert Kuntz, the Cuban Minister of Industry stated that "we must think everyday that we work here, that we're producing for our people to consume, that this is saying: our siblings, our parents or our children, all the Cuban people. Therefore, the struggle for the quality of the product is both revolutionary and vanguard. And can never be mistaken for thinking that, being a revolutionary, one can provide a poor quality product to the people. That would be making an attempt against the revolution." See Pérez-Galdós (1987, p.106-107).

[7]In the "scientific communism dictionary", by Rumiántsev, (1981, p.387-389) widely read in Cuba, that represented the official Soviet position, "Trotskyism" is described as an opportunistic petty-bourgeois political-ideological trend hostile to Marxism-Leninism, which reflected the ideas of a faction of the petty-bourgeois urban intellectuals with a tendency to a rhetorical revolutionarism, but that remained separate from the classist battles and spread capitulating conceptions of all the basic themes of the revolutionary struggle. According to the dictionary, "the ideological basis of Trotskyism was the 'theory of the permanent revolution', which fed parasitically on the idea of the permanent revolution of Marx and Engels, pointed against the Leninist doctrine of the transformation of the democratic-bourgeois revolution into socialist revolution. Some characteristics of this 'theory' are: the lack of faith in the capacity of the working class to gather allies around it; the denial of the revolutionary role of the peasants; the adventurer trend to 'lash' the revolution, to leap over unfinished phases of the latter; the denial of the general democratic movements; the guidance of a development of 'revolutionary wars'; the denial of the possibility of building socialism in a single country. In the 1920's and 1930's, this 'theory' gathered another crucial element, a rough anti-Sovietism and it became the unifying platform of the most heterogeneous anti-socialist forces [...] Trotsky's voluntaristic proposals about the transference of the revolution from one country to another excluded the possibility of a long-lasting co-existence of governments with different social systems with the capitalist world, to take full risk, until its own sacrifice, thus 'encouraging' the revolution in other countries [...] Trotskyism is a harmful element for the revolutionary, liberating and international movement, and one that objectively serves the interests of the reaction. For that reason, to the communist parties, fighting against Trotskyism is an important ideological task".

---

[8]According to a document by the CIA, "despite his dependence on the Soviet Union for economic help, Guevara seems to follow the ideological line of the Chinese Communist Party. His threat, though without basis, during the October crisis of 1962, to launch missiles against the United States was an indication of his militancy and his disdain for the Soviet politics. An admirer of Mao Tse-tung, he persistently encouraged the expansion of guerrilla warfare in all Latin America." (ESTADOS UNIDOS DA AMÉRICA, 1964)

---

[9]While most Latin American countries witnessed a gradual reduction in travel to China, between 1959 and 1961 Cuba increased it substantially. Most of the visitors went to the

celebrations of May 1st or October 1st. Many Latin Americans were invited by Chinese organizations, such as the Federation of Literature and Art, the Trade Union Federation, the Peace Committee, the Popular Association for Cultural Relations with Foreign Countries, the Chinese and Latin American Friendship Association, among others.

---

[10] It's worth noting that in the coup by Hugo Banzer, on August 21st, 1971, the POR participated in the Anti-imperialist Revolutionary Front together with the CP, the PC-ml, the other faction of POR, the ELN, the MIR, the PS, the PRIN and General Torres.

Conclusions

Observar, aprender y pensar, no copiar a nadie, y después empezar a caminar, tal es la forma que nosotros aplicamos.

Che Guevara

In order to elaborate a general analysis about the Cuban economic debate and its results, it's necessary to briefly summarize the different themes discussed throughout this work. The transition to socialism was a controversial goal, extremely popular in academic and political circles during much of the 20th Century, and was the center of intensive disputes among Marxists of different positions and trends. Based on concrete experiences and ideal models, different authors expressed their opinions about the paths that a socialist revolution should take.

In the specific case of Cuba, Che Guevara might have stood out the most in the debates that took place concerning that subject. Other intellectuals, however, were also paramount in the discussions about the economic development of Cuba and the creation of a New Man, non-alienated and aware of his role in the building of a new model of social relations in that concrete historical experience. Thus, from the plan made by the ECLA and its unfolding on the island, based on prominent figures that were active inside the Commission, such as Regino Boti and Juan Noyola, and the positions of the endogenous communists, represented mainly by Blas Roca and Carlos Rafael Rodríguez, we have a picture, in the first few years of the revolution, which certainly favored debate and an opening for the expression of the most varied opinions about the basic changes that were taking place in the country at that moment.

The presence of Latin American, Soviet and Eastern European technical advisors and aides enriched the environment of discussions and exchanges of experiences among the several interlocutors in that period. During the "economic debate" taking place in the magazines and journals of Cuban governmental institutions, we can see the participation of important personalities such as Charles Bettelheim and Ernest Mandel, while theoreticians who didn't directly participate in the matter, such as Leo Huberman, Paul Sweezy and other members of *Monthly Review,* constantly went to the country, and supported the new government through articles in their publications.

As it is known, Guevara was neither an economist nor an academic theoretician. Due to his position as a political leader and his own objective nature, he had more practical than intellectual concerns, and although he made an effort to be precise and serious in his writings — demonstrating that he had read important Marxist authors and that he was aware of what was going on in the socialist world — he showed that his main intention was to act based on a concrete reality and to try to rebuild the social pattern of the island, at the same time making an effort to impel the full development of the productive forces in the country.

In the discussions that took place in Cuba in that period, the positions of each of the individuals involved in the debate were clear. While one group theoretically sought more pragmatic solutions to the treatment of the state apparatus, by means of an overvaluation of material incentives, administrative decentralization, financial self-management and the use of profit figures as the main factor in evaluating the performance of the enterprise, another group praised aspects that supposedly presented an idealist cover and that were theoretically less efficient in economic terms, with the use of moral stimuli and greater management centralization of the Cuban industrial apparatus, but which, didn't necessarily correspond to reality, since the defense of those positions was intrinsically tied to a historical moment and a specific reality in the transition to socialism on the island. That is to say that those assumptions could be modified and adapted as the conjectural reality required.

Guevara was extremely critical of the process going on in the Soviet Union and in several Eastern European countries. According to him, building socialism with elements of capitalism, without changing them, would lead to an unfeasible political and economic model, which would gradually impose new concessions and slowly return the system to capitalism. (GUEVARA apud BORREGO, 2001a, p.410) That was clear in the book he wrote attacking the manuals of political economy of the Soviet Union, which he considered full of mistakes. Che believed that if that country continued to follow the path it was taking, in a few decades it would degenerate completely and would turn away, for good, from the path to communism. For that reason, there was a constant need to work with ideological mechanisms that promoted raising the consciousness of the workers, with moral incentives, socialist emulation and voluntary work.

In the beginning of the revolution, one of the main objectives was to industrialize the country at any cost. That meant giving priority to an agricultural diversification and promoting the construction of a solid industrial base. These factors promoted the destruction of large portions of farmland, which eventually led to a substantial reduction in the sugarcane harvest and a lower sugar production, even if there was, at the same time, a relative increase in the production of other food products. Some years later, noting the difficulties of industrializing the nation without enough capital in reserve, from the government, and knowing that traditional products of the country would provide greater yield in the short and medium term through exports, there was an effort by the rulers of the island to change the direction of investments and the agricultural and industrial production policy, with the return of sugar as the main product of the Cuban economy. It can be said that Cuba witnessed a significant increase in its trade with the socialist block, as well as the growth of its global productivity, even though it didn't reach the levels necessary for turning the island into a developed country.

Cuba had to convert almost all its machinery to the Soviet system. JUCEPLAN technicians, on the other hand, recommended that entire plants be bought from the Soviet Union and from the Eastern European countries. These industries, in general, worked with obsolete technology and produced low quality articles. The lack of many raw materials forced the Cubans to import the materials necessary to the operation of their factories. On the other hand, the bureaucracy, the delay in investments and the lack of technical knowledge led much of the equipment and materials that came from abroad to remain in warehouses, rotting or unused. Only with time and with greater preparation by the Cuban experts, was it possible to make the industrial apparatus work better. By the end of the 1960's, the country could already rely on their own technicians to make modern machines work, mainly those inherited from the former American monopolies. That advanced technology was hard to handle even for the experts from the Soviet Union who were in the country. Some of the industries that were so desired by the government were never built or didn't work to their full capacity, while others, such as the industry of home utensils, bought from Czechoslovakia, which took a long time to be completed, didn't produce competitive products in terms of quality, even within the socialist world.

Guevara himself criticized the quality of the Soviet products and the efficiency of their enterprises in the socialist system. According to him, it was crucial to use the capitalist techniques — which were more efficient — as well as to use the technology of the developed countries, without fearing that there would be ideological "corruption". That is, it was crucial to create mechanisms that ensured industrial modernization at the same time that one should work to raise the consciousness of the workers. The training of Cuban technicians and experts, the use of computers and technological development were always a concern for Che, who encouraged the priorization of all those aspects for building socialism on the island. Thus, he promoted the creation of several government institutions that, theoretically, should ensure the development of scientific research on the island, such as the Cuban Institute for the Research of Sugarcane By-Products (ICIDCA), the Cuban Institute for the Development of the Chemical Industry (ICDIQ), the Cuban Institute for Technological Research (ICIT), the Cuban Institute for the Development of Machinery (ICDM), the Cuban Institute for Mineral Resources (ICRM), the Cuban Institute for Researches on Mining and Metallurgy (ICIMM) and the Management of Automation and Electronics, among others.

The organization and management of the Cuban economy gradually changed over the years, while Guevara's assumptions concerning the structure and management of the enterprises were slowly left aside. Several ministries were created from the institution run by Che. In 1964, there was the creation of the Ministry of Sugar Industry; next, the Ministry of Basic Industry, the Ministry of Light Industry and the Ministry of Food Industry; and in 1974, at last, the Ministry of Steel and Mechanical Industry. For some time, the budgetary finance system and the economic accounting system coexisted in the country. From 1976 on, however, the *Sistema de Dirección de la Economía,* which was based primarily on the economic accounting system, was established in Cuba. (PÉREZ-ROLO, 1989, p.279) Even so, critics of the budgetary finance system in the beginning of the 1960's, such as Carlos Rafael Rodríguez, would later admit the efficiency and the quality of the system proposed by Che.

According to Guevara, as well as other heterodox Marxists of his time, discussion of the "laws" of socialism was complicated. If there were a true law in that system, it would be the planning of the economy itself. (BORREGO, 2001a, p.407) According to him, the plan wouldn't only be made up of technical elements, but mainly based on the development of the consciousness of the entire population. (BORREGO, 2001a, p.408) Moving away from an efficient plan and promoting an open market would also mean moving away from socialism itself. The plan should include several levels of decision-making, from the workers in the plants to the highest tiers of the government. As for the trade unions, the Minister of Industry was categorical when he stated that they should fulfill a role different from the traditional one during the transition period to socialism. Guevara placed special importance on the technical aspects of managing the industries and he believed that some original mechanisms could work for Cuba. The trade unions, therefore, would work in close cooperation with the CTAs and with the directors of the enterprises. According to him, the trade unions should also make an effort to avoid strikes and to encourage a better relationship with the authorities of the country, as well as striving for the best possible quality of the products and the increase of productivity.

Socialism in Cuba underwent several different phases. With the entrance of the island in the CEMA, in the beginning of the 1970's, there was an even greater attempt at working together with other planned economies. The efficiency of the plans in this period is doubtful at best, but, despite the disintegration of the Soviet block, the country remained firm, trying to adapt itself to the new times as best it could. Cuba still had several material difficulties and without the help of its former allies, it needed, once again, to convert the machinery inherited from the previous period and redirect much of its investments to the tourism sector. Even though many current measures by the government give the impression of a gradual redirection towards capitalism, the Cuban leaders still believe in the importance of Guevara's image to the younger generations as a way to encourage the continuity of the socialist system in the country.

REFERENCES

ACADEMIA DE CIÊNCIAS DA UNIÃO SOVIÉTICA. **La historia de Cuba.** Moscow, 1980.

______. **La política exterior de la Cuba Socialista.** Moscow: Editorial Progreso, 1982.

______. **Lénine, biografia.** Moscow: Edições Progresso; Lisbon: Avante, 1984.

ADAMS, Jerome R. **Latin American Heroes.** New York: Ballantine Books, 1993.

AFANÁSSIEV, V. **Os fundamentos do comunismo científico.** Moscow: Edições Progresso, 1985.

ALARCÓN DE QUESADA, Ricardo; ÁLVAREZ SÁNCHEZ, Miguel. **Bloqueo, guerra económica de Estados Unidos contra Cuba.** Havana: Editora Política, 2001.

ALMEYRA, G.; SANTARELLI, E. **Guevara:** il pensiero ribelle. Rome: Datanews, 1994.

ALONSO JÚNIOR, Odir. A esquerda cubana antes da revolução: anarquistas, comunistas e trotskistas. In: COGGIOLA, Osvaldo (Org.). **Revolução Cubana:** história e problemas atuais. São Paulo: Xamã, 1998. p. 29-50.

ALONSO TEJADA, Aurélio. **Interview.** By: Luiz Bernardo Pericás. Havana, jan. 1999.

ALTHUSSER, Louis. **Por Marx.** Havana: Edición Revolucionaria, 1966.

ALTMANN, Werner. **México e Cuba, revolução, nacionalismo, política externa.** São Leopoldo: Unisinos, 2001.

ALVAREZ BATISTA, Geronimo. **Che:** una nueva batalla. Paris: Pablo de la Torriente, 1994.

ANDERSON, Jon Lee. **Che Guevara, uma biografia.** Rio de Janeiro: Objetiva, 1997.

ARICÓ, José. **Marx e a América Latina.** São Paulo: Paz e Terra, 1982.

______. La sed de absoluto. **La Ciudad Futura,** Buenos Aires, n. 7, p. 32, out. 1987.

ARIET, Maria del Carmen. **Che, pensamiento político.** Havana: Editora Política, 1988.

AROCA, Santiago. **Fidel Castro, el final del camino.** Mexico City: Planeta, 1992.

BABY, Jean. **As grandes divergências do mundo Socialista.** São Paulo: Senzala, [ca. 1970].

BAILEY, Paul. Maoísmo. In: OUTHWAIT, William; BOTTOMORE, Tom. (Org.). **Dicionário do pensamento social do século XX.** Rio de Janeiro: Zahar, 1996. p. 441-445.

BALIÑO, Carlos et al. **La Revolución de Octubre y su repercusión en Cuba.** Havana: Instituto del Libro, 1967.

BALOYRA, Enrique A.; MORRIS, James A. (Org.). **Conflict and Change in Cuba.** Albuquerque: University of New Mexico Press, 1993.

BANDEIRA, Luiz Alberto Moniz. **De Martí a Fidel:** a Revolução Cubana e a América Latina. Rio de Janeiro: Civilização Brasileira, 1998.

______. **Interview.** By: Luiz Bernardo Pericás. St. León, Germany, ago. 2001. Via Internet.

BARAGAÑO, J. A. La Historia los condenará. **Lunes de Revolución,** Havana, n. 79, p. 4-7, 3 out. 1960.

BARÁIBAR, Carlos de. Ante el desafío económico comunista. **Estudios sobre el Comunismo,** Santiago de Chile, ano V, n. 16, p. 1-8, abr./jun. 1957.

BARAN, Paul. La planificación social y económica. **Monthly Review,** New York, ano 2, n. 20, p. 6-16, 1965.

______; SWEEZY, Paul. **Capitalismo monopolista.** Rio de Janeiro: Zahar, 1974.

BARROS FILHO, Omar de. **Bolívia:** vocação e destino. São Paulo: Versus, 1980.

BARTON, Paul. La legislación del trabajo en la URSS. **Estudios sobre el Comunismo,** Santiago de Chile, ano VII, n. 25, p. 46-52, jul./set. 1959.

BARTRA, Alberto. La reforma agraria y el proceso económico. **Lunes de Revolución,** Havana, n. 38, p. 2-5, 7 dez. 1959.

BASMÁNOV, M.; LEIBZÓN, B. **Vanguardia revolucionaria:** problemas de la lucha ideológica. Moscow: Editorial Progreso, 1978.

BATÁLOV, E. **La teoria leninista de la revolución.** Moscow: Editorial Progreso, 1985.

BAUDIS, Dieter; GARCÍA, Gloria. La planificación a largo plazo de la Cuban Electric Company. In: GARCÍA BRITO, Horacio (Ed.). **Monopolios norteamericanos en Cuba.** Havana: Editorial de Ciencias Sociales, 1973. p. 77-167.

BEKARÉVICH, Anatoli; MANCILLA, Anastásio. Transformaciones Socialistas y problemas del período de transición en Cuba. In: ACADEMIA DE CIÊNCIAS DA UNIÃO SOVIÉTICA. **La historia de Cuba.** Moscow, 1980. p. 24-71.

BELOÚSSOV, R. **Gestão planificada da economia Socialista.** Moscow: Edições Progresso, 1986.

BENACHENHOU, Abellatif. For Autonomous Development in the Third World. **Monthly Review,** New York, v. 32, n. 3, p. 43-52, july/aug. 1980.

BETTELHEIM, Charles. La planificación y el mercado. **Monthly Review,** New York, ano 2, n. 21, p. 42-49, May 1965.

______. **Cálculo económico y formas de propiedad,** Mexico City: Siglo XXI, 1972.

______. **A luta de classes na União Soviética.** Rio de Janeiro: Paz e Terra, 1976a.

______. **Planificação e crescimento acelerado.** Rio de Janeiro: Zahar, 1976b.

BETTELHEIM, Charles.. Formas e métodos do planejamento Socialista e nível de desenvolvimento das forças produtivas. In: GUEVARA, Ernesto. **Textos econômicos.** São Paulo: Edições Populares, 1982. p. 226-240.

______. The Specificity of Soviet Capitalism. **Monthly Review,** New York, v. 37, n. 4, p. 43-61, Sept. 1985.

______. More on the Nature of the Soviet System. **Monthly Review,** New York, v. 38, n. 7, p. 31-41, Dec. 1986.

______. L'autocritica. **Quaderni della Fondazione Ernesto Che Guevara,** Bolsena, n. 4, p. 153-154, 2001.

BOITO JÚNIOR, Armando et al. (Org.). **A obra teórica de Marx:** Atualidade, problemas e interpretações. São Paulo: Xamã; IFCH/Unicamp, 2000.

BONACHEA, Rolando E.; VALDÉS, Nelson P. (Org.). **Cuba in Revolution.** New York: Anchor Books; Doubleday & Company, 1972.

BONSAL, Philip W. Cuba, Castro and the United States. **Foreign Affairs,** New York, v. 45, n. 2, p. 260-276, jan. 1967.

BORREGO, Orlando. El Che y el Socialismo. In: CENTRO DE ESTUDIOS SOBRE AMÉRICA. **Pensar al Che:** los retos de la transición Socialista. Havana: Centro de Estudios sobre América; Editorial José Martí, 1989. t. 2. p. 283-344.

______. **Che, el camino del fuego.** Havana: Imagen Contemporanea, 2001a.

______. **Interview.** By: Luiz Bernardo Pericás. Havana, nov. 2001b.

BOTTOMORE, Tom et al. **A Dictionary of Marxist Thought.** Cambridge: Harvard University Press, 1983.

BOURNE, Richard. **Political Leaders of Latin America.** Baltimore: Pelican Books, 1969.

BROWN, J. F. Economics and Politics: III, Reforms in Bulgaria. **Problems of Communism,** Washington, n. 3, v. XV, p. 17-18, may/jun. 1966.

BRZEZINSKI, Zbigniew K. **The Soviet Bloc, Unity and Conflict.** New York: Frederick A. Praeger, 1965.

BUCH RODRÍGUEZ, Luis M. **Gobierno revolucionario cubano:** génesis y primeros pasos. Havana: Editorial de Ciencias Sociales, 1999.

CABRERA, Guillermo. **Memories of Che.** Secaucus, New Jersey: Lyle Stuart, 1987.

CABRERA, Olga. **El antiimperialismo en la historia de Cuba.** Havana: Editorial de Ciencias Sociales, 1985.

CASTAÑEDA, Jorge. El Che aún guarda enigmas. **Clarín,** Buenos Aires, 24 dec. 1995.

______. **Che Guevara, a vida em vermelho.** São Paulo: Companhia das Letras, 1997.

CASTRO, Fidel. **La Revolución Cubana, 1953/1962.** Mexico City: Era, 1976.

______. **Che.** Edited by David Deutschmann. Melbourne: Ocean Press, 1994.

CASTRO, P. G. Villas-Bôas. Che Guevara economista. **ADB:** Boletim da Associação de Diplomatas Brasileiros, Brasília, ano 2, n. 9, p. 5, jan. 1994.

CENTRO DE ESTUDIOS SOBRE AMÉRICA. **Pensar al Che:** desafíos de la lucha por el poder político. Havana: Centro de Estudios sobre América; Editorial José Martí, 1989a. t. 1.

______. **Pensar al Che:** los retos de la transición Socialista. Havana: Centro de Estudios sobre América; Editorial José Martí, 1989b. t. 2.

CEPERO BONILLA, Raul. **Escritos económicos.** Havana: Editorial de Ciencias Sociales, 1983.

______. **Escritos históricos.** Havana: Editorial de Ciencias Sociales, 1989a.

______. El convenio cubano-soviético. In: ______. **Escritos históricos.** Havana: Editorial de Ciencias Sociales, 1989b. p. 321-341.

CHAMBRE, Henri. **El marxismo en la Unión Soviética.** Madrid: Tecnos, 1960.

______. **De Marx a Mao Tse Tung.** São Paulo: Duas Cidades, 1963.

CHAVANCE, Bernard. Sobre as relações de produção na URSS. **Teoria & Política,** São Paulo, ano I, n. 3, p. 92-104, 1980.

CHÁVEZ ÁLVAREZ, Ernesto (Ed.). **Los obreros hacen y escriben su historia.** Havana: Editorial de Ciencias Sociales, 1975.

CHÁVEZ LIMA, Israel. **Interview.** Interviewer: Luiz Bernardo Pericás. Havana, nov. 2001.

CHIROT, Daniel. **Social Change in the Twentieth Century.** New York: Harcourt Brace Jovanovich, 1977.

CHITARIN, Atilio. Consideraciones "ideológicas" sobre la transición. **Cuadernos de Pasado y Presente,** Córdoba, n. 46, p. 15-25, 1973.

______. Problemas de la transición del capitalismo al Socialismo en la URSS. **Cuadernos de Pasado y Presente,** Córdoba, n. 46, p. 125-140, 1973.

CHVIRTOV, I. M. **O planeamento económico de Estado.** Moscow: Edições Progresso, 1989.

CLAUDÍN, Fernando. **A oposição no "Socialismo real".** Rio de Janeiro: Marco Zero, 1983.

COGGIOLA, Osvaldo (Org.). **Trotsky, ontem e hoje.** Belo Horizonte: Oficina de Livros, 1990.

______. (Org.). **Revolução Cubana, história e problemas atuais.** São Paulo: Xamã, 1998.

______. **Imperialismo e guerra na Iugoslávia.** Radiografia do conflito nos Bálcãs. São Paulo: Xamã, 1999.

______; PAULINO, Robério. **O fim do "Socialismo real" em debate.** São Paulo: [s. n.], 2001.

COLE, Ken. **Cuba from Revolution to Development.** London: Pinter, 1998.

CONNEL-SMITH, Gordon. **The United States & Latin America.** London: Heinemann, 1974.

COOKE, John William. La revolución y su ética. **Lunes de Revolución,** Havana, n. 76, p. 2-4, 12 set. 1960.

CORMIER, Jean. **Che Guevara, compagnon de la révolution.** Paris: Gallimard, 1996.

CUBA. Ministério da Fazenda; Gabinete da Presidência. **Decreto n.º 2.261,** de 26 de novembro de 1959. Nomeação de Ernesto Guevara para o cargo de presidente do Banco Nacional. Havana, 1959.

______. Ministério das Relações Exteriores. **Carta a Daniel M. Braddock** (encarregado de negócios dos Estados Unidos em Havana). Havana, 18 mar. 1960a.

______. Ministério das Relações Exteriores. **Carta a Daniel M. Braddock** (encarregado de negócios *ad-interin* dos Estados Unidos em Havana). Havana, 22 fev. 1960b.

______. **Decreto n.º 2.950,** de 27 de fevereiro de 1961. Nomeação de Ernesto Guevara para o cargo de ministro das Indústrias. Havana, 1961.

DEBRAY, Régis. **Revolução na Revolução.** Havana: Casa de las Américas, 1967.

______. Latin America: some problems of revolutionary strategy. In: HOROWITZ, I. L.; CASTRO, J.; GERASSI, J. (Org.). **Latin American Radicalism.** London: Jonathan Cape, 1969. p. 499-531.

DEL ROSAL, Amaro. **Los congresos obreros internacionales en el siglo XX.** Barcelona: Grijalbo, 1973.

DEL TORO, Carlos. **El movimiento obrero cubano en 1914.** Havana: Instituto del Libro, 1969.

DEMAITRE, Edmund. The Wonders of Marxology**. Problems of Communism,** Washington, v. XV, n. 4, p. 29-35, jul./ago. 1966.

DE SANTIS, Sergio. Debate sobre la gestión Socialista en Cuba. In: ______ et al. **La economía Socialista:** debate. Barcelona: Terra Nova, [197-?].

DETROIT, Mark. Cuba in the 1960's: Bureaucrats Head to "Communism" Without the Workers. **Communist Voice,** v. 4, n. 2, 20 abr. 1998. Disponível em: <http://www.home.flash.net/~comvoice/17cCuba60s.html>. Acesso em: 27 out. 2000.

DEUTSCHER, Isaac. **Soviet Trade Unions.** London: Royal Institute of International Affairs, 1950.

______. **The Unfinished Revolution, 1917/1967.** New York: Oxford University Press, 1967.

______. A falência do krushevismo. In: ______ et al. **Problemas e perspectivas do Socialismo.** Rio de Janeiro: Zahar, 1969a.

______ et al. **Problemas e perspectivas do Socialismo.** Rio de Janeiro: Zahar, 1969b.

DEVLIN, Kevin. The Permanent Revolutionism of Fidel Castro. **Problems of Communism,** Washington, v. XVII, n. 1, p. 1-11, jan./fev. 1968.

DINERSTEIN, Herbert. Moscow and the Third World, Power Politics or Revolution? **Problems of Communism,** Washington, v. XVII, n. 1, p. 52-56, jan./fev.1968.

DJILAS, Milovan. **A nova classe.** Rio de Janeiro: Agir, 1958.

DOBB, Maurice. **Socialist Planning:** Some Problems. London: Lawrence & Wishart, 1970.

DOZER, Donald Marquand. **América Latina, uma perspectiva histórica.** Porto Alegre: Globo; USP, 1966.

DRACHKOVITCH, Milorad M. (Org.). **O marxismo no mundo moderno.** Rio de Janeiro: Zahar, 1966.

DRAPER, Theodore. Castrismo. In: DRACHKOVITCH, Milorad M. (Org.). **O marxismo no mundo moderno.** Rio de Janeiro: Zahar, 1966a. p. 271-316.

______. **Castrismo, teoria e prática.** Rio de Janeiro: GRD, 1966b.

DREIER, John C. (Org.). **A Aliança para o Progresso.** Rio de Janeiro: Fundo de Cultura, 1962.

DUMONT, René. **Cuba:** Socialism and Development. New York: Grove Press, 1970.

______.; MAZOYER, Marcel. **Desarrollo y Socialismos.** Caracas: Tiempo Nuevo, 1969.

DUTRA, Hélio. **Querida ilha.** São Paulo: Mandacaru, 1988.

EASTMAN, Lloyd. Mao, Marx, and the Future Society. **Problems of Communism,** Washington, v. XVIII, n. 3, p. 21-26, maio/ jun. 1969.

ELLMAN, Michael. **Planejamento Socialista.** Rio de Janeiro: Zahar, 1980.

ESCOBAR, Froilán; GUERRA, Félix. **Che sierra adentro.** Havana: Editora Política, 1988.

ESCOSTEGUY, Jorge. **Cuba hoje:** 20 anos de revolução. São Paulo: Alfa-Omega, 1978.

ESTADOS UNIDOS DA AMÉRICA. Central Intelligence Agency. CIA Biographic Register on Che. Ago. 1964. Disponível em: <http://www.parascope.com/articles/1197/chedoc.htm>. Acesso em : 2 out. 2001.

FARIA, Octavio de. **Destino do Socialismo.** [São Paulo]: Ariel, 1933.

FAVROD, Charles-Henri (Coord.). **Os soviéticos.** Lisbon: Dom Quixote, 1978. (Enciclopédia do Mundo Atual, v. 16)

FENGHI, Francesco. Economía de transición y superación del "modelo Socialista" en China. **Cuadernos de Pasado y Presente,** Córdoba, n. 46, p. 141-165, 1973.

FERNANDES, Florestan. **Da guerrilha ao Socialismo:** a Revolução Cubana. São Paulo: TAQ, 1979.

FERNÁNDEZ FONT, Marcelo. Desenvolvimento e funções do sistema bancário Socialista em Cuba. In: GUEVARA, Ernesto. **Textos econômicos.** São Paulo: Edições Populares, 1982. p. 202-213.

FERNANDEZ RÍOS, Olga. **Formación y desarollo del Estado Socialista en Cuba.** Havana: Editorial de Ciencias Sociales, 1988.

FERRERA DIAZ, Jorge. **Interview.** By: Luiz Bernardo Pericás. Havana, nov. 2001.

FISCHER, Ernst. **Marx in His Own Words.** London: Penguin Books, 1978.

FITZGERALD, Frank T. Cuba and the Problem of Socialist Development. **Monthly Review,** New York, v. 33, n. 11, p. 48-51, abr.1982.

FLORES CASAMAYOR, Bárbara. Aspectos económicos del período de transición en Cuba. **Cuba Socialista,** Havana, n. 35, p. 105-125, set./out. 1988.

FORNET-BETANCOURT, Raúl. **O marxismo na América Latina.** São Leopoldo: Unisinos, 1995.

FRANQUI, Carlos. Cultura y revolución. **Lunes de Revolución,** Havana, n. 19, p. 11-12, 26 jul. 1959.

______. **Retrato de família com Fidel.** Rio de Janeiro: Record, 1981.

FUNG RIVERÓN, Thalia M. **En torno a las regularidades y particularidades de la revolución Socialista en Cuba.** Havana: Editorial de Ciencias Sociales, 1982.

FURTADO, Celso. **A fantasia organizada.** Rio de Janeiro: Paz e Terra, 1985.

FURTAK, Robert K. Revolución mundial y coexistencia pacífica. **Foro Internacional,** Mexico City, 25-26, v. VII, n. 1 e 2, p. 1-28, [1971?].

GÁLVEZ, William. _____. **Camilo, señor de la vanguardia.** Havana: Editorial de Ciencias Sociales, 1979.

______. **Viajes y aventuras del joven Ernesto.** Havana: Editorial de Ciencias Sociales, 1997.

Camilo en Camilo. Havana: Verde Olivo, 1998a.

______. **El joven Camilo.** Havana: Gente Nueva, 1998b.

______. **Interview.** By: Luiz Bernardo Pericás. Havana, jan. 1999.

GARCÍA BRITO, Horacio (Ed.). **Monopolios norteamericanos en Cuba.** Havana: Editorial de Ciencias Sociales, 1973.

GERRATANA, Valentino. Estado Socialista y capitalismo de Estado. **Cuadernos de Pasado y Presente,** Córdoba, n. 46, p. 81-123, 1973.

______. Formación económico-social y proceso de transición. **Cuadernos de Pasado y Presente,** Córdoba, n. 46, p. 45-79, 1973.

GIACOBETTI, Francis. **Che's Compañeros:** Witnesses to a Legend. Paris: Assouline, [entre 1997 e 1999].

GIRARDI, Giulio. Critica rivoluzionaria del "Socialismo reale" e critica marxista del marxismo dogmatico. **Quaderni della Fondazione Ernesto Che Guevara,** Bolsena, n. 4, p. 73-95, 2001.

GLUCKSMANN, André. **Althusser:** un estructuralismo ventrílocuo. Barcelona: Anagrama, 1971.

GONZALEZ CARBAJAL, Ladislao. **El ala izquierda estudiantil y su época.** Havana: Editorial de Ciencias Sociales, 1974.

GOODMAN, Elliot R. **O plano soviético de Estado mundial.** Rio de Janeiro: Presença, 1965.

GORENDER, Jacob. **Interview.** By: Luiz Bernardo Pericás. São Paulo, jul. 2001.

GORKIN, J. G. (Org.). **La transición del capitalismo al comunismo.** Madrid: Akal, [197-?]

GRESPAN, Jorge. O estruturalismo da Cepal na obra de Raúl Prebisch. **História Unisinos,** São Leopoldo, v. 5, n. 3, p. 105-125, jan./jun. 2001.

GRIGULÉVICH, Iósif. **Luchadores por la libertad de América Latina.** Moscow: Editorial Progreso, 1988.

GUEVARA, Ernesto. _____. **Carta a Regino Boti.** Havana, 28 out. 1963.

______. **Carta a Charles Bettelheim.** Havana, 24 out. 1964a.

______. **Carta a José Medero.** Havana, 26 fev. 1964b.

______. **Cartas.** São Paulo: Edições Populares, 1980a.

______. **Diário da guerrilha boliviana.** São Paulo: Edições Populares, 1980b.

______. **Sierra Maestra:** da guerrilha ao poder. Passagens da guerra revolucionária. São Paulo: Edições Populares, 1980c.

______. **Por uma revolução internacional.** São Paulo: Edições Populares, 1981a.

______. **Reflexões sobre a história cubana.** São Paulo: Edições Populares, 1981b.

______. **Textos políticos e sociais.** São Paulo: Edições Populares, 1981c.

______. **Textos econômicos.** São Paulo: Edições Populares, 1982.

______. **Che Guevara Speaks.** New York: Pathfinder Press, 1985a.

______. **Escritos y discursos.** v. 5. Havana: Editorial de Ciencias Sociales, 1985b.

______. **Che Guevara and the Cuban Revolution.** Sydney: Pathfinder, 1987a.

______. **Textos revolucionários.** São Paulo: Edições Populares, 1987b.

______. **Che periodista.** Havana: Pablo de la Torriente, 1988a.

______. **Temas económicos.** Havana: Editorial de Ciencias Sociales, 1988b.

______. **A New Society:** Reflections for Today's World. Melbourne: Ocean Press, 1991.

______. **Notas de viaje.** Havana; Madrid: Abril; Sodepaz, 1992.

GUEVARA LYNCH, Ernesto. **Meu filho Che.** São Paulo: Brasiliense, 1986.

GUIJARRO DÍAZ, Gabriel. **La concepción del hombre en Marx.** Salamanca: Sígueme, 1975.

GUNTHER, John. **A Rússia por dentro.** Porto Alegre: Globo, 1959.

GUTELMAN, Michel. Cuba's Lessons on Economic Policies. In: BONACHEA, Rolando E.; VALDÉS, Nelson P. (Org.). **Cuba in Revolution.** New York: Anchor Books, 1972. p. 231-237.

GÚZMAN, Oscar. **Interview.** By: Luiz Bernardo Pericás. Havana, jan. 1999.

HAGELBERG, G. B. Cuba: A First Hand Account. **Monthly Review,** New York, v. 20, n. 5, p. 87-93, out. 1968.

HALPERIN, Ernst. Beyond Libermanism. **Problems of Communism,** Washington, n. 1, v. XVI, p. 47, jan./fev. 1967.

HALPERIN DONGHI, Túlio. **História da América Latina.** São Paulo: Paz e Terra, 1989.

HANSEN, Joseph. **Dynamics of the Cuban Revolution.** A Marxist Appreciation. New York: Pathfinder, 1994.

HARNECKER, Marta. **Cuba:** democracia ou ditadura? São Paulo: Global, [197-?].

HARRIS, Seymour E. **Economic Planning:** The Plans of Fourteen Countries With Analyses of the Plans. New York: Alfred A. Knopf, 1949.

HARRISON, James P. Peking's Remembrance of Things Past. **Problems of Communism,** Washington, v. XV, n. 3, p. 11-16, maio/jun. 1966.

HART DAVALOS, Armando. Che, un eccelente ammistratore Socialista. **Quaderni della Fondazione Ernesto Che Guevara,** Bolsena, n. 4, p. 118-120, 2001.

HERNÁNDEZ GONZÁLEZ, Enrique et al. **Cuestiones fundamentales de la dirección económica.** Havana: Editora Politica, 1984.

HOOK, Sidney. Marx's Second Coming. **Problems of Communism,** Washington, v. XV, n. 4, p. 26-29, jul./ago. 1966.

HOUGH, Jerry. The Soviet Elite: I, Groups and Individuals. **Problems of Communism,** Washington, v. XVI, n. 1, p. 28-35, jan./fev. 1967.

HOY. **Periódico Hoy, aclaraciones.** Havana: Editora Política, 1966.

HUBERMAN, Leo. Preguntas sobre el Socialismo. **Monthly Review,** New York, ano 2, n. 16, p. 17-28, [1965?].

______. Why Socialism is Necessary. **Monthly Review,** New York, v. 20, n. 8, p. 1-14, jan. 1969.

HUBERMAN, Leo; SWEEZY, Paul. **Cuba, Anatomy of a Revolution.** New York: Monthly Review Press, 1960.

______. El futuro de la economía cubana. **Monthly Review,** New York, ano 1, n. 9, p. 5-22, 1964.

______. **Socialism in Cuba.** New York: Modern Reader, 1970.

IGNÁTIEV, V. (Ed.). **La lucha del partido bolchevique contra el trotskismo después de la Revolucion de Octubre.** Moscow: Editorial Progreso, [197-?]

ITIN, L. I. **Economía de la industria Socialista.** Havana: Pueblo y Educación, 1983. t. 1.

JAGUARIBE, Hélio et al. **A dependência político-econômica da América Latina.** São Paulo: Loyola, 1976.

JACKSON, Bruce D., Whose Men in Havana? **Problems of Communism,** Washington, v. XV, n. 3, p. 1-10, maio/jun. 1966.

JAMES, Joel. **Interview.** By: Luiz Bernardo Pericás. Santiago de Cuba, jan. 1999.

JOBIC, Bernard. La revolución cultural y la crítica del economicismo. **Cuadernos de Pasado y Presente,** Córdoba, n. 46, 1973. p. 167-201.

KAMENITZER, S. E. **Organización, planificación y dirección de la actividad de las empresas industriales.** Havana: Pueblo y Educación, 1981. Segunda parte.

KAROL, K. S. **Les guérilleros au pouvoir.** Paris: Robert Laffont, 1970.

KAUFMAN, Edy. **The Superpowers and Their Spheres of Influence.** London: Croom Helm, 1976.

KELLNER, Douglas. **Che Guevara.** São Paulo: Nova Cultural, 1990.

KLÁREN, Peter F.; BOSSERT, J. (Org.). **Promise of Development.** Boulder, Colorado: Westview Press, 1986.

KLOFÁC, Vladimir. Guevara e la Cecoslovacchia. **Quaderni della Fondazione Ernesto Che Guevara,** Bolsena, n. 4, p. 65- 68, 2001.

KOHAN, Néstor. El Che Guevara y la filosofía de la praxis. **Debates Americanos,** Havana, n. 3, p. 55-70, jan./jun. 1997.

KOONT, Sinan. Cuba: An Island Against All Odds. **Monthly Review,** New York, v. 46, n. 5, p. 1-18, out. 1994.

KOWALEWSKI, Zbigniew Marcin. Il riferimento a Guevara nella Polonia degli anni 60. **Quaderni della Fondazione Ernesto Che Guevara,** Bolsena, n. 4, p. 51-58, 2001.

KUCZYNKI, Jurgen et al. Los pronósticos económicos de la Esso Standard Oil de Cuba. In: GARCÍA BRITO, Horacio (Ed.). **Monopolios norteamericanos en Cuba.** Havana: Editorial de Ciencias Sociales, 1973. p. 53-76.

KUX, Ernst. El utópico plan de Khrushev. **Estudios sobre el Comunismo,** Santiago de Chile, ano VII, n. 25, p. 1-9, jul./set. 1959.

LANDAU, Saul. Un análisis de la Revolución Cubana. **Lunes de Revolución,** Havana, n. 76, p. 5-6, 12 set. 1960.

LANDAUER, Carl. **Sistemas econômicos contemporâneos.** Rio de Janeiro: Zahar, 1966.

LANGE, Oskar. A economia política do Socialismo. In: SINGH, V. B. et al. **Da economia política.** Rio de Janeiro: Zahar, 1966a. p. 79-95.

______. O marxismo e a economia burguesa. In: SINGH, V. B. et al. **Da economia política.** Rio de Janeiro: Zahar, 1966b. p. 53-78.

LANGE, Oskar. Da economia política. In: POMERANZ, Lenina (Org.). **Oskar Lange.** São Paulo: Ática, [198-]a. p. 49-76.

______. Planejamento e teoria econômica. In: POMERANZ, Lenina (Org.). **Oskar Lange.** São Paulo: Ática, [198-]b. p. 93-109.

______.; TAYLOR, Fred M. **Sobre la teoría económica del Socialismo.** Barcelona: Ariel, 1970.

______. ; TINBERGEN, J. **Ensaios sobre planificação econômica/política econômica:** princípios e planejamento. São Paulo: Nova Cultural, 1986.

LASSERRE, Georges. **A empresa Socialista na Jugoslávia.** Lisbon: Morais, 1966.

LAURAT, Lucien. Estadísticas soviéticas. **Estudios sobre el Comunismo,** Santiago de Chile, ano V, n. 16, p. 54-57, abr./jun. 1957.

LAVRETSKI, I. **Che Guevara.** Moscow: Editorial Progreso, 1975.

LEAL SPENGLER, Eusebio. La resurrección del Che: una victoria del ideal revolucionario. **Tricontinental,** Havana, ano 30, n. 138, p. 33-36, 1997.

LECHÍN, Juan. **Interview.** By: Luiz Bernardo Pericás. La Paz, jan 1995.

LÊNIN, V. I. Cartas de longe. In ______. **Obras escolhidas.** Lisbon: Avante; Moscow: Edições Progresso, 1978. v. 2. p. 1-9.

______. Mais uma vez sobre os sindicatos, o momento atual e os erros dos camaradas Trótsky e Bukhárine. In: ______. **Obras escolhidas 3.** Lisbon: Avante; Moscow: Edições Progresso, 1979a. v. 3. p. 433-462.

______. Projeto de resolução, as tarefas dos sindicatos e os métodos da sua realização. In: ______. **Obras escolhidas 3.** Lisbon: Avante; Moscow: Edições Progresso, 1979b. v. 3. p. 408.

______. Uma grande iniciativa. In: ______. **Obras escolhidas 3.** Lisbon: Avante; Moscow: Edições Progresso, 1979c. v. 3. p. 152-158.

LENK, Kurt. **Teorías de la revolución.** Barcelona: Anagrama, 1978.

LEÓN COTAYO, Nicanor. **El bloqueo a Cuba.** Havana: Editorial de Ciencias Sociales, 1983.

LEÓN EXPÓSITO, Roberto. 1 de mayo de 1919 en La Habana. In: CHÁVEZ ÁLVAREZ, Ernesto (Ed.). **Los obreros hacen y escriben su historia.** Havana: Editorial de Ciencias Sociales, 1975. p. 327-336.

LEONHARD, Wolfgang. **O futuro do comunismo soviético.** Rio de Janeiro: Nórdica, 1977.

LE RIVEREND, Julio. Orígenes de la propiedad agraria en Cuba. **Lunes de Revolución,** Havana, n. 19, p. 14-15, 26 jul. 1959.

______. **Historia económica de Cuba.** Havana: Instituto del Libro, 1967.

LESAGE, Michel. **As instituições soviéticas.** Coimbra: Almedina, 1976.

LEVESQUE, Jacques. **O conflito sino-soviético.** Varzim, Portugal: Estúdios Cor, 1974. LEVI, Arrigo et al. **Os homens do Kremlin.** Rio de Janeiro: Editora Três, 1974.

LEZCANO PÉREZ, Jorge. **Interview.** By: Luiz Bernardo Pericás. Brasília, dez. 2001a.

______. **O sistema político cubano.** Rio de Janeiro: [s. n.], 2001b.

LINDSAY, Jack. **Marxism and Contemporary Science.** London: Dennis Dobson, [195-].

LINHART, Robert. **Lenin, os camponeses, Taylor.** Rio de Janeiro: Marco Zero, 1983.

LISS, Sheldon B. **Marxist Thought in Latin America.** Berkeley: University of California Press, 1984.

LOBAINA, Esther. **Interview.** By: Luiz Bernardo Pericás. Havana, nov. 2001.

LOCKWOOD, Lee. **Castro's Cuba, Cuba's Fidel.** Boulder, Colorado: Westview Press, 1990.

LÓPEZ-FRESQUET, Rufo. **Fui ministro de Fidel.** Rio de Janeiro: Laudes, 1969.

LOPEZ SEGRERA, Francisco. **Cuba:** capitalismo dependiente y subdesarrollo (1510-1959). Havana: Casa de las Américas, 1972.

LORA, Guillermo. **Revolución y foquismo.** Buenos Aires: Documentos, 1978.

______. La guerrilla y las masas. In: SORIA GALVARRO, Carlos (Org.). **El Che en Bolivia 3:** análisis y reflexiones. La Paz: Cedoin, 1994. p. 179-192.

LOSADA ALDANA, Ramón. **Dialética do subdesenvolvimento.** Rio de Janeiro: Paz e Terra, 1968.

LOSOVSKY, D. **Marx e os sindicatos.** São Paulo: Anita Garibaldi, [198-?].

LOURENÇO, Maria José. Introdução. In: BARROS FILHO, Omar de. **Bolívia:** vocação e destino. São Paulo: Versus, 1980. p. 3-7.

LOVEMAN, Brian; DAVIES JUNIOR, Thomas M. (Org.). **The Politics of Antipolitics.** Lincoln: University of Nebraska Press, 1989.

LÖWY, Michael. **O pensamento de Che Guevara.** Lisbon: Bertrand, 1976.

______. (Org.). **Le marxisme en Amérique Latine de 1909 à nous jours.** Paris: François Maspero, 1980.

______. **Nacionalismos e internacionalismos** – Da época de Marx até nossos dias. São Paulo: Xamã, 2000.

______. Ni calco ni copia: Che Guevara en busca de un nuevo Socialismo II. **La Insignia,** 29 jun. 2001. Disponível em: <http://www.lainsignia.org>. Acesso em: 2 out. 2001.

______.; BENSAÏD, Daniel. **Marxismo, modernidade, utopia.** São Paulo: Xamã, 2000.

MACHADO, Nery. **Cuba, vanguarda e farol da América.** São Paulo: Fulgor, 1962.

MAGDOFF, Fred. Impressions of the Cuban Agriculture. **Monthly Review,** New York, v. 32, n. 2, p. 35-40, jun. 1980.

MAGDOFF, Harry. Are There Economic Laws of Socialism? **Monthly Review,** New York, v. 37, n. 3, p. 112-127 jul./ago. 1985.

MAHIEU, Jaime Maria de. La filosofía marxista. **Estudios sobre el Comunismo,** Santiago de Chile, ano V, n. 16, p. 45-49, abr./jun. 1957.

MAIDANIK, Kiva et al. **El pensamiento revolucionario del "Che".** Buenos Aires: Seminário Científico Internacional; Ediciones Dialectica, 1988.

MALLORQUÍN, Carlos. **Ideas e historia en torno al pensamiento económico latinoamericano.** Mexico City: Plaza y Váldes, 1998.

MANDEL, Ernest. La teoría económica yugoslava. **Monthly Review,** New York, ano IV, n. 41, p. 19-32, ago. 1967.

______. **Introducción a la economía marxista.** Lima: Fondo de Cultura Popular Editores, 1973.

______. **Da Comuna a Maio de 68.** Lisbon: Antídoto, 1979.

______. As categorias mercantis no período de transição. In: GUEVARA, Ernesto. **Textos econômicos.** São Paulo: Edições Populares, 1982a. p. 241-260.

______. O debate econômico em Cuba durante o período 1963-1964. In: GUEVARA, Ernesto. **Textos econômicos.** São Paulo: Edições Populares, 1982b. p. 165-171.

MANKIEWICZ, Frank; KIRBY, Jones. **With Fidel:** A Portrait of Castro and Cuba. Chicago: Playboy Press, 1975.

MARGOLIN, M. S. **Planificación financiera.** Havana: Ministerio de Hacienda Publicaciones, 1962.

MARKUS, Gyorgy. **Teoria do conhecimento no jovem Marx.** Rio de Janeiro: Paz e Terra, 1974.

MARTÍNEZ, Osvaldo. Notas sobre el pensamiento de Ernesto Che Guevara en las relaciones económicas internacionales. **Cuba Socialista,** Havana, n. 35, p. 69-92, set./out. 1988.

MARTÍNEZ HEREDIA, Fernando. **Interview.** By: Luiz Bernardo Pericás. Havana, jan. 1999.

MARX, Karl. A questão judaica. In: ______. **Manuscritos económico-filosóficos.** Lisbon: Edições 70, 1964a. p. 35-73.

______. **Manuscritos económico-filosóficos.** Lisbon: Edições 70, 1964b.

______. Teses sobre Feuerbach. In: ______.; ENGELS, Friedrich. **Obras escolhidas.** Lisbon: Avante; Moscow: Edições Progresso, 1982. t. 1. p. 1-3.

______. Critique of the Gotha Program. New York: International Publishers, 1979.

______; ENGELS, Friedrich. **A ideologia alemã.** São Paulo: Hucitec, 1986.

MASSARI, Roberto. **Che Guevara, grandeza y riesgo de la utopia.** Navarra: Txalaparta, 1993.

MASSARI, Roberto. **Interview.** By: Luiz Bernardo Pericás. Bolsena, dez. 2001a. Via Internet.

______. Nahuel Moreno, Che Guevara, héroe y mártir de la revolución. **Quaderni della Fondazione Ernesto Che Guevara,** Bolsena, n. 4, 2001b. p. 348.

______. Periodizzare il Che e il Socialismo. **Quaderni della Fondazione Ernesto Che Guevara,** Bolsena, n. 4, p. 96-101, 2001c.

______. Sequenza del "debate económico" dal 1963 in Poi. **Quaderni della Fondazione Ernesto Che Guevara,** Bolsena, n. 4, p. 121-123, 2001d.

MATOS, Almir. **Cuba:** a revolução na América. Rio de Janeiro: Vitória, 1961.

MCFARLANE, Bruce. Iugoslávia: perspectivas políticas atuais. In: DEUTSCHER, Isaac et al. **Problemas e perspectivas do Socialismo.** Rio de Janeiro: Zahar, 1969b. p. 104-129.

MCLELLAN, David; **Marx Before Marxism.** New York: Harper & Row Publishers, 1970.

______. **Marxism After Marx.** Boston: Houghton Miffin Company, 1979.

MEDEIROS, Rui. **A Rússia de hoje.** Rio de Janeiro: Jalkh, 1979.

MEHNERT, Klaus. **Stalin Versus Marx,** the Stalinist Historical Doctrine. London: George Allen and Unwin, 1952.

MENDONÇA, Paulo. **Brezhnev.** Rio de Janeiro: Editora Três, 1975.

MENDOZA DÍEZ, Alvaro. The Lessons of the Cuban Revolution. In: AGUILAR, Luis E. (Org.). **Marxism in Latin America.** New York: Alfred A. Knopf, 1968. p. 180-185.

MESA-LAGO, Carmelo. Economic Significance of Unpaid Labor in Socialist Cuba. In: BONACHEA, Rolando E.; VALDÉS, Nelson P. (Org.). **Cuba in Revolution.** New York: Anchor Books; Doubleday & Company, 1972. p. 384-412.

______. **The Labor Sector and Socialist Distribution in Cuba.** New York: Frederick A. Praeger, [197-].

MILLS, C. Wright. **A verdade sobre Cuba.** Rio de Janeiro: Zahar, 1961.

MINÀ, Gianni. **An Encounter With Fidel.** Melbourne: Ocean Press, 1991.

MIRANDA, Basílio. Estado e partido na transição para o Socialismo. **Teoria & Política,** São Paulo, ano I, n. 3, p. 145-174, 1980.

MIRANDA FERNÁNDEZ, Lucinda. **Lazaro Peña, capitan de la clase obrera cubana.** Havana: Editorial de Ciencias Sociales, 1984.

MORRIS, George. **A CIA e o movimento operário americano.** Rio de Janeiro: Civilização Brasileira, 1967.

MOSCATO, Antonio. Le critiche all'URSS e al sistema sovietico. **Quaderni della Fondazione Ernesto Che Guevara,** Bolsena, n. 4, p. 29-50, 2001.

MUNSLOW, Barry. Is Socialism Possible in the Periphery? **Monthly Review,** New York, v. 35, n. 1, p. 25-39, maio 1983.

MYRDAL, Gunnar. **El Estado del futuro.** Mexico City: Fondo de Cultura Económica, 1961.

NEPOMUCENO, Eric. **Cuba:** anotações sobre uma revolução. São Paulo: Alfa-Omega, 1981.

NORMANO, J. F. **A economia na Rússia.** São Paulo: Atlas, 1945.

NOYOLA, Juan. **Carta a Raul Prebisch.** Havana, out. 1960.

______. Aspectos económicos de la Revolución Cubana. In: ______. **La economía cubana en los primeros años de la revolución.** Mexico City: Siglo XXI, 1978a. p. 111-134.

______. **La economía cubana en los primeros años de la revolución.** Mexico City: Siglo XXI, 1978b.

______. Principios de economía. In: ______. **La economía cubana en los primeros años de la revolución.** Mexico City: Siglo XXI, 1978c. p. 142-252.

NUIRY SÁNCHEZ, Nuria; FERNÁNDEZ MAYO, Graciela (Org.). **Pensamiento y política cultural cubanos.** Havana: Pueblo y Educación, 1986. t. 1.

NUÑEZ JIMENEZ, Antonio. **En marcha con Fidel.** Havana: Letras Cubanas, 1982.

______.; SOUCHY, Agustín. **Cooperativismo y colectivismo.** Havana: Lex, 1960.

NUÑEZ RODRÍGUEZ, Mauricio. Che más alla de la imagen. **Tricontinental,** Havana, ano 31, n. 138, p. 22-24, 1997.

O'CONNOR, James. Revolution and the Cuban Workers. **Monthly Review,** New York, v. 21, n. 1, p. 52-56, maio 1969.

______. Cuba: It's Political Economy. In: BONACHEA, Rolando E.; VALDÉS, Nelson P. (Org.). **Cuba in Revolution.** New York: Anchor Books, 1972. p. 52-81.

OELGART, Bernd. **Ideólogos e ideologias da nova esquerda.** Lisbon: Presença, [ca. 1970].

OIZERMAN, Teodor. **El problema de la alienación en los trabajos de Marx en su juventud.** Havana: Editorial de Ciencias Sociales, 1985.

OLTUSKI, Enrique; FRANQUI, Carlos; HART, Armando. Filosofía revolucionaria. **Lunes de Revolución,** Havana, n. 19, p. 62, 6 jul. 1959.

OQUENDO BARRIOS, Leyda et al. **Las clases y la lucha de clases en la sociedad neocolonial cubana.** Havana: Editorial de Ciencias Sociales, 1981.

OUTHWAIT, William; BOTTOMORE, Tom. (Org.). **Dicionário do pensamento social do século XX.** Rio de Janeiro: Zahar, 1996.

PARRA BARRERO, Jesús. **Interview.** By: Luiz Bernardo Pericás. Havana, nov. 2001.

PARTIDO COMUNISTA CUBANO. The Communist Party and the Cuban Revolutionary Situation. In: AGUILAR, Luis E. (Org.). **Marxism in Latin America.** New York: Alfred A. Knopf, 1968. p. 112-117.

PÉREZ, Humberto. **El subdesarrollo y la vía del desarrollo.** Havana: Editorial de Ciencias Sociales, 1975.

PÉREZ-GALDÓS, Víctor. **Un hombre que actúa como piensa.** Manágua: Vanguardia, 1987.

PÉREZ-ROLO, Martha. La organización y la dirección de la industria Socialista en el pensamiento y la acción de Ernesto Che Guevara. In: CENTRO DE ESTUDIOS SOBRE AMÉRICA. **Pensar al Che:** los retos de la transición Socialista. Havana: Centro de Estudios sobre América; Editorial José Martí, 1989. t. 2. p. 257-282.

PERICÁS, Luiz Bernardo. **Che Guevara e a luta revolucionária na Bolívia.** São Paulo: Xamã, 1997.

______.; BARSOTTI, Paulo (Org.). **América Latina:** história, crise e movimento. São Paulo: Xamã, 1999.

PETRAS, James. Problems in the Transition to Socialism. **Monthly Review,** New York, v. 35, n. 1, p. 14-24, maio 1983.

PINO-SANTOS, Oscar. **El asalto a Cuba por la oligarquia financiera yanki.** Havana: [s. n.], 1972.

POMERANZ, Lenina. (Org.). **Oskar Lange.** São Paulo: Ática, [198-?].

______. **Interview.** By: Luiz Bernardo Pericás. São Paulo, set. 2001.

PORCARO, Mimmo. Charles Bettelheim, um longo adeus. **Outubro,** São Paulo, n. 5, p. 59-81, 2001.

PRADO JÚNIOR, Caio. **O mundo do Socialismo.** São Paulo: Brasiliense, 1962.

PREBISCH, Raúl. Aspectos econômicos da Aliança para o Progresso. In: DREIER, John C. (Org.). **A Aliança para o Progresso.** Rio de Janeiro: Fundo de Cultura, 1962. p. 55-102.

______. **Dinâmica do desenvolvimento latino-americano.** São Paulo: Fundo de Cultura, 1964.

______. Prefácio. In: RODRÍGUEZ, Octavio. **Teoria do subdesenvolvimento da Cepal.** Rio de Janeiro: Forense-Universitária, 1981. p. 7-12.

RADOSH, Ronald. Incentives, Moral and Material. **Monthly Review,** New York, v. 25, n. 10, p. 59-64, mar. 1974.

RAMOS, Jorge Abelardo. Dangers of Empiricism in Latin-American Revolutions. In: AGUILAR, Luis E. (Org.). **Marxism in Latin America.** New York: Alfred A. Knopf, 1968. p. 186-191.

RATLIFF, William E. Chinese Communist Cultural Diplomacy Toward Latin America, 1949-1960. **Hispanic-American Historical Review,** North Carolina, v. XLIX, n. 1, p. 53-79, fev. 1969.

REGALADO, Antero. **Las luchas campesinas en Cuba.** Havana: Comisión de Educación Interna del Comité Central del Partido Comunista de Cuba, 1973.

RIERA, Pepita. **Servicio de inteligencia de Cuba comunista.** Miami: Service Offset Printers, 1966.

RIMALOV, V. **La cooperación económica de la Unión Soviética con los países subdesarrollados.** Moscow: Ediciones de Lenguas Extranjeras, [1961 ou 1962].

RIVERO, Nicolas. **Fidel Castro, um dilema americano.** São Paulo: Dominus, 1963.

ROBINSON, Joan. Cuba-1965. **Monthly Review,** New York, v. 17, n. 9, p. 10-18, fev. 1966.

ROCA, Blas. **Los fundamentos del Socialismo en Cuba.** Havana: Ediciones Populares, 1961.

ROCA, Blas. Batista, Grau and the Roads to National Unity. In: AGUILAR, Luis E. (Org.). **Marxism in Latin America.** New York: Alfred A. Knopf, 1968. p. 133-138.

RODRIGUES, Miguel Urbano. **Opções de revolução na América Latina.** Rio de Janeiro: Paz e Terra, 1968.

RODRÍGUEZ, Carlos Rafael. **Cuba en el tránsito al Socialismo (1959-1963)/Lenin y la cuestión colonial.** Mexico City: Siglo XXI, 1978.

______. **La clase obrera y la revolución.** Havana: Vanguardia Obrera, 1960.

______. **Letra con filo.** Havana: Editorial de Ciencias Sociales, 1983a. t. 1.

______. **Letra con filo.** Havana: Editorial de Ciencias Sociales, 1983b. t. 2.

______. **Letra con filo.** Havana: Unión, 1987. t. 3.

______. **Palabras en los setenta.** Havana: Editorial de Ciencias Sociales, 1984.

______. Sobre la contribución del Che al desarrollo de la economía cubana. **Cuba Socialista,** Havana, n. 33, p. 1-29, maio/jun. 1988.

RODRÍGUEZ, José Luis. Quarenta años de planificación en Cuba, nuestro modelo no es el que falló en los ex-Socialistas. Entrevistadora: Arleen Rodriguez Derivet. **El Economista de Cuba,** Havana, n. 38, 2000. Disponível em: <http://www.eleconomista.cubaweb.cu>. Acesso em: 14 dez. 2001.

RODRIGUEZ, Octavio. **Teoria do subdesenvolvimento da Cepal.** Rio de Janeiro: Forense-Universitária, 1981.

RODRÍGUEZ, Rolando. **Interview.** By: Luiz Bernardo Pericás. Havana, jan. 1999.

RODRIGUEZ FARIÑAS, Ricardo. **Apuntes sobre la planificación de la economía nacional.** Havana: Universidad de la Habana, 1986. t. II.

RODRÍGUEZ FERREYRO, Zobeida. **Interview.** By: Luiz Bernardo Pericás. Havana, nov. 2001.

RODRÍGUEZ GARCÍA, José Luis et al. **Cuba:** revolución y economía 1959-1960. Havana: Editorial de Ciencias Sociales, 1985.

ROJO, Ricardo. **Meu amigo Che.** São Paulo: Edições Populares, 1983.

ROMUALDI, Serafino. **Relatório à American Federation of Labor sobre a situação política e sindical de Cuba.** Havana, abr. 1959.

______. **Presidents and Peons.** New York: Funk & Wagnalls, 1967.

ROSSANDA, Rossana. Poder y democracia en la sociedad de transición. **Cuadernos de Pasado y Presente,** Córdoba, n. 46, p. 27-43, 1973.

ROTHMAN, Stanley. Understanding Marxism. **Problems of Communism,** Washington, v. XV, n. 4, jul./ago. 1966.

ROTHSTEIN, Andrew. **Man and Plan in Soviet Economy.** London: Frederick Muller Ltd., 1948.

ROUGIER, Louis. La mística soviética y sus consecuencias económicas. **Estudios sobre el Comunismo,** Santiago de Chile, ano VII, n. 25, p. 25-30, jul./set. 1959.

RUMIÁNTSEV, A. **Comunismo científico.** Moscow: Editorial Progreso, 1981. Dicionário.

SACHS, Ignacy. **Obstáculos al desarrollo y planificación.** Havana: Edición Revolucionaria; Instituto del Libro, [entre 1967 e 1969].

SADER, Emir (Org.). **Fidel Castro.** São Paulo: Ática, 1986.

SALAZAR MONTEJO, Carlos. The "Stalinist" Parties in Bolivia and Cuba. In: AGUILAR, Luis E. (Org.). **Marxism in Latin América.** New York: Alfred A. Knopf, 1968. p. 232- 239.

SALVADORI, Massimo. **Desenvolvimento do comunismo moderno.** Rio de Janeiro: Ipanema, [195-].

SAMBÓRSKI, G. **União Soviética, 1959/1965.** Rio de Janeiro: Vitória, 1960.

SANTA PINTER, José Julio. La educación y su reforma en la URSS. **Estudios sobre el Comunismo,** Santiago de Chile, ano VII, n. 25, p. 77-79, jul./set. 1959.

SAVIN, S. L.; FONTE, R. S.; JORSOV, S. E. **Breve diccionario de economia concreta.** Havana: Editora Política, 1981.

SERGUERA RIVERI, Jorge. **Interview.** By: Luiz Bernardo Pericás. Havana, jan. 1999.

SETTEMBRINI, Domenico. **Socialismo y revolución después de Marx.** Salamanca: Sígueme, 1978.

SHER, Gerson S. (Org.). **Marxist Humanism and Praxis.** New York: Prometheus Books, 1978.

SILVA, Arnaldo. **Interview.** By: Luiz Bernardo Pericás. Havana, jan. 1999.

SINCLAIR, Andrew. **Guevara.** London: Fontana, 1970.

SINGH, V. B. et al. **Da economia política.** Rio de Janeiro: Zahar, 1966.

SKIDMORE, Thomas E.; SMITH, Peter H. **Modern Latin America.** New York: Oxford University Press, 1989.

SMOLINSKI, Leon. Economics and Politics: IV, Reforms in Poland. **Problems of Communism,** Washington, n. 4, v. XV, p. 8-12, jul./ago. 1966.

SOLER, Rafael. **Interview.** By: Luiz Bernardo Pericás. Santiago de Cuba, jan. 1999.

SOLGANICK, Allen. Las reformas económicas soviéticas, el peligro de los incentivos materiales. **Monthly Review,** New York, ano IV, n. 37, p. 41-49, abr. 1967.

SOLIUS, G. **Economía política del Socialismo.** Havana: Orbe, 1976.

SORIA GALVARRO, Carlos (Org.). **El Che en Bolivia 3:** Análisis y reflexiones. La Paz: Cedoin, 1994.

STÁLIN, Joseph. **Problemas econômicos do Socialismo na URSS.** Rio de Janeiro: Vitória, 1953.

______. **Em defesa do Socialismo científico.** São Paulo: Anita Garibaldi, 1990.

STEELE, Jonathan. **The Limits of Soviet Power.** Middelsex: Penguin Books, 1984.

STRUMILIN, Stanislav G. **Ensayos sobre la economía Socialista.** Havana: Publicaciones Económicas, 1966.

SUÁREZ SALAZAR, Luis. Inmortalidad del Che: un reencuentro Tricontinental con el comandante Manuel Piñero Losada. **Tricontinental,** Havana, ano 30, n. 138, p. 41-49, 1997.

SUCHLICKI, Jaime. **Historical Dictionary of Cuba.** Metuchen, New Jersey: The Scarecrow Press, 1988.

SURGANOV, Boris. **Socialismo e capitalismo, perspectivas econômicas.** Lisbon: Prelo, 1975.

SWEEZY, Paul. Czechoslovakia, Capitalism and Socialism. In: ______; BETTELHEIM, Charles. **On the Transition to Socialism.** New York: Modern Reader, 1972.

______. Hacia un programa de estudio de la transición al Socialismo. **Cuadernos de Pasado y Presente,** Córdoba, n. 46, p. 1-13, 1973.

______. A réplica de Paul Sweezy a Bernard Chavance. **Teoria & Política,** São Paulo, ano I, n. 3, p. 105-111, 1980.

SWEEZY, Paul; BETTELHEIM, Charles. **On the Transition to Socialism.** New York: Modern Reader, 1972.

SZULC, Tad. **Fidel, a Critical Portrait.** New York: Avon Books, 1987.

TABARES DEL REAL, José. **Interview.** By: Luiz Bernardo Pericás. Havana, jan. 1999.

TABLADA, Carlos. **Che Guevara: Economics and Politics in the Transition to Socialism.** Sydney: Pathfinder, 1989.

TABLADA PÉREZ, Carlos. La creatividad en el pensamiento económico del Che. In: CENTRO DE ESTUDIOS SOBRE AMÉRICA. **Pensar al Che:** los retos de la transición Socialista. Havana: Centro de Estudios sobre América; Editorial José Martí, 1989. t. 2. p. 217-256.

TAIBO II, Paco Ignácio. **Ernesto Guevara, também conhecido como Che.** São Paulo: Scritta, 1997.

TANGRI, Shanti S. China and Peaceful Coexistence: Some Considerations. **Problems of Communism,** Washington, v. XVI, n. 1, p. 76-80, jan./fev. 1967.

TATU, Michel. **O poder político na URSS.** [S. l.]: Expressão e Cultura, 1970.

TCHERKESOFF, Varlan. **O marxismo antes e depois de Marx.** São Paulo: Biblioteca Prometeu, 1935.

TENNANT, Gary. Che Guevara e os trotskistas cubanos. In: COGGIOLA, Osvaldo (Org.). **Revolução Cubana, história e problemas atuais.** São Paulo: Xamã, 1998.

TOPOROWSKI, Jan. The Contradictions of Market Socialism. **Monthly Review,** New York, v. 46, n. 11, p. 1-7, abr. 1995.

TOURAINE, Alan. **Palavra e sangue.** São Paulo: Unicamp; Trajetória Cultural, 1989.

TRAPÉZNIKOV, S. **En los grandes virajes de la Historia.** Havana: [s. n.], 1977.

TRÓTSKY, León. El ejército del trabajo en la Rusia de los soviets. **Cuadernos de Pasado y Presente,** Córdoba, n. 15, p. 161-170, 1972.

______. **Escritos latinoamericanos.** Buenos Aires: Centro de Estudios, Investigaciones y Publicaciones León Trotsky, 2000.

TUTINO, Saverio. Ricerca e dibattito critico sullo sviluppo economico a Cuba. **Quaderni della Fondazione Ernesto Che Guevara,** Bolsena, n. 4, p. 196-198, 2001.

ULAM, Adam B. **A nova face do totalitarismo soviético.** Rio de Janeiro: Record, 1964.

______. **Expansion & Coexistence:** The History of Soviet Foreign Policy, 1917-1967. New York: Frederick A. Praeger, 1968.

______. **Lenin and the Bolsheviks.** London: The Fontana Library, 1969.

UREÑA, Enrique. **Karl Marx economista.** São Paulo: Loyola, 1981.

VAIL, John J. **Fidel Castro.** São Paulo: Nova Cultural, 1987.

VAKHRUCHEV, V. **O neocolonialismo e os seus métodos.** Lisbon: Prelo, 1975.

VALDÉZ PAZ, Juan. **Interview.** By: Luiz Bernardo Pericás. Havana, jan. 1999.

VÁSQUEZ, Euclides. En torno al movimiento 26 de Julio. **Lunes de Revolución,** Havana, n. 19, p. 4-5, 26 jul. 1959.

VENABLE, Vernon. **Human Nature:** the Marxian View. London: Dennis Dobson, 1946.

VERA SOSA, Julio. El "Che", teórico de la violencia y la guerrilla. **El Mundo,** La Paz, p. A6, 24 fev. 1996.

VIGNIER, E.; ALONSO, G. **La corrupción política y administrativa en Cuba.** Havana: Editorial de Ciencias Sociales, 1973.

VILABOY, Sergio Guerra; DE LA NUEZ, Iván. Che: una concepción antiimperialista de la historia de América. In: CENTRO DE ESTUDIOS SOBRE AMÉRICA. **Pensar al Che:** desafíos de la lucha por el poder político. Havana: Centro de Estudios sobre América; Editorial José Martí, 1989. t. 1. p. 285-334.

VILLEGAS, Abelardo. **Reformismo y revolución en el pensamiento latinoamericano.** Mexico City: Siglo XXI, 1986.

VÓLKOV, G. N. (Ed.). **Fundamentos da doutrina marxista-leninista.** Moscow: Edições Progresso, 1984.

VOROCHILOV, K. **Stalin y las fuerzas armadas de la URSS.** Moscow: Ediciones en Lenguas Extranjeras, 1953.

WILKERSON, Loree. **A filosofia política de Fidel Castro.** Rio de Janeiro: O Cruzeiro, 1966.

WOLFF, Eric R. **Peasant Wars of the Twentieth Century.** New York: Harper Torchbooks/Harper & Row Publishers, [1970?].

WOLFF, Lenny. **Guevara, Debray y revisionismo armado.** Chicago: RCP Publications, 1986.

YRARRAZAVAL CONCHA, Eduardo. **América Latina en la guerra fría.** Santiago de Chile: Nascimento, 1959.

ZEA, Leopoldo. El Che y el hombre nuevo. **Casa de las Américas,** Havana, ano XXXVII, n. 206, jan./mar. 1997.

ZEITLIN, Maurice. **La política revolucionaria y la clase obrera cubana.** Buenos Aires: Amorrortu, 1970.

ZIMBALIST, Andrew. A Synthesis of Dependency and Class Analysis. **Monthly Review,** New York, v. 32, n. 1, p. 27-31, may 1980.

— *books available from Atropos Press*

Teletheory. Gregory L. Ulmer

Philosophy of Culture-Kulturphilosophie: Schopenhauer and Tradition. Edited by Wolfgang Schirmacher.

Virilio: Grey Ecology. The La Rochelle Workshop.
Edited by Hubertus von Amelunxen. Translated by Drew Burk

The Tupperware Blitzkrieg. Anthony Metivier

Talking Cheddo: Teaching Hard Kushitic Truths. Manga Clem Marshall

Che Guevera and the Economic Debate in Cuba. Luiz Bernardo Pericás

Follow Us or Die. Vincent W.J. van Gerven Oei and Jonas Staal

Just Living: Philosophy in Artificial Life. Collected Works Volume 1.
Wolfgang Schirmacher

Think Media: EGS Media Philosophy Series

Wolfgang Schirmacher, editor

The Ethics of Uncertainty: Aporetic Openings. Michael Anker

Trans/actions: Art, Film and Death. Bruce Alistair Barber

Literature as Pure Mediality: Kafka and the Scene of Writing. Paul DeNicola

Imaginality: Conversant and Eschaton. A. Staley Groves

Hospitality in the age of media representation. by Christian Hänggi

The Organic Organisation: freedom, creativity and the search for fulfilment. Nicholas Ind

Can Computers Create Art? James Morris

The Art of the Transpersonal Self: Transformation as Aesthetic and Energetic Practice.
Norbert Koppensteiner

Community without Identity: The Ontology and Politics of Heidegger. Tony See

Sonic Soma: Sound, Body and the Origins of the Alphabet. Elise Kermani

Mirrors triptych technology: Remediation and Translation Figures.
Diana Silberman Keller

Printed in the United States
145769LV00001B/7/P

9 780981 946283